MW01087978

CIVIL WAR SPECIAL FORCES

CIVIL WAR SPECIAL FORCES

The Elite and Distinct Fighting Units of the Union and Confederate Armies

Robert P. Broadwater

 PRAEGER

AN IMPRINT OF ABC-CLIO, LLC
Santa Barbara, California • Denver, Colorado • Oxford, England

Copyright 2014 by Robert P. Broadwater

All rights reserved. No part of this publication may be reproduced, stored in a retrieval system, or transmitted, in any form or by any means, electronic, mechanical, photocopying, recording, or otherwise, except for the inclusion of brief quotations in a review, without prior permission in writing from the publisher.

Library of Congress Cataloging-in-Publication Data

Broadwater, Robert P., 1958–
  Civil War special forces : the elite and distinct fighting units of the Union and Confederate armies / Robert P. Broadwater.
    pages cm
  Includes bibliographical references and index.
  ISBN 978–1–4408–3057–0 (hard copy : alk. paper) — ISBN 978–1–4408–3058–7 (ebook) 1. United States—History—Civil War, 1861–1865—Regimental histories. 2. Special forces (Military science)—United States—History—19th century. 3. Special forces (Military science)—Confederate States of America. 4. United States. Army—History—Civil War, 1861–1865. 5. Confederate States of America. Army. I. Title.
  E492.7.B76   2014
  973.74—dc23   2014015661

ISBN: 978–1–4408–3057–0
EISBN: 978–1–4408–3058–7

18 17 16 15 14   1 2 3 4 5

This book is also available on the World Wide Web as an eBook.
Visit www.abc-clio.com for details.

Praeger
An Imprint of ABC-CLIO, LLC

ABC-CLIO, LLC
130 Cremona Drive, P.O. Box 1911
Santa Barbara, California 93116-1911

This book is printed on acid-free paper ∞

Manufactured in the United States of America

To Mary Brunner:
a longtime friend, supporter, and fellow historian

CONTENTS

INTRODUCTION

The U.S. Civil War is regarded by historians as being the first modern war. Technological advances, from the minié ball to the telegraph and from iron-clad naval vessels to the chemical corps, made this a conflict that forever changed the manner in which battles and wars were fought. The Civil War witnessed the formation of the first balloon corps, and, in the case of the Confederates, the first use of a naval aircraft carrier. Heavy-caliber railroad guns and trench warfare foretold the terrible carnage that would shock the world in the Great War, while the use of hospital trains and ships provided a medical response to the ever-increasing human devastation technological advances brought about. The CSS *Hunley* proved that submarine warfare was possible and paved the way for the dreaded wolf packs of the German navy that terrorized Allied shipping in two world wars. Snipers and sharpshooters, armed with the most advanced weaponry and optics of the era, fought war at a distance and forever changed the notion that war was a valorous and manly contest waged between men who could look one another in the eye. In typical U.S. fashion, women stepped forward to prove that they were not the weaker sex. The Nancy Harts, of Georgia, formed a militia company to protect their homes from the advance of the Federal army, while vivandières served on both sides with valor and devotion.

But the Civil War was also a period of transition. Advances in military science and technology were to be found side by side with relics from a bygone era. This age of fearful firepower also witnessed antiquated forms of warfare more in keeping with knights of old than a modern conflict. Cavalry units, armed only with lances, fought against enemies having the most sophisticated long-range rifled muskets in the world. Infantrymen carrying pikes seemed more like men-at-arms assaulting a castle than soldiers in a modern army, while miners and sappers performed variations of jobs that had been done for centuries. Signalmen still sent messages with flags, as had been done since ancient times, but now there were elaborate codes to disguise those messages from the enemy, and signalmen bridged the ties from ancient to modern times through the military application of the telegraph.

The Civil War was a blend of old and new, as the past and future came face to face on the battlefield. It witnessed the creation of methods and weapons of warfare that are still in use today while bidding farewell to outdated units and armaments whose time had passed. In the following pages, you will read about the elite and unusual military organizations that were created by and used in the Civil War. You will also discover many of the units that were made obsolete by the technology of the industrial age. There will be chapters giving the history of units unusual because of their composition, as well. Old men and young boys, far above and below the draft age, were banded together into the Junior and Senior Reserves of North Carolina and fought in the final battles of the war. Native American troops fought in both Eastern and Western Theaters, and U.S. Colored Troops fought to secure their freedom and win their citizenship.

In the following pages, the reader will discover that Civil War armies were far more diverse than merely infantry, cavalry, and artillery. Civil War navies were more complex than sailing ships and paddle-wheeled steamers. The Civil War was an American drama viewed by the world, and its effects influenced all military conflicts to follow. This is not to say that military professionals around the globe always used the lessons of the Civil War to their greatest advantage. The carnage of World War I gave evidence to that. While armies adopted trench warfare and machine guns that had been introduced in the Civil War, their leaders failed to understand the benefits these innovations provided defending troops and continued to order massed, frontal assaults that were as futile as they were bloody.

There is an old saying that military tactics are always one war behind military technology. That was certainly true in the Civil War. Napoleonic tactics seemed almost suicidal when used against artillery and small arms whose effective killing range was several times longer than the weapons used a generation before. Troops marching shoulder to shoulder against such weaponry seems suicidal and foolish to us today. Lancers and pikemen seemed archaic next to machine gunners and balloonists, but they served together in this war that closed out a bygone era and introduced the world to military operations in the industrial age.

The focus of this book is to provide the reader with a glimpse of the many special units employed in the Union and Confederate armies and navies.

Some enjoyed elite status and were on the cutting edge of mid-nineteenth-century military technology. Others were unusual because of their outdated character or the nature of their makeup or function. I hope you will enjoy this look at some of the unique military organizations that made up the Union and Confederate armies and navies.

In many instances, the units depicted in the following pages serve as a representation of like units that were enrolled during the war. It is not the intention of this work to provide a comprehensive history of any of these units, but rather to provide the reader with a vignette of the varied and unusual nature of the service performed by them during the war.

CHAPTER 1

THE ZOUAVES

Zouaves was the name given to light infantry units of the French army serving in French North Africa. Their first organization was in 1831, when the French military raised two battalions of volunteers from among the local Berber tribe. These troops were expert skirmishers and served the role of light infantry with the French army operating in the region. Their most distinguishing feature was the colorful uniforms in which they were adorned. The typical Zouave uniform included short, open-fronted jackets, with baggy, balloon-legged pants, a sash, and oriental headgear, usually a tasseled fez. By 1838, the Zouaves had transformed into a completely French unit. These soldiers earned a reputation as superb skirmishers and dogged fighters, and by 1852 two more regiments of Zouaves had been added to the French army.

Elmer Ellsworth was the person most responsible for bringing the Zouave craze to the United States. A clerk in a patent agency by trade, Ellsworth was also an active member of several militia companies and an avid student of military tactics. Ellsworth had read accounts of the French Zouaves in North Africa and was impressed by their reported fighting abilities. When he moved to Chicago, Illinois, a few years before the Civil War, Ellsworth was made colonel of the city's National Guard Cadets. He immediately transformed the unit into a Zouave organization, complete with the gaudy, colorful uniforms. His experience as a former drillmaster paid dividends, and the men under his command quickly became one of the finest precision units in the country.

Ellsworth and his company toured the nation, thrilling spectators with their highly disciplined drill maneuvers. As a result, militia companies across the country decided to adopt the Zouave style of dress and instruction, as the fashion became far more popular in the United States than it would ever be in the French army. Ellsworth would go on to write a drill manual for Zouave

Colonel Elmer Ellsworth. The person most responsible for making Zouaves popular in the United States, he was commander of the 11th New York Infantry, know as Ellsworth's Zouaves. (Library of Congress)

companies, *Complete Instructions for the Recruit in the Light Infantry Drill: As Adapted and Arranged for the United States Zouave Cadets,* a 76-page manual published in 1861. As such, Ellsworth lays claim to being the father of Zouave units in the Union and Confederate armies.

The fad quickly spread, and there were literally hundreds of Zouave units, of varying size, in both North and South by the outbreak of the war. Pennsylvania and New York were especially caught up in the craze, as those two states fielded by far the largest number of Zouave organizations. In fact, the only states that did not have at least a company of Zouaves at the outbreak of the war, or raise one once it started, were Missouri, North Carolina, New Hampshire, Connecticut, and Florida. Even the District of Columbia boasted a company of Zouaves.

At the beginning of the war, most Zouave militia companies were folded into regiments. The 61st Pennsylvania had six Zouave companies among its ten-company organization. In other cases, Zouave companies banded together to form Zouave regiments, or regiments were to be Zouave organizations.

In April of 1861, Lew Wallace, a lawyer from Indianapolis, Indiana, raised a regiment of Zouaves for Federal service. The 11th Indiana Zouaves were mustered in for 90 days' service and assigned to duty at Cumberland, Maryland. On June 26, a portion of this regiment took part in one of the first engagements of the war. A scouting detachment from the 11th Indiana ran into a force of 40 to 50 Virginia cavalry 11 miles east of Cumberland, setting off a firefight that resulted in one dead and one wounded for the Zouaves and twenty-three dead and seven wounded for the Confederates. Though hardly a skirmish, the affair was reported as a major battle in the Cumberland newspaper, which heralded the action as "one of the most daring achievements in modern warfare."[1] When this regiment was mustered out of the service in August 1861, Wallace immediately recruited another 11th Indiana Zouaves to serve for three years or the duration of the war. This unit would become known as Wallace's Zouaves. Wallace would go on to become a major general in the Union army and governor of the New Mexico Territory following the end of the war. He is best known, however, as the author of the best-selling novel *Ben Hur: A Tale of the Christ*.

Elmer Ellsworth also raised a regiment of Zouave troops at the beginning of the war. The men for the regiment came from the many volunteer fire departments in New York City, leading to the regiment often being called the New York Fire Zouaves. Ellsworth was a personal friend to Abraham Lincoln, who gave him a commission as colonel in the volunteer service to raise the regiment.[2] Ellsworth put out a call for volunteers on April 15, and four days later 2,300 men had answered the appeal. Ellsworth selected the best 1,100 from among these to fill his regiment. He raised $60,000 to arm and equip the regiment with uniforms, provisions, and several models of the latest Sharps rifles.[3] The regiment arrived in Washington on May 2 and was officially sworn into Federal service five days later. When Virginia passed the ordnance of secession on May 23, the 11th New York Zouaves, along with seven other regiments, was ordered to cross the Potomac River and seize Arlington and Alexandria.

The 11th landed on the Virginia shore on May 24, with no opposition from the enemy. Ellsworth, along with a detachment of men, set out to secure a telegraph station to communicate with Washington. On the way, the party passed by the Marshall House, a local inn, above which flew the Confederate flag. Ellsworth led a detachment of men into the hotel to cut down the flag from its roof. They accomplished their mission and were descending the stairs when they were accosted by James Jackson, the proprietor of the inn. Jackson shot Colonel Ellsworth in the chest with a shotgun, killing him instantly. Corporal Francis Brownell responded by shooting Jackson.[4] Ellsworth became the first martyr of the country and its first national hero. The slogan "Remember Ellsworth" soon became a watchword for the Union cause.

Group of Zouaves in camp. (Library of Congress)

The 11th New York would play a prominent role in the battle of First Manassas, making four charges against Henry House Hill and serving as a rear guard for the Union army when it retreated from the field. The regiment suffered high casualties in this engagement, with 35 men killed, 74 wounded, and 68 captured.[5]

The 11th New York was mustered out of the service on June 2, 1862. Efforts were later made to reorganize the original regiment as a three-year unit, but the required number of men could not be raised. The regiment had been among the first to occupy enemy territory in the war, and Colonel Ellsworth had been the Union's first casualty and martyr. They had fought valiantly at Manassas and had earned a colorful reputation for themselves within the army, but their existence as a unit lasted only about a year.

Perhaps the most famous Zouave regiment to serve in the Union army was the 5th New York Infantry, more commonly known as Duryee's Zouaves. Abram Duryee raised the regiment in May of 1861 and became its colonel. Like Ellsworth, Duryee had served extensively in the prewar militia and had been a colonel in the state of New York. Duryee's Zouaves most closely adopted the attire of the French Zouaves, wearing a dark blue jacket with red trim, a dark blue vest with red trim, a red sash with light blue trim, baggy red pantaloons, a red fez with a yellow tassel, and white gaiters. The 165th New York, which was recruited between August and December of 1862, was considered to be the sister regiment of the 5th and wore exactly the same uniform, with the exception that the tassel on their fez was blue.

Duryee's Zouaves were assigned to duty at Fortress Monroe, Virginia, on May 24. They were employed in numerous scouting missions against the

Confederate forces in the area, and Duryee's insistence on constant drilling was causing them to be regarded as one of the finest regiments in the Union army. On June 10, 1861, the regiment took part in the first real land battle of the war, when Union forces under the command of Major General Benjamin Butler clashed with Confederate forces led by Brigadier General John B. Magruder at Big Bethel, Virginia. Butler, with 3,500 men, had planned a surprise attack against the Confederate camp, numbering only about 1,400. All hope of surprise was lost, however, when the 7th New York Infantry mistook the 3rd New York Infantry for the enemy in the early morning darkness and opened fire on them. The 3rd New York was greatly demoralized, and the Confederates were alerted to the presence of the Union army, but Butler determined to continue with his offensive. Duryee's Zouaves were sent ahead of the main body to scout the Southern position, and they reported that Magruder's men were well positioned behind strong fieldworks at Big Bethel.[6] When the Federals advanced, a portion of the 5th New York was able to make a lodgment in the Confederate line but was unable to hold the gain when their supporting units retired and left them facing the enemy alone. Another portion of the regiment was roughly handled when it tried to march around the Confederate flank, forcing them to retire. The battle did not go well for Duryee's Zouaves or for the Union army. The Confederates sustained only 8 casualties in the affair, while inflicting 76 on the Federals. By later war standards, Big Bethel was a minor affair, of little consequence, but in these opening days of the conflict, it served as the first test of might on the battlefield, and the Confederates had emerged victorious.

The regiment participated in the Peninsula Campaign and the Seven Days Battles in front of Richmond in 1862. At Gaines's Mill, one-third of the men were shot down, but despite these losses, the regiment showed superb discipline and resolve. At one point, while still under fire, the men counted off to ensure that their movements would not be effected by the casualties they had sustained. The 5th New York won its greatest distinction at Second Manassas, where it received the dubious honor of sustaining the greatest number of battlefield deaths suffered by any Union regiment in the entire war. On that field, Duryee's Zouaves had been assigned to provide infantry support for a Federal battery being attacked by Brigadier General John B. Hood's Texas brigade. The regiment was overpowered and driven from the field, but not before putting up a terrific struggle. Of the 490 men in the regiment who entered the battle, 117 were killed. The regiment was held in reserve at the battle of Antietam, but took an active part at both Fredericksburg and Chancellorsville. On May 14, 1863, Duryee's Zouaves were mustered out of the service at the expiration of their term of enlistment.[7]

Two more notable Northern Zouave organizations were the 114th Pennsylvania, known as Collis's Zouaves, and the 76th Pennsylvania, known as the Keystone Zouaves. In August of 1861, Charles H. T. Collis was granted permission from Major General Nathaniel P. Banks to raise a company of Zouaves in the city of Philadelphia. Banks intended the company to serve as his personal bodyguard. The unit trained for a month at Fort Delaware before joining Banks in the Shenandoah Valley. On May 24, 1862, the company was ordered to cover the retreat of Banks's army, toward Winchester, and fought a successful delaying action against a full brigade of the enemy, despite the fact there were only 76 men in the company. General Banks was so impressed by the conduct of the Zouaves that he granted Collis permission to expand the organization to regimental strength. Collis returned to Philadelphia to open recruiting stations, while the company remained with Banks's army and took part in the battles of Cedar Mountain, Second Manassas, Chantilly, and Antietam. In five weeks, Collis was able to secure enough volunteers to fill nine new companies.

The regiment performed heroically at Fredericksburg, and at Chancellorsville, where 24 of its 27 officers fell as casualties. At Gettysburg, the regiment held a position along the Emmitsburg Pike, near Little Round Top. On July 2, it was forced to retire in the face of General James Longstreet's massed assault against the Federal left, but not before making a dogged defense of its position. In the spring of 1863, Major General George G. Meade selected the 114th Pennsylvania to serve as his personal headquarters guard, in recognition of its "discipline and soldierly bearing" displayed on several fields of battle. The Collis Zouaves served as the nucleus for a headquarters guard that would grow to include six regiments. During General Ulysses S. Grant's Overland Campaign of 1864, these regiments were constantly relied upon to save the day on the field of battle, being continually committed to hard-pressed points on the line. Rapidity of movement and gallantry in the attack became their watchwords. At Guinea Station, Virginia, the Collis Zouaves successfully repulsed an attack on General Grant's headquarters by the cavalry of Major General Fitzhugh Lee. On April 2, 1865, the regiment was successful in carrying a portion of the enemy's Petersburg works, opposite Fort Hell, which had been the scene of repeated failures by other troops. The following day, the 114th became the first unit to raise the U.S. flag above the Petersburg courthouse. The Collis Zouaves missed the surrender of Lee's army at Appomattox Court House, having been assigned to escort the six thousand prisoners captured at Sailor's Creek back to City Point. The regiment was mustered out of the service on May 29, 1865.[8]

The 76th Pennsylvania Infantry, also known as the Keystone Zouaves, was raised between August and October 1861. John M. Power was commissioned colonel for the regiment. It was mustered into the service on October 18 and sent to Fortress Monroe before being assigned to duty in South Carolina. The Keystone Zouaves participated in the Union operations against Fort Pulaski at Savannah, Georgia, culminating with the siege of that place on April 10–11, 1862. The 76th had been selected to be one of the regiments to storm the works following a Union artillery bombardment, but the infantry assault became unnecessary when the walls of the fort were breeched by the barrage and its defenders were forced to surrender on April 11. Private Alexander Gwin wrote, "This day one year ago the Rebels captured Ft. Sumter . . . Today Ft. Pulaski fell into our hands."[9]

The Keystone Zouaves performed duty in South Carolina, operating against the Confederate defenses of Charleston throughout 1862 and 1863, and took an active role in the two assaults against Fort Wagner. On July 11, 1863, the Keystone Zouaves were among the spearhead of a Union attack against the Confederate stronghold that resulted in a bloody repulse. The Zouaves suffered terrible casualties, sustaining 234 killed or wounded in the assault. One week later, on July 18, the Keystone Zouaves were once more ordered to attack the fort, this time in support of the spearhead led by the Colored 54th Massachusetts Regiment. This attack was also repulsed with terrible casualties. In May of 1864, the regiment was transferred to General Benjamin Butler's Army of the James, where it participated in the capture of Bermuda Hundred on May 5. From May 14 to 16, it fought in the battle of Drewry's Bluff, then in the Cold Harbor Campaign before taking part in the siege of Petersburg. In December of 1864, the Keystone Zouaves were assigned to the failed expedition against Fort Fisher, North Carolina, at Wilmington. They were also part of the second expedition against that place, which resulted in the capture of Fort Fisher on January 15, 1865. From that time until the end of the war, the 76th Pennsylvania cooperated with Major General William T. Sherman's march through the Carolinas that culminated with the surrender of General Joseph E. Johnston's army at Bennett Place, North Carolina, on April 26, 1865. The Keystone Zouaves were mustered out of the service on July 18, 1865.[10]

The most famous Zouave unit to fight for the Confederacy during the Civil War was undoubtedly the 1st Louisiana Special Battalion, more commonly known as the Louisiana Tigers, or Wheat's Tigers. The battalion was raised by Chatham Roberdeau Wheat, a Virginia-born adventurer who had served in the Mexican-American War, been elected to the state assembly of Louisiana, earned a law degree, and hired out regularly as a mercenary. The outbreak of hostilities found Wheat in Italy, offering his services to Giuseppe Garibaldi in his second war for Italian independence. When word arrived in Europe that Virginia was planning to secede from the Union, Wheat returned to the United States with all haste to offer his services to the Confederacy. On April 18, 1861, the New Orleans *Crescent* ran an announcement that Wheat was seeking recruits for a company he planned to raise. Wheat named his company the Old Dominion Guards, in honor of the state of his birth, and within a few days he had more than 50 volunteers.

In the meantime, he was successful in convincing four other companies that were in the process of forming to come under his command as a battalion of infantry. These companies were the Walker Guards, the Delta Rangers, the Rough and Ready Rangers, and the Tiger Rifles. The last company was being raised as a Zouave unit and was the only one that was so designated. Most of the men in Wheat's battalion had been recruited from the New Orleans waterfront, and they had a reputation as "the lowest scum of the lower Mississippi ... adventurous wharf rats, thieves, and outcasts ... and bad characters generally."[11] To be sure, they were an unruly and perhaps unsavory group of ruffians, but they were fighters, one and all.

As previously stated, only the Tiger Rifles were raised as a Zouave unit. Three of the other regiments were uniformed in red flannel battle shirts, with jean-wool pants. Most of the men in the entire battalion preferred to wear straw hats in the field, to combat the heat. The Tiger Rifles usually reserved wearing their trademark fez headgear for camp. The fact that one of the companies of the battalion was a Zouave unit combined with the colorful attire of the rest of the unit led to the misconception that the entire battalion was a Zouave organization.

The battalion completed its organization by June 6, 1861. Its five companies totaled 416 officers and men. Orders came through for Wheat and his Tigers to report to Virginia, and the unit arrived in time to take an active role in a skirmish at Seneca Falls, along the Potomac River, on June 28, making them the first Louisiana unit to engage in combat in the war. At the battle of First Manassas, Wheat's men fought like the tigers they were named for, holding a portion of the Confederate line against a strong attack until other Southern units could be brought up in support. Following the battle, Wheat's Tigers were brigaded together with five other Louisiana regiments to form Brigadier General Richard Taylor's Louisiana Brigade. The men performed picket duty and drilled in the school of the soldier, but that was hardly enough to occupy all of their idle hours. Fights were common in Wheat's battalion, and when they could not find members of other Confederate units willing to engage in fisticuffs, they often battled among themselves. One such internal scuffle led to two of the Tigers being executed on December 9, 1861, and gave Wheat's men the distinction of being the first soldiers in the Army of Northern Virginia to be shot before a firing squad. General Taylor's brigade was assigned to General Thomas J. "Stonewall" Jackson's army, operating in the Shenandoah Valley, in the spring of 1862. Wheat's Tigers took an active part in Jackson's Valley Campaign, helping to capture Front Royal on May 23 and distinguishing itself at the battle of Port Republic on June 9. Jackson's forces joined with Robert E. Lee's army to take part in the Seven Days Battles around Richmond, and Wheat's Tigers were heavily engaged at the battle of Gaines's Mill on June 27. Major Wheat was killed in that battle, which led the Confederate high command to make a difficult decision regarding his Tigers. The battalion had been greatly reduced in numbers during the campaigning in the Valley and around Richmond, but the undersized status of the unit is not what concerned headquarters. Following Major Wheat's death, the men became even more unruly and undisciplined than they had been before. It was as if no one but Wheat could command them or enforce any measure of military protocol. They were fighters, no one in the Confederate army questioned that, but their conduct off the field was becoming too much of a problem to be ignored. Accordingly, it was decided that the unit be disbanded, which took place on August 15, 1862. Wheat's Tigers had existed as a military unit for slightly more than a year, but their fame would become eternal. The reckless courage they showed on the battlefield had made them famous, so much so that General Taylor's entire brigade was soon being called Louisiana Tigers and would continue to be known by this name long after Wheat's Tigers ceased to exist.[12]

While some Zouave units retained their colorful attire and performed the duties of light infantry for the duration of the war, many more became swallowed up in the larger units of which they were a part. The specialized clothing associated with the Zouaves became harder to obtain as the war went along, and many units were forced to adopt the standard blue army issue the rest of the Union forces wore. But Zouave units, regardless of their uniform or whether they were used as light or heavy infantry, generally earned for themselves a reputation as hard, courageous fighters, and that reputation was upheld on battlefields across the nation throughout the four bloody years of the war.

CHAPTER 2

THE LANCERS

A lancer is a cavalryman who fights with a lance, a long pole tipped with a metal blade or point. The use of lances in combat first took place about 700 BC, and they continued to be employed by military units around the world until well into the twentieth century. The poles were usually about 10 feet in length, providing increased reach over mounted soldiers carrying swords and giving a line of charging lancers a clear advantage on the battlefield. This held true only when lancers were on the offensive, making a charge. In close combat, the long lances were unwieldy and clumsy to use, and all advantage passed to the soldiers using swords. But lancers were intended to be shock troops, and their primary function was to break an enemy's line through both the application and intimidation of their weapons, at which time other cavalry or infantry units were moved forward to support and exploit the gains they had achieved. The introduction of firearms greatly reduced the efficiency of lancers, and by the seventeenth and eighteenth centuries their use had declined in most of the armies of Europe. Mounted troops carrying a pistol and a sword were more than a match for the lance, and the weapon fell out of favor with most military commanders. By the beginning of the nineteenth century, the lance experienced a resurgence in European warfare. The Napoleonic armies discovered that the weapon still had the power to unnerve enemies when massed cavalry formations used them in thundering charges against lines of battle. The sight of a thousand galloping horses, riders leaned forward, with their long, death-tipped poles horizontal and pointing at their intended victims, had a terrifying effect on defenders. It was also discovered that a rapid charge by the lancers would usually limit the enemy to one volley from their muskets before the horsemen would be upon them. This proved to be the factor that made lancer charges most effective. After firing their initial shot, most infantrymen would become seized with panic trying to reload while the seemingly resistless charge of the lancers bore down upon them. All European nations adopted lancer units into their military, and after more than two thousand years, the lancer was once more a member of an elite fighting unit.

In the few short decades that separated the Napoleonic Wars of Europe with the U.S. Civil War, military technology had advanced to the point where lances were once more antiquated and unacceptable combat weapons. The rifling of muskets and improvements made in small arms conical ammunition meant that an infantryman's shoulder weapon now had an effective killing range several times that of Napoleonic arms. Simply put, this meant that a line of defending infantry could fire several accurate volleys at a line of charging lancers before they came close enough to put their lances to work, instead of the one volley that could accurately be fired a few decades before. The extended range of the rifled musket could allow its wielder to shoot down a line of lancers before their fearful weapons could ever be brought to bear. As with most wars, however, military technology had advanced faster than military tactics, and several lancer units would be raised for service on both sides during the Civil War.

The oldest lancer organization in the country at the beginning of the war was the National Lancers. This unit was formed in Boston, Massachusetts, in 1836 in response to Governor Edward Everett's desire for a mounted, ceremonial escort. They were also charged with maintaining order and defending Massachusetts in case of invasion. At the outbreak of the Civil War, the National Lancers were designated as a home guard unit and were not incorporated into the Federal army. They did, however, see limited action during the course of the war, when they were called out to quell the Boston Draft Riots of 1863. The National Lancers played a prominent role in putting down the riot and in preventing the rioters from seizing the arms and munitions stored in the armory of the Boston Light Artillery.[1] Though some of the younger members of the National Lancers enlisted in other cavalry units to serve in the war, the draft riot was as close as this organization ever came to combat. The National Lancers continue to this day as a ceremonial unit under the auspices of the Massachusetts National Guard.

Colonel Arthur Rankin was an interesting officer who proposed to raise a regiment of lancers in Michigan. Rankin was an avid abolitionist, but he was also a Canadian on active duty in the Ninth Military District of West Canada. Nonetheless, he proposed to Washington that he be granted permission to raise a lancer regiment from the Detroit, Saginaw, and St. John regions of Michigan. Permission was granted, and in November of 1861 recruitment was begun. By the latter part of February 1862, Rankin had been successful in raising 903 men for what he was calling the 1st U.S. Lancers. All seemed to be progressing in good order, but circumstances quickly unraveled for Rankin. Weapons for the lancers were hard to obtain, and by the end of February the regiment was still unarmed. Rankin came under personal criticism by Canadian officials and was accused in the Toronto press of trying to violate the Neutrality Act between the United States and Canada. Furthermore, his superiors refused to grant him leave from his responsibilities in Canada to command the 1st U.S. Lancers. Because of all these difficulties, the regiment was disbanded on March 20, 1862.[2]

George Washington Carter, a Methodist minister serving as president of Soule University at Chappell Hill, Texas, was granted permission to raise a regiment of lancers in the spring of 1862. Carter proposed to raise his regiment from the counties of central Texas, and he found the residents there enthusiastic supporters of his idea. Many Texans wanted to fight in the war, but the thought of plodding over the countryside as infantry left them cold. Texans liked to ride, and Carter's proposed cavalry regiment seemed to many the best way to go to war. Enlistments were so brisk that Carter detailed two of his subordinate officers to raise two additional regiments, with Carter being the senior colonel and commander of the brigade that would thus be formed. Carter named his regiments the 1st, 2nd, and 3rd Texas Lancers, but they were later designated the 21st, 24th, and 25th Texas Cavalry. The Texas Lancers faced the same problem that beset the 1st U.S. Lancers in having difficulty obtaining lances for the troopers. Because of this, the 1st Texas Lancers (21st Texas Cavalry) was converted to traditional cavalry and armed with swords and pistols. The 2nd Texas Lancers (24th Texas Cavalry) and 3rd Texas Lancers (25th Texas Cavalry) were both dismounted and served the rest of the war as infantry. Though Colonel Carter continued to call his regiment the Texas Lancers, they were lancers in name alone.

One of the more famous cavalry regiments to emerge from the Civil War, and the only one on either side to fight with lances in battle, was the 6th Pennsylvania Cavalry, commonly known as Rush's Lancers. The regiment was raised by Richard H. Rush and Clement B. Barclay, two prominent citizens of Philadelphia. Rush was the grandson of Benjamin Rush of Philadelphia, signer of the Declaration of Independence and the Constitution. His father had served as an ambassador to England, where Rush was born. Rush himself was a graduate of the famed West Point class of 1846 that produced such notables as George B. McClellan, Stonewall Jackson, George E. Pickett, Ambrose P. Hill, and John Gibbon. Following graduation, he had served as a second lieutenant of artillery in the Mexican-American War. After eight years in the regular army and a promotion to first lieutenant, Rush resigned from the army in 1854. Clement Barclay was a member of one of Philadelphia's leading families. He was also a member of Philadelphia's elite First City Troop, a militia cavalry unit tracing its origins

The 6th Pennsylvania Cavalry, known as Rush's Lancers. Though a number of units were issued lances during the war, Rush's Lancers was the only one to actually go into battle armed with them. (Library of Congress)

back to the American Revolution, where it served as George Washington's bodyguard. Membership in the First City Troop was a great distinction and could only be obtained through being elected to occupy vacancies when they occurred. As such, membership in the elite unit was a symbol of social distinction among the city's best families. Barclay had great political influence and was a personal friend and advisor to Governor Andrew G. Curtin.[3]

The Commonwealth of Pennsylvania had shown patriotic fervor in responding to President Lincoln's call for volunteers following the Confederate firing on Fort Sumter. In the first several months of the war, Pennsylvania raised 41 regiments of infantry, 5 batteries of artillery, and 12 regiments of cavalry for the Union cause. All told, nearly 100,000 men had answered the call. In fact, more men volunteered than there were arms and uniforms for, placing Governor Curtin in a predicament. Most other states had accepted only the number of volunteers needed to meet their quota to the Federal government, sending all surplus volunteers home. Curtin decided to take a different course of action. He determined to retain all Pennsylvania volunteers in service, subsidizing those over the Federal quota by means of funds allocated by the Pennsylvania legislature. In doing so, he created a Pennsylvania Reserve Corps, paid for by the state but subject to any call by the Federal government for their services.

On July 27, 1861, Governor Curtin authorized Rush and Barclay to raise a volunteer regiment in Philadelphia to serve for three years. Recruiting was conducted throughout the summer, and by September 3, enough men had been enrolled to establish a camp of instruction, known as Camp Meigs. Many of the recruits for the regiment came from the ranks of the First City Troop, and the officer corps of the regiment was well represented by the best families in Philadelphia. Robert Morris Jr., grandson of Robert H. Morris, the esteemed financier of the Revolution, was named major of the regiment. Other prominent officers included George G. Meade Jr., son of the eventual commander of the Army of the Potomac; Charles E. Cadwalader, a relative of Revolutionary War General John Cadwalader; and Thomas Gregg, brother of General David McMurtrie Gregg and relative to Governor Andrew Curtin.[4]

At the suggestion of Major General George B. McClellan, commander of the Army of the Potomac, Governor Curtin approached Colonel Rush with a proposal to arm the regiment with lances. Curtin had previously obtained a contract from the War Department for a manufacturer to produce one thousand lances of Austrian design. The weapons consisted of a nine-foot staff of Norway fir, tipped with a three-sided blade, nearly twelve inches in length, and weighing eight pounds. Rush responded to McClellan, "The material of my regiment is fully equal to the lance. I would consider the selection an honor."[5] In reality, Rush and his men had little choice in the matter. There were no weapons available to arm his troopers with other than the lances, so he might as well be gracious about accepting the assignment. Training of the men in the proper usage of the lances began as soon as the weapons arrived. Rush was an able administrator and drillmaster. In short order, he was able to report that the troopers had attained a reasonable degree of proficiency with their weapons and were ready for duty with the army. A small number of carbines were distributed to the regiment, to be used in scouting missions. On October 30, the regiment was presented its colors and a set of guidons by the ladies of Germantown.[6]

The Lancers had received orders to report to Washington without delay on October 28, but it took more than six weeks for the regiment to comply, and they did not arrive in the capital until December 16. The regiment was inspected by Brigadier General George Stoneman, chief of cavalry for the Army of the Potomac, and on January 1, 1862, it was paraded through the city, presenting a thrilling scene for local spectators. On March 10, the Lancers took part in the army's movement on Manassas, Virginia, which revealed that the Confederates had abandoned their defensive positions and moved further south. The regiment then took part in the Peninsula Campaign, moving to Fortress Monroe and thence to New Market Bridge, Virginia.[7]

The regiment arrived at Yorktown just prior to the evacuation of that place by the Confederates, and then it made a series of marches up the Peninsula until it reached Hanover Court House. On May 23, 1862, the Lancers were reconnoitering the enemy when they discovered the Confederates to be massing near the courthouse. On May 25, the regiment made a lance charge against the advance cavalry of the enemy, driving them back upon their infantry support. Two days later, when Major General Fitz-John Porter attacked the Confederates and drove them back from the vicinity of

Hanover Court House, the lancers harassed the retreating foe and captured eighty men and two officers.[8]

Rush's men took no part in the battle of Fair Oaks at the end of the month, but they played a significant role in one of the most spectacular cavalry achievements of the war. On June 10, Major General James "Jeb" Stuart was summoned to General Lee's headquarters and ordered to scout the right flank of the Union army to provide the commander with much-needed intelligence. Stuart had previously presented a plan to ride around the Army of the Potomac, and he decided to expand his orders to implement his original scheme. On June 12, he led 1,200 troopers on a raid that would go completely around McClellan's 105,000-man army. It was an audacious move that would place the Confederate cavalrymen behind enemy lines and in constant danger of being cut off and captured by overwhelming numbers. But luck was with Stuart. The Federal response to the raid was both uncoordinated and tardy. The Union pursuit always seemed one step behind Stuart's band. In three days, the Confederate troopers traveled 150 miles around the Union army, capturing 165 Federal soldiers and 260 horses and mules. The ride brought Stuart international fame and was a source of deep embarrassment to the North. One of the few Union units able to catch up to the Southern horsemen was Rush's Lancers. When Stuart's men were about 35 miles from their own lines, the Lancers caught up to their rear guard. A charge with their lances was not possible, however, and Rush's men had to be content with firing a few shots at their rapidly withdrawing foes.[9]

A portion of the regiment took part in the battle of Beaver Dam Creek in support of a Union battery that kept the Confederates at bay long enough to keep a retreat from the field from turning into a rout. Another portion of the regiment fought in the engagement at White Oak Swamp and served as the rear guard for the retrograde movement to Malvern Hill. The regiment missed the second battle of Manassas, but it took an active part in the Antietam Campaign. During the battle of Fredericksburg, the Lancers were given the responsibility of guarding one of the pontoon bridges across the Rappahannock River and detailed to act as the provost guard for the left wing of the Union army. In October the Lancers once more found themselves chasing Jeb Stuart's cavalry, during the Confederate raid on Chambersburg, Pennsylvania. A portion of the regiment did make contact with Stuart's force, but the Confederates were able to make it safely back to their own lines before sufficient force could be gathered to stop them.

In accordance with orders from the War Department that all cavalry regiments have 12 companies, several members of the regiment were sent back to Philadelphia to recruit two new companies to bring the Lancers up to the required level. The new companies were drilled and quickly brought up to standard in using their lances. They would not have long to enjoy their distinction, however. During the Chancellorsville Campaign, Rush's Lancers took part in General George Stoneman's cavalry raid against Richmond. On April 20, 1863, Company A made a lance charge against enemy forces holding Warrenton, Virginia, causing the Confederates to flee. The regiment then took possession of the town, remaining there for one week. On April 27, Colonel Rush resigned his commission due to illness. Rush had contracted a chronic disease while serving in the Mexican-American War, and the constant exposure of the last three weeks had taken its toll on his health and rendered him incapacitated to continue in command. Leadership of the regiment devolved to Major Robert Morris Jr. The regiment proceeded to Louisa Court House, where telegraph lines and track from the Virginia Central Railroad were torn up. After destroying all Confederate contraband in the area, it was decided on the evening of May 4 to return to the Army of the Potomac. Intelligence was slow in coming to the troopers, and no one in Stoneman's command was aware that Hooker's army had been defeated in the battle of Chancellorsville and compelled to retreat back across the Rappahannock River.[10]

In May of 1863, the Lancers officially lost the thing that had made them an elite unit in the Army of the Potomac. They traded in their lances for Sharps carbines and were assigned to the cavalry division of Major General John Buford. On June 9, the regiment played a significant role in the battle of Brandy Station, the only great all-cavalry engagement to be fought in the war. The Lancers were then assigned to detached duty, which prevented them being with General Buford on the first day at Gettysburg, but they arrived on the field in time to take part in the fighting on July 2 and 3. They then took an active part in the pursuit of Lee's retreating army and in the engagement that took place at Williamsport, Maryland, on July 6. The regiment served with the Army of the Potomac through the remainder of the war and continued to be called the Lancers, despite the fact they no longer carried the weapons for which they had been named. On August 7, 1865, the regiment was mustered out of the service, and Rush's Lancers faded into Civil War lore. The regiment had been an experimental unit, and although their performance in battle and on the march seemed to justify the time and effort expended, lancers were just not the direction either army desired to pursue in regard to their cavalry. Officers like Joe Wheeler, Nathan Bedford Forrest, and John Buford were perfecting the tactics of deploying cavalry more in the fashion of mounted infantry, using horses to move quickly from point to point on the battlefield but dismounting to fight as infantry once they got where they were going. Lancers would continue to be used in the armies of Europe until World War I, but Rush's Lancers would prove to be the only effort the U.S. Army ever made at fielding a regiment of lancers on the battlefield. As such, they hold a special place not just in the annals of the Civil War but in the country's military history as a whole.

CHAPTER 3

THE PIKEMEN

The pike is a weapon that can trace its ancestry back to ancient times, when spears were a mainstay of many armies. The pike was employed in great numbers during the Middle Ages, by footmen massed for close-order combat. Consisting of a lance or bayonet affixed to the end of a long wooden shaft, the pike was an effective weapon against both cavalry and infantry and could be effectively used by men with little or no formal military training. By the early 1700s, the pike had been abandoned in most of the armies of Europe because of the ever-increasing technology of firearms. It would be revived in the 1800s during the Napoleonic Wars, by insurrectionist movements in Ireland, and in several other conflicts around the world. Though archaic and obsolete, the pike was still a cheap and effective way to place a formidable weapon in the hands of inexperienced fighters.

John Brown planned to use pikes in his proposed slave insurrection of 1859, and contracted a Connecticut firm, C. Hart, to manufacture 10,000 of them at a cost of $1.25 each. Brown planned to arm slaves with these weapons, which could readily be used by men who had no previous experience with firearms. When John Brown and his followers raided Harpers Ferry, Virginia, in an attempt to seize the government arsenal there, approximately 950 pikes were taken along to arm the slaves that Brown was sure would rally to his banner. Brown's attempt at instigating a slave war failed, however, and he and his followers were killed or captured by Federal troops and Virginia militia. A large number of pikes were captured when Brown's force was taken, and these were stored in the Harpers Ferry Arsenal. Later, when the arsenal was captured by the Confederates, these weapons were sent south, where they eventually found their way into the hands of a Texas regiment.[1]

During the Civil War, the Confederacy was often plagued by a shortage of weapons with which to arm its soldiers. Having few factories capable of the production of such arms, the Confederacy was forced to address its needs by purchasing a large portion of its weapons from European markets. The Union naval blockade of Southern ports increasingly made this means of acquiring arms a risky and undependable venture. Captured Union weapons helped to ease the shortage from time to time, but the deficiency of arms for its troops was a problem that bedeviled the Confederacy from the beginning of the war till its conclusion.

The pike was a logical solution to the arms shortage that beset the South, and their limited production had begun even before the Confederacy entered into open hostilities with the North. Easy to manufacture and inexpensive to produce, pikes seemed to many in the South to be a feasible way to put weapons in the hands of volunteers until more suitable arms could be procured. The first pikes produced for the Confederate military were manufactured by Ross Winans of Baltimore, Maryland. The firing on Fort Sumter caused a massive mobilization of military forces on both sides of the Mason-Dixon line. Neither side had sufficient weapons with which to arm the multitude of volunteers that came forward to serve their country, but the Union was far better equipped to address the shortage. In June of 1861, the mayor of Memphis, Tennessee, announced that pikes were being issued to a newly raised company in the city. They were "ten feet long with a bayonet head for thrusting and a hook for cutting." In August of 1861 the Richmond *Examiner* reported, "It is proposed to arm some companies with the Polish scythes. A scythe fastened to the end of an 8 or 10 foot staff."[2]

By 1862 many notable Confederate leaders, like Robert E. Lee, "Stonewall" Jackson, Joseph E. Johnston, and Josiah Gorgas, chief of Confederate ordnance, advocated the manufacture and distribution of pikes as a stopgap measure to deal with the shortage of weapons in the South. In January of 1862, several regiments assigned to coastal defense were issued pikes as their side arms. Since the primary duty of these troops was defending against incursion by the Union navy, they were usually to be found in coastal fortifications, where they served as gun crews for the artillery. As such, they would generally do battle at long range with the ships of the Union fleet and would only be called upon to use their pikes if an amphibious force was landed on the beach to assault the fort. Their weapons were reported to be "Alabama pikes, manufactured under appropriation of the State Legislature," and having a "keen, two-edged steel head like a Bowie-knife blade near 18 inches long with a sickle-like hook, very sharp, bending back from near the socket." Indeed, this would have proved to be an intimidating weapon against sailors armed with swords, but it would have provided little protection for the defenders against an enemy armed with pistols or muskets.[3]

The 12th Battalion, Louisiana Heavy Artillery was one of the few early war units to actually be on the field of battle while armed with pikes. The battalion was organized at Yorktown, Virginia, and served in the Yorktown defenses during the initial phase of the Peninsula Campaign. It is said that a portion of the unit fired the last shot from Yorktown before the place was evacuated. The battalion was then ordered to Richmond, where it manned batteries in the capital's defenses. While the members of the battalion carried pikes as their side arms, they were never called upon to use them in close combat.[4]

One company of pikemen was raised in the mountains of Habersham County, Georgia, under the command of Captain Littleton Stephens. The company was raised to aid in the defense of Savannah in February of 1862 and was armed with pikes having blades in the shape of a cross, with six sharp edges. A newspaper in Athens, Georgia, reported the pikes to be "intimidating weapons, and in the hands of brave men, as they are, will do good execution." The company was assigned to the Savannah Brigade, under the command of Colonel William H. T. Walker, where it was said it quickly became a favored unit of its commander.[5]

Pikes were issued to other troops performing guard duty, or serving in the capacity of home guard units, far removed from the front lines. Members of the 56th Georgia Infantry were issued pikes while performing guard duty at Camp McDonald, near Kennesaw, Georgia, in the spring of 1862. When James J. Andrews and his Union raiders hijacked the locomotive "General" during their failed raid to destroy the Western and Atlantic Railroad link to Chattanooga, on April 12, 1862, the soldiers of the 56th Georgia who were on guard duty at the station were powerless to stop them, owing to the fact they were armed only with pikes, and Andrews's men had pistols.[6]

The 31st Georgia Infantry was another regiment armed with pikes. This regiment was raised in November of 1861 and was mustered into Confederate service, despite the fact that suitable weapons were not available with which to arm it. Unlike the 56th Georgia, which had been assigned to guard duty at Camp McDonald, the 31st Georgia had orders to report to Virginia, where it would be employed in frontline duty against General George B. McClellan's Army of the Potomac, then threatening Richmond. The men of the 31st Georgia knew that they were soon to be pitted against an enemy armed with modern muskets and pistols, and they felt their pikes to be little better than sharpened sticks against such weaponry. The troops protested the issuing of pikes almost to the point of open rebellion, and a mutiny in the ranks was only avoided by the timely acquisition of a sufficient supply of muskets with which to arm them before they departed for the North.[7]

It was not a matter of coincidence that the last three units mentioned all came from Georgia. The state's governor, Joseph E. Brown, was one of the strongest supporters of the use of pikes in the Confederacy. On February 20, 1862, Governor Brown issued an appeal to the blacksmiths and machine shop owners of his state to produce 10,000 pikes to arm Georgia troops. In a tone of patriotic fervor, Brown proclaimed his intention that "every army have a large reserve, armed with a good pike, and a long heavy side knife, to be brought upon the field, with a shout for victory, or when the time comes for a charge with bayonets."[8]

Major Lachlan H. McIntosh, chief of ordnance for the state of Georgia, issued specifications for the pikes to potential contractors. McIntosh directed that the pikes have heads "made of steel, well tempered, the staff to be of ash, white oak, or hickory, well seasoned—to be straight stuff, not crossgrained." McIntosh informed the potential manufacturers that they would be paid $5 for each pike that was accepted, and he provided samples that had been forged at the state arsenal and armory, at Milledgeville.[9]

Between March and September of 1862, 7,099 pikes were delivered to the state arsenal. The pikes were of two styles, with about a half dozen subtypes. The first was a cloverleaf pattern having three blades. The main blade was 10 inches long, with a leaf-shaped blade on either side, to be used as bridle cutters when pitted against cavalry. The second style featured a retractable, sword-like blade that was spring-loaded and released with great force to impale an enemy. Due to the inability of manufacturers to produce a service-able spring, these pikes rarely performed properly and were used with the blades in an exposed, fixed position. Numerous blacksmiths and artisans throughout the state manufactured pikes, but one of the prime contractors was Griswold & Gunnison, the same firm that produced 3,700 Colt Navy-pattern revolvers for the Confederate army.

By the end of 1862, the state of Georgia was able to procure an adequate number of muskets with which to arm its soldiers, and the need to issue the pikes had passed. Members of the Georgia State Assembly called Governor Brown to task to explain why the weapons had been purchased and how much public money had thus far been spent. The public was already derisively referring to the weapons as "Joe Brown Pikes," and the governor was being heavily criticized for squandering the state's limited financial resources on such antiquated weapons. Brown appeared before the legislative body on December 12, 1862, to make a full disclosure of the project. He informed the body that 7,099 pikes had been purchased for state use. Of those, 1,229 had been shipped west, at the request of President Jefferson Davis, to be used by home guard units in Alabama and Mississippi. The remaining 5,870 pikes were stored in the arsenal at Milledgeville. Brown went on to silence his crit-ics by giving historic precedent for his ordering the pikes to be manufactured, citing their successful use against Napoléon by Spanish forces serving under Wellington in 1808 and 1809. In an impassioned statement, he asked if pikes could be used to rout the troops of Napoléon, why could they not be effective in the hands of Georgia troops.[10]

There is no record of any troops engaging in combat with "Joe Brown Pikes" during General William T. Sherman's Atlanta Campaign or in his March to the Sea, both of which took place in 1864. It is probable that all of them remained stored in the Georgia State Arsenal and Armory at Milledgeville, because when that place was captured, on November 22, 1864, the 3rd Wisconsin Mounted Infantry reported burning about 5,000 pikes, along with various other supplies.[11]

In 1863, an Alabama regiment was reported to have arrived at Knoxville, Tennessee, armed only with pikes. One of these pikes can be found among the artifacts offered for sale by Army of Tennessee Civil War Artifacts, of Knoxville. The pike blade bears a very old tag with the following inscription: "Knoxville, Tenn, a whole regiment of 'Alabama Tigers' came here armed with only these 'manchets'. Before the charge on Fort Sanders on the hill overlooking the city, they were armed with rifles." This is but another example of a Confederate unit that was armed with pikes that were never used in actual combat.

There is no record of pikes ever being issued to soldiers in the Union army, but that does not mean that the North shunned them. Pikes were commonly issued to sailors in both the Union and Confederate navies. According to U.S. naval regulations, "one-fourth of the number of men composing a gun's crew ... and all the men of the Master's division on the spar deck, except those designated as boarders" were to be issued pikes to be used to repel potential boarders. This number would be multiplied by the number of guns on a ship. The pikes were to be 8 feet long, and the metal tips varied in length from 6 to 24 inches. According to regulations, the pikes were to be stored until such time as an enemy ship was to be boarded or when it was evident that the enemy was about to attempt boarding your ship. Then, they were to be handed out to the pikemen, who, along with sailors armed with cutlasses and marines armed with muskets, do close combat with the enemy. The fact is that improved technology in naval firepower made the pikes obsolete and unnecessary. Battles between naval ships during the Civil War were almost always settled, one way or another, by the cannon of the opposing vessels, and the need to board or repel boarders was not a part of Civil War maritime combat.[12]

In the final analysis, the usage of pikes in the Civil War served as a stopgap measure that put weapons in the hands of volunteers until more suitable arms could be obtained. Home guard units and garrison troops, far removed from the front lines, were the most likely candidates to be issued pikes, and even then, they were carried only until muskets or pistols could be obtained in sufficient quantity to replace them. No accounts were recorded during the war of a Confederate soldier bearing a pike actually being employed in combat. That being said, the pike, and the men who carried them, still became an integral part of Confederate military history, and the pike itself served as a symbol of Southern resolve. General John B. Gordon paid tribute to all Confederate pikemen when he wrote in his reminiscences about first seeing troops armed with the weapons. "Of course, few if any of these pikemen ever had occasion to use these warlike implements, which were worthy of the Middle Ages, but those who bore them were as gallant knights as ever leveled a lance in close quarters."[13]

Despite the fact that the Civil War proved that pikes were no longer an effective weapon in the arsenal of a modern nation's army, they continued to be used around the world well into the twentieth century. In fact, their issuance was suggested as late as World War II, when the British considered distributing them in an effort to put weapons into the hands of home guard soldiers, who were performing guard duty at various military instillations throughout the country.

CHAPTER 4

THE HORSE ARTILLERY

Horse artillery, sometimes referred to as flying artillery, was a combination of cavalry and artillery to form a fast-moving, hard-striking unit capable of being deployed quickly on a battlefield to provide either offensive or defensive support to infantry and cavalry troops. The distinguishing features of horse artillery that separated it from the rest of the artillery arm of an army were the use of light cannon or howitzers, pulled by light, two-wheeled caissons or limbers. The gun crew rode to battle atop the limber or the horses, unlike traditional artillery where many of the members of the crew marched on foot. The crews were able to reach a point on a battlefield much more quickly than traditional field artillery, and they were trained to rapidly deploy, or unlimber, their guns and bring them into action. Speed was of the essence, and the crews could re-limber and hurry off to another point on the battlefield with equal dispatch.

The first usage of the horse artillery took place in the seventeenth century, during the Thirty Years' War. Lennart Torstensson, a field marshal and military engineer for King Gustavus Adolphus of Sweden, was placed in charge of Swedish artillery. Torstensson developed a system of providing the Swedish cavalry with artillery fire support to deal with enemy infantry that served as the basis of what would later become horse artillery.

In the early eighteenth century, Russian cavalry experimented with small units of horse artillery equipped with two-pound cannon and three-pound mortars. The effectiveness of these units was observed by Frederick the Great of Prussia, who formed the first regular unit of horse artillery in 1759. The Prussian model established that every artilleryman in horse artillery service must be a part-time cavalryman. Speed and mobility was stressed through special training and drill, until the artillerists achieved lightning quickness in moving and deploying their guns. During the Seven Years'

War, the effectiveness of the Prussian horse artillery was duly observed by all the belligerents, and over the next 40 years most of the armies of Europe adopted horse artillery units of their own.

Horse artillery reached its highest point of development during the Napoleonic Wars. All of the warring countries had adopted horse artillery units by this time, but it was with the French army that this branch of service became most popular. Napoléon's army boasted eight full regiments of horse artillery, each containing six batteries of six guns. With a full complement of 288 cannon, the French horse artillery became the largest such force ever assembled by any army.[1]

England was quick to follow the example of the French. During the French Revolutionary Wars, in 1793, England organized its first unit of horse artillery, the Royal Horse Artillery. The basic unit was referred to as a troop instead of a battery, but, like the French, it contained six 6-pounder cannon. The Royal Horse Artillery initially used civilian drivers to ride the horses pulling the cannon, but by 1794, a Driver Corps was raised from within the ranks of the military. By the time of the Napoleonic Wars, the British military boasted 11 troops of horse cavalry—an imposing array of firepower, but still only about a quarter of the cannon the French had committed to their own horse artillery units.[2]

The advantages of horse artillery became quickly evident to officers in the U.S. Army as they watched with interest the employment of this new military tactic in the wars in Europe. One Continental observer chronicled the advantages horse artillery provided in an 1802 article on the subject. He noted that "the ease with which it is able to cover a certain distance compared with other artillery, and as such to occupy any given position quickly, being able to leave such a position quickly again, and to deploy in another position" resulted in the horse artillery being especially useful in numerous ways. Horse artillery was indispensable when forming the nucleus of an artillery reserve, as it could be quickly dispatched to any point on the battlefield where artillery support was needed. It was also without peers when it came to speedily occupying any favorable position to the front or flank of an army's line of battle. During a reconnaissance, the horse artillery was able to provide speedy support, and, in the case of a retreat of the reconnaissance force being needed, could cover that retreat, being able to quickly extricate itself, unlike the slow-moving foot artillery. For the same reason, horse artillery could be effectively used to cover the retreat of infantry from a battlefield, as well as rapidly covering infantry during a charge. "In support of light infantry, the horse artillery can mean a big advantage. As again, most operations are based on speed, only to be executed by the horse artillery. No other artillery is able to execute such operations."[3]

Even though U.S. officers were paying close attention to this new development in artillery warfare, no steps were taken to incorporate it into the U.S.

Officers of Battery A, 2nd U.S. Light Artillery. This unit was part of the Horse Artillery Brigade in the Army of the Potomac. (Library of Congress)

Army. At the outbreak of the War of 1812, the U.S. artillery service was in a dismal state of affairs. Many officers and men assigned to artillery units were actually serving as infantrymen on the frontier, and the weapons and equipment of the artillery were mostly in a neglected condition. In 1813, Captain Henry Thompson of Baltimore, Maryland, formed a mounted company called the 1st Baltimore Horse Artillery. Thompson's unit saw little action as horse artillery, however. A shortage of dragoon forces prompted Brigadier General John Striker to use Thompson's troopers to act as messengers, providing information on British movements between Washington and Bladensburg. In 1814, the 1st Baltimore Horse Artillery served as the personal guard to General Samuel Smith, commander of the defenses of Baltimore during the British attack on that city and Fort McHenry.[4]

Over the next 30 years, improvements were made to the artillery arm of the U.S. Army, but it was not until the Mexican-American War that the military fully embraced horse artillery as an integral part of its organization and tactics. The driving force behind the improvements in the artillery service came primarily from Captain Samuel Ringgold, a graduate of the Military

Academy at West Point in 1818. Ringgold was assigned to the artillery and, in the early 1820s, was assigned to the staff of General Winfield Scott. Ringgold attended the newly established Artillery School for Practice, at Fort Monroe, Virginia, showing such appetite for the service that he was later sent to Europe to study at the French École Polytechnique in Paris and the Military Institution at Woolwich in England. When Ringgold returned to the United States in 1838, he was instructed by the secretary of war to organize and equip a battery of light horse artillery. Over the next few years, Ringgold set to work modifying Robert Anderson's manual for artillery tactics to include the innovations for horse artillery. In his work, Ringgold combined the best tactics of the French and the British and established a truly American approach to this mobile artillery service. Following the European pattern, he organized his battery with six 6-pounder cannon and began work on training his gun crews. In a relatively short period of time, Ringgold's artillerists had attained a level of speed and efficiency in the handling of their guns that rivaled any of the horse artillery units of Europe. His unit became commonly known as Ringgold's Flying Artillery, and Ringgold himself became known as the father of modern artillery in the U.S. Army.

Despite his personal reputation and the excellent work of his battery, Ringgold was not able to convince his superiors that the new tactic of direct artillery support would work on the battlefield. Most U.S. officers still clung to the belief that the bayonet was the primary weapon of an army and felt that all other weapons were used only in an effort to get the opposing combatants close enough to engage in hand-to-hand combat. Ringgold's horse artillery got the chance to prove its worth in the Mexican-American War, when U.S. forces under the command of General Zachary Taylor were attacked by a superior Mexican force at the battle of Palo Alto on May 8, 1846. The Mexican army formed in line of battle in front of Taylor's troops, awaiting the anticipated charge of the U.S. infantry. Instead, Taylor advanced his infantry, halting them just out of range of the enemy's muskets. He then pushed forward his artillery 20 yards in advance of his line of battle, opening on the Mexican line of battle with a barrage of shot and shell. The execution of the U.S. artillerists was swift and deadly. Ulysses S. Grant, who was a junior officer in Taylor's command, noted, "The infantry stood at order arms, as spectators, watching the effect of our shells on the enemy." He observed that the U.S. artillery "cleared a perfect road" through the Mexican formation, causing the bulk of the more than 250 casualties sustained by the enemy army. When darkness brought about an end to the fighting, the Mexican army withdrew from the field, giving a complete victory to Taylor and his men. U.S. casualties were minimal in number, but they included Major Ringgold, who had been shot through both legs by an enemy artillery shell. He would die a few days later, but not before he had proved the value of his flying artillery

Ringgold's Battery unlimbered in the field. (National Archives)

on the battlefield. U.S. horse artillery would give the U.S. Army an edge in almost every engagement in the war and would prove to be the deciding factor in the battles of Buena Vista and Vera Cruz, in both of which contests the U.S. forces were severely outnumbered.[5]

The great success of the horse artillery in the Mexican-American War caused it to become an integral part of the U.S. Army, and by the outbreak of the Civil War, direct artillery support tactics had become a mainstay of battlefield planning and operations. The opening of hostilities saw the U.S. Army holding some 4,167 pieces of artillery, of which 163 were field pieces and howitzers. The Confederacy, attempting to build an army from scratch, found itself at a severe disadvantage in regard to artillery and had to initially rely on what ordnance supplies could be obtained from Federal arsenals seized within its borders. Though the South captured a large number of cannon and supplies, only 35 of them were light field pieces.[6] Though the Confederacy went to great lengths to increase the number of cannon available for its armies in the field, it was never able to close the gap between itself and the Union forces. Northern armies would hold a decided advantage in artillery throughout the war, and this superiority would be one of the strategic keys to final Union victory. Union artillery was not just superior in the number or quality of guns that it possessed, it also held an edge based on the quality of the men making up the gun crews. The U.S. Army started the war with a large corps of regular army artillerists who had been well trained and disciplined and were professionals in their craft. Though a large number of Southern artillery officers resigned their commissions to fight for the Confederacy, a significant number of Confederate batteries were made up of militia soldiers or raw recruits that had volunteered once the war began. These men would learn their

craft over the course of the next four years, but they would have to do so
against Union artillery that was largely a professional organization from the
outset of hostilities. Despite these disadvantages, the most famous commander of horse artillery and the most celebrated horse artillery unit to serve
in the war would come from the Confederate army.

John Pelham was a 22-year-old cadet at West Point when the Civil War
broke out. Being from Alabama, his sympathies were with the South, causing
him to leave the academy a few weeks prior to his graduation to offer his services to the Alabama militia, where he received a commission as a lieutenant
and was assigned to the artillery. He and his battery were ultimately sent to
Virginia, where they came under the eye of Brigadier General Joseph E.
Johnston and Colonel Jeb Stuart. At the battle of First Manassas, Pelham
handled his battery with cool efficiency and was conspicuous in averting a
crisis to the Confederate army by beating back a Union attack on Henry
House Hill. His performance on the field earned him a promotion to the rank
of captain, and, at the recommendation of General Johnston, he and his battery were assigned to Colonel Stuart to serve with his cavalry in the capacity
of horse artillery.[7]

Pelham's battery consisted of eight cannon: two 6-pounder howitzers, four
12-pounder howitzers, a 12-pounder Napoleon, and a Blakely cannon manufactured in England. There were 150 officers and men and 130 horses in the
unit to serve the eight guns. Over the winter of 1861–62, Pelham constantly
drilled and trained his artillerists until they had achieved a level of competence that equaled the most elite cannoneers in the world. Stuart's Horse
Artillery, under the command of the youthful Pelham, would undertake active
campaigning in the spring of 1862 as one of the finest artillery units on either
side. During the Peninsula Campaign, Pelham's guns covered the retreat of
General Johnston's army from Yorktown. When Union forces under the command of Major General Joe Hooker attacked Johnston's rear guard at
Williamsburg, Pelham deployed three cannon to halt the enemy advance. In
less than three hours, his gunners expended an amazing 360 rounds of ammunition into the ranks of the Federals, significantly contributing to the repulse
of Hooker's forces and allowing Johnston's army to continue its withdrawal
unimpeded. During the Seven Days Battles, Pelham's Horse Artillery accompanied General Stuart on a mission to cut McClellan's line of supplies. Upon
reaching White House on the Pamunkey River, Stuart spotted the USS
Marblehead. Two boatloads of sharpshooters were rowing toward shore,
covered by the 11-inch guns on the Union warship. Stuart ordered Pelham
to take one of his howitzers, find a favorable position, and open fire on the
Northern warship. Pelham took the gun to an elevated location with a commanding field of fire and opened a deadly barrage of shells on the deck of
the ship. His fire was so accurate that the captain of the ship recalled the

sharpshooters and sailed back down the river. Pelham pursued, stopping several times to deploy his howitzer and keep the *Marblehead* moving down the Pamunkey.[8]

During its first two campaigns of the war, Pelham's Horse Artillery had performed magnificently. In his official report, General Stuart stated "Captain John Pelham of the Horse Artillery displayed such signal ability as an artillerist, such heroic example and devotion in danger, and indomitable energy under difficulties in moving his battery, that, reluctant as I am at the chance of losing such a valuable limb from the brigade, I feel bound to ask for his promotion with the remark that either in the cavalry or artillery, no field grade is too high for his merit and capacity." Stuart's superiors agreed with his assessment, and later that summer Pelham was promoted to the rank of major. He was also given command of two more batteries: Chew's Virginia Light Artillery and Hart's South Carolina Light Artillery. By the middle of August, all three batteries of Pelham's new Horse Artillery Battalion were ready for action. The battalion performed well at the battle of Groveton and all through the Second Manassas Campaign before participating in the Confederate invasion of Maryland. At South Mountain, one of Pelham's batteries vigorously contested the advance of the Federals at Fox's Gap. On the field of Antietam, Pelham's Horse Artillery was placed on the extreme left of Lee's line of battle. When Hooker's troops advanced through Miller's cornfield against Jackson's line at daybreak on September 17, they were greeted by a destructive enfilade fire from Pelham's guns. Hooker ordered some of his cavalry and infantry to drive off the Confederate artillerists, but Pelham's gunners beat them back and continued to harass the Federal flank. When Colonel Henry Hunt brought up a battery of 20-pounder Parrott guns, the Federals finally gained the advantage. But Pelham merely limbered up his cannon and moved them a few hundred yards to the right, where they unlimbered and continued punishing the Union advance. When Hooker's corps retired, it was replaced by Major General Robert K. Mansfield's corps and then by the corps of Major General Edwin V. Sumner. Pelham's guns punished the flank of all three Federal units, contributing mightily to their repulse by inferior numbers of Confederate infantry. The historian of General Lee's artillery in the Army of Northern Virginia went so far as to state that Pelham's placement of his guns in a position that commanded the approaches to Jackson's line was one of the key tactical maneuvers of the battle.[9]

Already one of the most famous artillery commands on either side, the Pelham Horse Artillery Battalion won its greatest laurels at the battle of Fredericksburg, on December 13, 1862. On that day, the audacious artillerist took one of his 12-pounder Napoleons, along with his Blakely gun, and positioned them one-half mile in advance of Stonewall Jackson's line of battle, on the flank of Major General William B. Franklin's Grand Division. When the fog lifted from the countryside, at approximately 9:00 a.m., Pelham's two exposed guns roared into action, just as Franklin's lead division, under the command of General George G. Meade, was preparing to advance on Jackson's line. The gunners worked their pieces so rapidly that the Federal officers were convinced that two full batteries of Confederate cannon were arrayed against them. The attack against Jackson was halted as Meade turned to respond to the threat on his flank. A brigade of infantry and three artillery batteries were ordered to silence the Confederate guns. Two more batteries, from General Abner Doubleday's division, immediately behind Meade, were also ordered to join in the attack. When a detachment of Union troops tried to flank Pelham's position, they were greeted with a torrent of shot and shell that caused them to take cover and conceal themselves for the duration of the fighting. Pelham moved his cannon adroitly from position to position as he continued the unequal contest and prevented Franklin's divisions from moving forward. When his Blakely gun was knocked out of commission, a messenger arrived from General Stuart directing him to retire. Pelham told the messenger to "Tell the general I can hold my ground." Increasing the rate of fire from his remaining Napoleon, he continued to stymie the Federals, ignoring a second directive from Stuart to remove himself from harm's way. By the time Stuart's third order to retire arrived, it was 11:00 a.m. Pelham was almost out of ammunition, and he decided it was finally time to heed his superior's instructions. He and his two guns had single-handedly delayed the advance of half of the Union army for two hours. His feat was witnessed by General Lee, who declared, "It is glorious to see such courage in one so young." In his official report of the battle, Lee described him as "the gallant Pelham," and for the rest of his short career, he was known throughout the South as the Gallant Pelham.[10]

Pelham's career came to an end on March 17, 1863. He was at the home of his sweetheart, in Culpepper, when Brigadier General William W. Averell's Federal cavalry advanced on Kelly's Ford. Pelham rode with General Stuart, who was going to Kelly's Ford, where Brigadier General Fitzhugh Lee's cavalry had been ordered to contest Averell's advance. On arriving at the ford, the pair watched as the 3rd Virginia Cavalry prepared for an assault to drive the Union troopers back across the Rappahannock River. Pelham became carried away in the moment and decided to take part in the charge. He was struck in the neck by a shell, and the wound proved to be mortal. The horse artillery of Stuart's cavalry would continue to serve for the remainder of the war, adding further laurels to their already famed stature, but the Confederacy had lost its most famous and possibly its best horse artillery commander.[11]

Another Confederate horse artillery battery that gained great fame during the war was Chew's Battery. Roger Preston Chew was an 18-year-old youth from Charles Town, Virginia, when the war broke out in 1861. Despite his tender years, he raised a battery of horse artillery that became attached to

Battery M, 2nd U.S. Light Artillery, limbered and ready to move. (Library of Congress)

Stonewall Jackson's famed Laurel Brigade. He and his battery served in every engagement fought by Jackson's command. All of the officers in Chew's command were cadets from the Virginia Military Academy, in Lexington, and had been thoroughly trained soldiers. Serving in the Shenandoah Valley under Colonel Turner Ashby, and then serving under Stonewall Jackson, it is believed that Chew's Battery was the first Southern horse artillery to be engaged against the enemy in the war. Over the course of the war, Chew's gunners served in more skirmishes and battles than any other battery in the Confederate service, and earned for themselves a reputation for bravery and efficiency that was second to none. Chew's Battery became part of Stuart's Horse Artillery Battalion in the summer of 1862, when it and Hart's Battery were combined with Pelham's Battery, all under the overall command of Pelham. When that officer was killed at Kelly's Ford early in 1863, Chew was promoted to take command of the battalion. By 1865, the Stuart Horse Artillery had been expanded to five battalions of two batteries each, all under the command of the youthful Chew, who had been promoted to the rank of lieutenant colonel.[12]

On both sides, horse artillery was much more prevalent in the Eastern Theater than in the West. A large reason for this was that the battlefields of the East were more favorable to the rapid deployment of this branch of service owing to a more developed system of roads. In the Army of the Potomac, Brigadier General William F. Barry, chief of artillery for the Army of the Potomac, developed a plan in 1861 for the creation of a brigade of horse artillery from the batteries of the regular army units already in the service. Under the command of Lieutenant Colonel William Hays, the brigade was made up of five batteries from the 2nd and 3rd U.S. Artillery and served with distinction during the Peninsula Campaign. By the time the battle of Gettysburg was fought, the organization had grown to two full brigades, containing twelve batteries from the 1st, 2nd, 3rd, and 4th U.S. Artillery, as well as the 9th Michigan Battery, Light Battery H of the 3rd Pennsylvania Heavy Artillery, and the Independent Battery of the 6th New York Light Artillery. The U.S. Horse Artillery Brigade would fight in most of the major battles in which the Army of the Potomac was engaged, earning for itself an enviable reputation for military efficiency and accuracy of fire. With its solid corps of professional artillery soldiers, the U.S. Horse Artillery Brigade was a model unit for the power of horse artillery on the battlefield, and it provided tactical advantage for Union forces on numerous occasions when its firepower was responsible for turning the tide of battle.

High-ranking U.S. officers had been slow to grasp the importance of horse artillery during the Mexican-American War. Samuel Ringgold had to convince them of the true worth of the innovative concept on the battlefield. During the Civil War, field officers on both sides fully grasped the tactical and strategic value of these flying messengers of death, as can be seen by the sheer number of such units existing in the contending armies. Rapidly deployed artillery became the mainstay of all offensive and defensive maneuvers on the battlefield. Lines of battle were often held or conquered due to the efficiency and accuracy of horse artillery supporting the infantry or cavalry action. The units discussed in this chapter are but a small sampling of the many horse artillery batteries that served in the war. The artillery made up a small portion of the overall size of the contending armies. It is estimated that they accounted for only 18 percent of the Confederate army. While they rarely attained the fame or notoriety many cavalry and infantry regiments enjoyed, their contribution to the outcome on the battlefield was greatly disproportionate to their small percentage of the aggregate total of troops engaged. The effects of their lightning-quick movements would be revisited in the mechanized era, when these same principles became the foundation for the German blitzkrieg of World War II.

CHAPTER 5

THE MACHINE GUNNERS

The machine gun can trace its earliest origins to the mind of James Puckle, a London lawyer, writer, and inventor who first designed a rapid-fire weapon in 1718. The "Defense Gun" or "Puckle Gun," as it came to be known, consisted of a flintlock revolver cannon capable of firing nine 1.25-inch rounds before needing to be reloaded. The weapon, having a three-foot barrel, was mounted on a tripod and featured a revolving cylinder, much like that later adopted for handguns by Colt and Remington. Puckle developed his weapon for use by the British navy, as a defense to prevent boarding by enemy sailors. The gun was capable of firing 63 rounds in seven minutes, almost three times the rate of fire that a soldier with a musket could produce. The weapon was never adopted by the British navy, however, and it fell to inventors and arms makers of later generations to perfect Puckle's design.

Philadelphia gunsmith Joseph Belton took up the gauntlet when he offered the Continental Congress a rapid-fire weapon in 1777 to assist the fledgling nation in its war against England. The weapon utilized a single barrel, loaded with a charge much like a Roman candle, containing a number of musket balls. A single lock ignited the fused chain of charges, discharging each round in sequence. Belton reported that his device could fire as many as 16 balls in as little as five seconds. Congress commissioned Belton to build or modify 100 "Belton Flintlocks" on May 3, 1777, but cancelled the contract less than two weeks later when the gunsmith turned in a bid that was felt to be exceedingly high and an "extraordinary allowance."[1]

The first half of the nineteenth century witnessed the introduction of numerous rapid-fire weapons of various design. Some, like the pepperboxes, were repeating weapons having a rotating grouping of barrels that could be fired independently, while others employed a line of barrels that were fired together in

Members of the 96th Pennsylvania Infantry gathered around an Ager machine gun.
(Library of Congress)

volley style. The outbreak of the Civil War brought with it a flurry of inventive
activity as gun makers attempted to design weapons that would be acceptable
for military use. One inventor, Wilson Ager (or Agar), developed a highly serv-
iceable machine gun that was ready for production in the early days of the war.

J. D. Mills of New York was engaged to sell the invention to the
government, and Mills was successful in setting up a demonstration of the
weapon with President Lincoln. In June of 1861, Lincoln and Mills met in
the loft of a carriage shop near Willard's Hotel. The machine gun was
mounted on artillery wheels, and above the barrel was a hopper filled with
blank cartridges. The turning of a hand crank to the rear of the barrel dropped
the shells into a revolving cylinder, one at a time, where they were struck by a
firing pin and ejected. Mills introduced the weapon as the Union Repeating
Gun, but when Lincoln examined the hopper and crank he quickly stated that
it put him in mind of a coffee mill. The name stuck. For the rest of the war this
machine gun would be known as the coffee mill gun.[2] The weapon fired a .58
caliber cartridge, had a range of 1,000 yards, and could maintain a sustained
fire of 120 rounds per minute.[3] Lincoln was favorably impressed by the
weapon and would end up placing an order for 10 of the machine guns on
his own initiative. The War Department would eventually order 54 additional
"coffee mill guns," with the vast majority going to General George B.
McClellan's Army of the Potomac.[4]

Ordnance Department officers quickly condemned the weapon for using
too much ammunition, and most army officers failed to realize the potential

the new innovation had on the battlefield. The machine guns were primarily used defensively, to guard bridges or narrow passes. They were always placed in the hands of infantrymen or artillerymen who had not been specifically trained to use them, as machine gun tactics had yet to be developed. Even so, a number of the coffee mill guns did find their way to the battlefield, where their performance paved the way for later development of the technology.

Two of the machine guns were issued to Colonel John Geary, commander of the 28th Pennsylvania Infantry, stationed at Harpers Ferry, Virginia. One of the soldiers in his regiment said the weapon looked like a "sausage machine" and stated it was "fired by turning a crank, the faster you turn it the more Rebels it will kill." Colonel Geary received his coffee mill guns the beginning of January 1862, and it is probable, though not recorded, that they were used in combat for the first time during some of the numerous skirmishes his regiment took part in during January and February of that year. There is proof of the weapon being used on March 29, 1862, at Middleburg, Virginia, when a coffee mill gun was used against Confederate cavalry, cutting the enemy to pieces at a range of 800 yards and causing their precipitate flight from the field. Despite this, Geary returned his guns to Washington on April 28, stating that they were "inefficient and unsafe to the operators."[5]

Major General John C. Frémont had an entirely different impression of Ager's invention. He had also received two of the machine guns for use with his forces operating in what would later become West Virginia. Frémont embraced the technology and felt that the weapons would be beneficial to his command, so much so that he petitioned the War Department that he be sent 16 more of them at once. His request was denied, as all of the coffee mill guns purchased by the government were already assigned, and there were no more available.[6]

General McClellan took several of Ager's machine guns along with the Army of the Potomac when it embarked on the Peninsula Campaign in the spring of 1862. In April of 1862, six of the coffee mill guns were deployed against the Confederate defenses of Yorktown by Colonel Charles Van Wyck's 56th New York Infantry. A *New York Post* reporter was on hand and wrote, "The balls flew thick and fast, and the Yankee invention must have astonished the other side." The weapons were used several more times during the course of the campaign. On June 28, 1862, Private George Wills of the 48th Pennsylvania Infantry became the first machine gunner to be wounded in combat when he was struck while firing his gun at an engagement at Golding's Farm, Virginia.[7]

Following the conclusion of the Peninsula Campaign, most of the Ager machine guns from the Army of the Potomac were returned to the Ordnance Department and were placed in storage in Washington. Major General William S. Rosecrans requested several of the weapons for his Army of the Cumberland during the Tullahoma Campaign of 1863. The guns were shipped west, but a delay in transit prevented them from arriving before Rosecrans's army had fought and lost the battle of Chickamauga. Captain David Porter of the Union navy ordered four of the guns to be used on ships performing duty on the Mississippi River. During the Vicksburg Campaign, Major General William T. Sherman became the first high-ranking casualty of machine gun fire when a sliver from a fired cartridge from an Ager gun struck him in the leg, causing a superficial wound.[8]

Another early machine gun was invented by Josephus Requa, a New York dentist who had been apprenticed to gunsmith William Billinghurst as a boy. Owing to this apprenticeship, Requa had long been fascinated with the construction of firearms. When the Civil War broke out, Albert Mack, a friend of Requa's, suggested that the Union army was in need of a rapid-fire weapon. After drawing a preliminary design, Requa went to see his old mentor Billinghurst. The design called for a battery of 25 two-foot rifle barrels mounted horizontally on a light frame, and mounted on a two-wheeled carriage. Twenty-five metallic cartridges of .52 caliber were mounted on a steel slip and loaded into the breech of the barrels as a unit. A single percussion cap fired all 25 rounds in a volley. A crew of three men was needed to service the weapon, and with minimal practice it was possible to fire 7 volleys or 175 rounds per minute. The individual barrels could be raised or lowered to account for distance and could be fanned out to create a larger firing pattern. This was also the first rapid-fire weapon to be designed to use cartridges with metal casings instead of the paper cartridges other inventors used in their creations. Billinghurst was intrigued by the design, and the two men constructed a scale model by July 11, 1861. The model proved to be acceptable, so the pair decided to build a full-sized gun, at the cost of $500. Requa traveled to Washington in April of 1862, hoping to secure an appointment with Brigadier General James Ripley, the chief of ordnance procurement, to sell his machine gun to the government. Requa found Ripley to be hesitant to embrace new technology, and his invention was dismissed without a trial as being too wasteful of ammunition. Requa then went to see President Lincoln, whom he found to be a more willing listener. Lincoln provided Requa with an introduction to Ripley, but it took the president's personal intervention to secure a test of the weapon. On May 12, 1862, the Billinghurst-Requa Volley Gun was finally put through its paces by the Ordnance Department. The results were favorable enough to schedule a second test on May 24. It was concluded that the weapon performed well in actual usage and would be an asset to the Union army.[9]

Requa had exhausted all of his financial assets in building and promoting his machine gun and was forced to seek backing for the project. He scheduled a demonstration of his weapon in Rochester, New York, for the purpose of convincing possible investors. The demonstration was a huge success, and

Requa obtained the money necessary to build a number of guns. Albert Mack, the man who had convinced Requa to construct the machine gun, was among the first to benefit from its invention. Mack had become a captain in the 18th Independent Battery, New York Light Artillery, and his unit was armed with the first Requa guns to be manufactured. The 18th Independent Battery was assigned to duty in New Orleans, which is where the Requa guns were deployed. Ammunition for the guns was shipped separately and failed to arrive in the city, making the guns nothing more than a curiosity, however. Mack would use the guns on other fields as the war progressed, putting them to use at Port Hudson, Mississippi, and at Mobile and Montgomery, Alabama. The U.S. government never purchased the guns, but a number of individual regiments secured them for use. Their most notable service came at Fort Sumter, South Carolina, in September of 1863 and at Cold Harbor, Virginia, in June of 1864.[10] Most Requa guns were used for defensive purposes. Their pattern of fire made them perfect to command narrow approaches through mountain passes or across bridges. Their usage in such circumstances became so common that they were nicknamed "covered bridge guns" by many in the military. The U.S. Army did not issue a final report on the efficiency of the Requa guns until 1866. This report confirmed the findings of the tests that had been conducted in 1862, prompting the government to order five of the weapons for its arsenal.

The Confederates were quick to counter Union efforts in the field of rapid-fire weapons, developing several different models of machine guns. Captain R. S. Williams invented a functional machine gun in the early days of the war that was adopted by the Bureau of Ordnance, C.S.A. The Williams Machine Gun fired a 1-pound, 1.57-caliber, paper cartridge shell. The four-foot barrel was mounted on a howitzer carriage. It was operated through the use of a hand crank on the right side of the weapon, which alternately retracted and pushed forward the breechblock. A striker would fire when the block was fully closed, discharging the cartridge. Self-consuming paper cartridges were fed by hand into the loading recess of the reciprocating breechblock. The machine gun had a rate of fire of 65 rounds per minute at a maximum range of 2,000 yards and proved to be highly reliable. Its only defect was that extended firing could cause the breech to expand from the heat, resulting in a failure of the lock to secure properly. When this took place, the machine gun would have to be allowed to cool for a sufficient time before firing again. Seven batteries of six guns each were manufactured by the Confederacy for military use.[11]

The first reported use of the Williams Machine Gun took place on May 31, 1862, at the battle of Seven Pines, Virginia. Captain Williams commanded a battery of the guns attached to Brigadier General George E. Pickett's brigade during that engagement. The weapons delivered a devastating fire against the

Union troops that faced them and proved completely successful in driving them from the field. The Williams Machine Gun was used throughout the war, seeing service in both Eastern and Western Theaters. From Blue Springs, Tennessee, to Petersburg, Virginia, the Williams Machine Gun was a scourge to Union troops who faced it. Captain T. T. Allen of the 7th Ohio Cavalry came face to face with the Williams Machine Gun at the battle of Blue Springs. He would later write in amazement of the deadly fire generated by these guns. One of the weapons was captured at Danville, Virginia, in April of 1865 and was sent to West Point as a trophy of war. The firing mechanism of the Williams Machine Gun was later adapted to create the first breech-loading field artillery adopted by the U.S. Army.[12]

The Vandenberg Volley Gun was invented by General Origen Vandenberg and was not really a machine gun, firing volleys of bullets instead of a sustained fire. It consisted of numerous individual barrels contained in a tube resembling a cannon. Vandenberg guns were constructed having from 45 to 451 individual barrels, firing a .45-caliber bullet at a maximum range of 2,500 yards. General Vandenberg offered the weapon to the U.S. Army, but ordnance tests were unfavorable. The gun was found to be difficult to load and took one man up to nine hours to clean. Vandenberg then offered the gun to the Confederacy, where it met with more favorable results. The Confederate government purchased a few, and Governor Zebulon Vance bought one for the state of North Carolina. The guns saw limited use in the war, but records indicate that one saw service during the siege of Petersburg.[13]

The South also adopted a rapid-fire cannon called the Confederate Cannon. The weapon was breech loading, firing a two-inch shell and using a five-shot cylinder. Only a few Confederate Cannon were built by the Confederacy, but one was definitely used during the siege of Petersburg. Major General Josiah Gorgas, C.S.A., chief of the Confederate Ordnance Department, invented an 18-shot machine gun of 1.25 caliber, having a single barrel and a horizontal magazine ring. The weapon performed well in tests but was not able to be put into production before the end of the war.

By far the most successful machine gun to come out of the Civil War was the Gatling Gun. Designed by Richard J. Gatling, an inventor from Indianapolis, Indiana, the weapon would become one of the most famous firearms of the nineteenth century. The machine gun he developed had six revolving barrels that were turned by a crank. Each barrel had its own bolt, and cocking and firing were performed by a gear-driven cam action. The original design used a paper cartridge of .58 caliber, but Gatling soon settled on adopting a copper-cased rim-fire cartridge instead. The machine gun could produce a sustained fire of 150 rounds per minute, and the fact that it utilized multiple barrels eliminated the problems of overheating from extended use. Gatling received a patent for his invention in November of 1862 and attempted to sell the guns to the Federal government. This proved to be an uphill battle. The Ordnance Department was not quick to incorporate new technology into the military and looked upon Gatling's invention with the same disparaging contempt it had viewed other rapid-fire weapon proposals. President Lincoln, usually a proponent of advanced weaponry, had become somewhat disillusioned with machine guns by this time. The Ager gun had not proved to be the master of the battlefield as Lincoln believed it would, and the president was not willing to personally back another such invention. Then there was the question of Gatling's loyalty to the cause. Originally born and raised in North Carolina, the inventor was accused of being a Southern sympathizer. He was also accused of being a leading member in the Order of American Knights, an organization of Southern supporters actively engaged in aiding the Confederate cause. Gatling had established his manufacturing facilities for constructing his Gatling Guns in Cincinnati, Ohio, and that provided further reason to question his allegiance. Cincinnati's position, just across the Ohio River from Kentucky, gave rise to the belief in some government sectors that Gatling intended to manufacture the weapons only to turn them over to the Confederacy. Suspicions over Gatling's loyalty served to keep his machine gun in limbo and deprived the Union army of the most efficient rapid-fire weapon devised during the Civil War.

Major General Ben Butler had no qualms about Gatling's political affiliations. After seeing a demonstration of the Gatling gun in action, he placed an order for 12 of the weapons, with 12,000 rounds of ammunition, at a cost of $12,000. Most of the Gatling Guns purchased by Butler were used aboard ships operating on the James River, but at least two of them were assigned to infantry with his Army of the James. Both of these guns saw service during the siege of Petersburg. The Gatling Gun was used with deadly effect in the streets of New York in the summer of 1863. Three of the weapons had been purchased to guard the *New York Times* newspaper building, and these guns were used against the mob that tried to storm the office during the New York Draft Riots. The U.S. government did not officially adopt the Gatling Gun until August of 1866, more than a year after the end of the war. Even so, the United States became the first country in the world to adopt a machine gun into its arsenal, and the course of future wars would be forever changed.[14]

It is apparent that neither side fully appreciated the tactical importance of a reliable machine gun on the battlefield during the Civil War, though it would seem those in the South had a firmer grasp of the realities than did their Northern counterparts. In the Union army, machine guns were typically given to infantry units, where they were serviced by soldiers unaccustomed to weapons more sophisticated than the standard-issue .58-caliber musket. There was no attempt made by the Union to develop any procedures or tactics specific to this new form of weapon, and it is little wonder that their

The Gatling gun could have dramatically altered the war if it had been embraced by the Union army. As it was, the gun would have to wait to prove its full value on the battlefield. (Photo by Max Smith)

performance on the field of battle was less than spectacular. In the South, the prevailing tendency was to issue machine guns to artillery units, not infantry. While this was still not the optimum use of the weapons, it did place them in the hands of soldiers accustomed to fighting with heavy ordnance instead of shoulder arms. This difference may account for the fact that, while the Ager Machine Gun had been retired from service long before the end of hostilities, the Williams Machine Gun continued to be used until the end of the war. In any event, the machine guns invented during the Civil War served to show the world what was possible in the field of military technology, and the world was watching. The Gatling Gun would serve as a staple in many of the armies of the world for half a century and would pave the way for the machine guns that would dominate the battlefields of World War I.

CHAPTER 6

THE ROCKET BATTALION

The development of the rocket battalions of the Civil War era traced their origins to ancient China and the discovery of gunpowder in the third century BC. As early as 1045, the Chinese recorded rockets, called fire arrows, as part of their military arsenal. In the thirteenth century, the Chinese were compelled to use rocket technology to combat the threat posed by the Mongolian hordes, and several new styles were developed. The Mongols quickly adopted rockets into their own military, and by 1241 they were used against Europeans at the battle of Sejo. By 1300, rockets were to be found in the arsenals of several European armies.

In 1647, *The Art of Gunnery* was published in London, containing 43 pages on the subject of rockets. Interest waned during the latter part of the seventeenth century, as rockets fell out of favor with most military professionals in Europe. For more than one hundred years, rocket technology remained dormant, as the armies of Europe concentrated their heavy firepower on more conventional artillery. Rockets were known to have a much longer range than artillery, but they were also highly inaccurate, and for that reason declined into disfavor. Rockets did not capture the imagination of the European military again until the dawn of the nineteenth century. British and French armies fighting in India were confronted by native forces relying heavily upon rockets for their artillery arm. While the French continued to rely almost solely on artillery, the British experimented with various designs of barrage rockets. Sir William Congreve developed a series of rockets weighing from 18 to 60 pounds. In order to improve the accuracy of his rockets, Congreve attached a stick or tail to the rocket tube. With an effective range of up to two miles, Congreve rockets became a favorite long-range weapon of the British military, though they remained largely inaccurate. They were used in the

Napoleonic Wars and in the War of 1812, where Congreve rockets at the battle of Fort McHenry provided the rockets' red glare for Francis Scott Key's Star-Spangled Banner. Americans adopted rockets of their own in the War of 1812, and General Winfield Scott used them in his campaign against Mexico City in the Mexican-American War.

Rockets once more fell into disfavor by the middle of the 1800s, as improvements in artillery increased the range and accuracy of those weapons. The outbreak of the Civil War brought with it a resurgence of interest in rocket technology. The old rockets in the Federal arsenal from the Mexican-American War were found to be deteriorated to the point of being useless, however, and new weapons had to be developed. Thomas W. Lion stepped forward to assume a role of leadership in this endeavor. Lion had been an officer in the British army, attached to the artillery. He was able to convince New York state officials that he could construct rockets, as well as a firing device, and was accordingly commissioned a major and given permission to raise a rocket battalion. Approximately 160 men enlisted. The men were later divided between two batteries of what was to become the New York Rocket Battalion, the first such unit raised by either side in the war. Lion made good on his claim to be able to construct rockets, and he oversaw the manufacture of a substantial number of the explosive devices, measuring from 12 to 20 inches long and from 2 to 3 inches wide. His delivery system consisted of metal tubes, several feet long, supported on a sort of "A" frame. Distance was accounted for by means of adjusting the elevation of the rocket and estimating the arc that was necessary to reach the target.[1]

The New York Rocket Battalion was organized in Albany, New York, on December 5, 1861, and was mustered into Federal service by December 7. The unit left the state on December 9, assigned for duty in the defenses of Washington. The New York Rocket Battalion served in the fortifications around the capital until May of 1862, during which time Lion had ample opportunity to test his rockets. Regrettably, many of the missiles proved to be defective. Some of them failed to gain altitude once ignited, wildly hissing along the ground before detonating far short of the targets. When the rockets did perform properly, it was reported that they could fly for a distance of three miles. The problem was that they rarely performed properly. The military quickly lost faith in both Major Lion and his rockets. The battalion was later transferred to North Carolina, where it was issued traditional artillery pieces and was redesignated the 23rd and 24th Batteries, New York Light Artillery. Lion subsequently resigned his commission and quit the service with the abandonment of the rocket project.[2]

The New York Rocket Battalion was the first unit to be armed with rockets, but the honor of being the first to use the weapons in combat went to other members of the Union army. Major General George B. McClellan took a substantial quantity of rockets with him when his Army of the Potomac embarked on the Peninsula Campaign in the spring of 1862. A few rockets were fired at the Confederate defenders of Yorktown by untrained and inexperienced artillerists in the spring of 1862, with minimal results. During the battle of Gaines's Mill, Virginia, on June 22, 1862, the Confederates captured 22 cannon and a number of rockets from the Army of the Potomac.[3] A quantity of these rockets ended up in the hands of Brigadier General James E. B. "Jeb" Stuart's cavalry, where they were turned over to Stuart's Horse Artillery, under the command of Captain John Pelham. Following the Confederate defeat in the battle of Malvern Hill, Stuart followed the retiring Federals to their base camp at Harrison's Landing. He discovered that an elevation known locally as Evelington Heights commanded the Union camp but was guarded by only a small detachment of Federal cavalry. On July 3, 1862, Stuart brushed aside these Union troopers and took command of the hill. Spread out before him on the ground below was a city of white tents belonging to the Army of the Potomac. Stuart decided to take the initiative, and he called Pelham forward with his artillery to shell the camp. But Pelham's guns had played a prominent part in the fighting that had taken place the preceding week, known as the Seven Days Battles, and he was critically short on ammunition. Pelham decided to augment his arsenal by using some of the captured rockets. When the barrage began, the hissing of rockets complemented the howitzer shells of Pelham's guns. Stuart reported that the rockets flew straight but when they struck the ground they often bounced and changed trajectory before exploding. Several of them hit in the camp and then whizzed back toward Evelington Heights to detonate. All in all, they caused more fear than damage. Several Union mules were wounded by the explosions, but only one Federal soldier was reported as being a casualty. Colonel James T. Kirk of the 10th Pennsylvania Reserves wrote that one of his men was wounded by a rocket fired from "a sort of gun carriage." Stuart was unimpressed by the performance of the rockets, and they were never again used by his horse artillery.[4]

Despite the lackluster performance of the rockets used against the Federals at Harrison's Landing, it would be the Confederates who continued to experiment with rocket technology during the war. Possibly this was because the Confederacy, facing overwhelming odds in Union manpower and materials, felt the need to make up for its deficiencies with scientific technology. Union artillery enjoyed a significant advantage in both numbers and quality of weapons throughout the war, and the development of reliable, inexpensive rockets could serve to offset that advantage and place the Confederate military on a more even footing.

Julius G. Kellersberger would become the commander of the Confederate Rocket Battalion in April of 1864, based in Houston, Texas. Little did anyone know at that time that Houston would become a center for NASA and the U.S. space program nearly a century later. Kellersberger was born in Switzerland in 1821 and received an education in engineering and military science at the military academy of Austria. At the age of 25, he was named superintendent of the Austrian Army Arsenal in Wiener Neustadt. Kellersberger resigned his position in 1847 to immigrate to the United States, where he hoped find fame and fortune. His engineering training quickly landed him a job as a surveyor in New York City's Central Park, but the position was short-lived. Kellersberger had met and fallen in love with Caroline Bauch during the voyage across the Atlantic, and he followed his heart to Texas, where the Bauch family had settled. Kellersberger married Caroline, and the couple moved to California, where Julius hoped to secure employment during the booming days of the gold rush. He was hired to survey the original town of Oakland and in 1853 was appointed engineer for the town. In 1855, Kellersberger was appointed deputy surveyor-general of California. He served in this capacity until 1857, when he was removed from office because of the political spoils system. Kellersberger then traveled to Mexico, where he accepted a position to survey the right of way for the Isthmus of Tehuantepec Railroad. Julius worked on the railroad until the outbreak of the Civil War, when he returned to Texas. Brigadier General Paul Hebert commissioned Kellersberger as a captain of artillery and assigned him to engineering duty constructing the defenses of Galveston.[5]

In the spring of 1862, Kellersberger was promoted to the rank of major and appointed chief engineer of East Texas. He was transferred to the Sabine area and charged with the responsibility of improving the defenses of the region. The improvements made to the fortifications in the Sabine area were instrumental in allowing the Confederate forces to maintain control of the region for the remainder of the war. Late in 1863, Kellersberger was reassigned to Austin, where he was once more to supervise the construction of fortifications. By April 1864 the defenses were completed, and Kellersberger was promoted to lieutenant colonel and transferred to Houston, where he was appointed superintendent of the Houston Foundry. It was at this time that he organized the first and only rocket battalion in the Confederate army. Kellersberger had previously made the acquaintance of a young lieutenant by the name of Schroeder who had served in a rocket battery in the German army. Schroeder had been a lieutenant in a rocket battery at the battle of Comorn in the Austro-Hungarian War and declared that he had learned all the secrets of constructing the weapons. Kellersberger had attended maneuvers while commanding the Austrian Army Arsenal, where he had witnessed displays of rocket technology. Intrigued by Schroeder's claims, he allowed the lieutenant to experiment with the project. A half-dozen rockets were manufactured, having grenade heads containing six pounds of explosive.

Schroeder also constructed a three-foot rocket stand from which to launch his missiles. Tests of the rockets were conducted in front of several high-ranking Confederate officers, including Major General John B. Magruder. All of the rockets performed with satisfactory results, and it seemed as if the Confederate rocket service was about to be born. The only problem was that the Confederacy was dreadfully short on many of the chemicals needed to construct the rockets. Saltpeter and brimstone were almost nonexistent in the South. Further experimentation with rockets would have to wait until some of these chemicals could be obtained or until suitable substitutes could be found. In the summer of 1864, a rich bed of saltpeter was discovered near San Antonio, and General Magruder directed that the rocket experimentation be resumed. Colonel Kellersberger built a workshop for Schroeder on the foundry grounds and assigned a crew of soldiers and slaves to him. Schroeder was forced to make numerous substitutions in the manufacturing of his rockets, including the use of tin to replace the normal copper-lead alloy usually used in making the rods. The fact that proper materials could not be obtained caused Kellersberger to quickly lose faith in the project, but Schroeder took to the work with a passion. In a relatively short period of time, Schroeder and his crew were able to construct more than one thousand rockets. Fifty soldiers were chosen to form the rocket battalion, under the command of two lieutenants, with Schroeder serving as the senior lieutenant. The unit was officially designated as Rocket Battery No. 1 in correspondence from General Magruder. The rocketeers drilled regularly with three-foot rockets and on the surface appeared to be perfecting their craft. When General Magruder ordered a demonstration of the weapons for himself, his staff, and a number of local ladies, Colonel Kellersberger became concerned over the reliability of the rockets. He directed Schroeder to conduct a test firing of the missiles prior to the demonstration for General Magruder. Twelve rockets were selected, without grenade warheads, and were placed in the launchers. Colonel Kellersberger stated that the "first rocket went correctly a hundred yards, hit the ground by a tree, ricocheted, struck directly behind my horse, and burrowed into the ground. I had great difficulty in controlling my horse and proceeded to take up a more conservative spot from which to observe. The second missile sank to earth immediately, making three or four zigzags— none of which were in the proper direction. A number of our rockets ran away. There was a hellish smoke and a deafening noise, which of course threw fear into man and beast alike. Our lieutenant [Schroeder] was the only one unperturbed. He apologized, saying that he was not able to secure the correct chemicals, a circumstance of which he was well aware prior to all this."[6]

Because of these failed results, Kellersberger tried to postpone the official demonstration of the weapons until such time as the necessary chemicals for the rockets could be obtained. General Magruder refused to grant the extension. He had already sent invitations to the event to a number of civilians and was not about to cancel. The demonstration would proceed as scheduled, regardless of Kellersberger's concerns. When the appointed day arrived, the men of the rocket battery eagerly prepared for their moment of glory. All anticipated that they would be officially recognized for their trailblazing work on the rocket project, and many probably looked forward to distinction on the field of battle. Colonel Kellersberger held no such delusions. In fact, he became so ill with a headache that he was forced to excuse himself from the proceedings. General Magruder, his staff, and a number of local ladies spread out the contents of picnic baskets as they prepared to watch the pyrotechnic display. Unfortunately, this demonstration proved to be even more disastrous than the first test had been. "One rocket burst on its launching stand, one tore the stand down with it, and a hellish chaos broke forth. No horse could be held and the picnic turned out to be a general flight to safety!" General Magruder had seen enough. That night he sent an order to Colonel Kellersberger stating, "Rocket Battery No. 1, the professor's army of Texas, is herewith dissolved. Officers and men will resume their previous assignments in their regiments; all material, equipment, tools, and munitions will be turned over to Lieutenant-Colonel Kellersberger, to whom Lieutenant Schroder will report for further duty." Kellersberger was obviously relieved that the project had been scuttled, for that "same night I directed that the remaining 1,200 rockets be tossed into the deepest part of the river, where they would have time to moulder away. So ended the first and last rocket battery in Texas."[7]

Given the fact that Lieutenant Schroeder's first rockets performed in a satisfactory manner, it is safe to conclude that the lack of suitable chemicals and materials led to the failure of the project. Had Kellersberger been able to provide Schroeder with the copper, lead, brimstone, and other items crucial for the manufacture of rockets, it is probable that the Confederate Rocket Battalion might have seen action against the Federal army. As it was, the experiment became more of a lesson on what did not work than a contributing chapter in the field of rocket development.

One last use of rockets in the Civil War concerns a story of questionable reliability, first reported in the 1950s. It seems that the 90-year-old son of a Confederate agent to England claimed that his father was able to convince Lord Kelvin to provide liquefied oxygen to go along with a turbine provided by German physicist Ernst Mach for the construction of a two-stage rocket by the Confederacy. According to the report, the rocket was constructed in a shed along the banks of the James River and, when completed, was to be fired at Washington, some one hundred miles distant. A deep hole was made in the riverbank into which was placed a tube made from the barrels of naval guns. Matthew Fontaine Maury, the chief of sea coast, river, and harbor defenses for the Confederacy, was supposed to have calculated the trajectory for the missile. The letters CSA were carved into the nose cone, and President Jefferson Davis and other officials were supposed to have signed their names on the warhead. In early March of 1865, the missile was to have been launched against Washington. A network of scouts were placed at intervals between Richmond and Washington to observe the flight of the rocket. According to the story, the first stage of the rocket was seen to fall off and was in fact recovered and returned to the shed where it had been constructed. No one ever witnessed the rocket fall to earth, however, and it definitely never reached its destination at Washington. Did the rocket clear the earth's atmosphere and become the first U.S. space junk to orbit our planet? While it is intriguing to speculate that somewhere out in space there is a satellite bearing the inscription CSA, most historians view this story to be nothing more than whim and fancy. The individual making the claim stated that he had documentary proof of the incident, but he did not want to make it public. As the records of the Confederate government were destroyed when Richmond fell in April of 1865, the ability to prove or disprove the story has forever been lost, and one is left to believe what one will. But the fact that liquefied oxygen was to have been used, at a date preceding the commonly accepted time of its discovery, tends to place this story in the category of folklore.[8]

CHAPTER 7

THE CHEMICAL CORPS

The use of chemicals in warfare dates back to ancient times, and it is unknown exactly when chemical agents were first used against an enemy. The first recorded usage is in the fourth century BC, when archers in India were reported to have dipped their arrows in snake venom. During this same time period, the Greeks and Chinese were reported to have used smoke to combat enemies that were digging tunnels.[1] During the Middle Ages and Renaissance, advances in chemical technology led to more sophisticated applications in the field of chemical warfare. During the siege of Belgrade in 1456, poison clouds were created through the burning of chlorine-soaked rags. Leonardo da Vinci even designed a shell containing arsenic and sulfur intended for use against enemy warships.[2]

By the time of the Civil War, advancements in chemical technology had produced a number of new agents that could be applied to warfare. These included hydrogen cyanide, phosgene, mustard gas, and cacodyl. Most of these chemicals found their origins in the fields of manufacturing or medicine, but they were quickly adapted to military use. Even so, chemicals were seldom used on the battlefield, as most countries viewed their employment to be barbarous and uncivilized.

Chemical and biological warfare was advocated by both sides during the Civil War, and there were a few instances where it was attempted. Neither side, however, formed a specific unit, a chemical corps, to facilitate the development and deployment of chemical or biological agents. Instead, the proposals for the use of such weapons came largely from individuals in the academic and medical fields. One such man was John W. Doughty, a New York City educator. Doughty wrote a letter to the War Department on April 5, 1862, proposing the use of artillery shells containing chlorine to drive Confederate soldiers away from their defensive works, making it easier for the assaulting Union troops to capture them.[3] Doughty wrote,

> If the shell should explode over the heads of the enemy, the gas would, by its great specific gravity, rapidly fall to the ground; the men could not dodge it, and their first intimation of its presence would be by its inhalation, which would most effectually disqualify every man for service that was within the circle of its influence; rendering the disarming and capturing of them as certain as though both their legs were broken.

Doughty also pointed out the benefits of using such shells against enemy warships, pointing out that they could be employed without placing Union soldiers or sailors in danger.

> It may be asked if the gas which drove the enemy from his guns, would not prevent the attacking party who used the gas, from taking possession of the abandoned position. I answer it would not. For this shell does not, like the Chinese stink-pots, deposit a material emitting a deleterious gas lighter than the atmosphere, but suddenly projects into the air, a free gas much heavier than the atmosphere, which does its work as it descends to the earth, where it is soon absorbed.

Doughty's proposed shell would go on to become a model for chemical weapons of the twentieth century. It contained two compartments, one filled with chlorine and the other with an explosive charge. The detonation of the explosives would release the chemical to do its work, making the powder charge a delivery system instead of an offensive weapon. Doughty provided the War Department with a detailed sketch of his proposed shell, which by all accounts should have worked precisely as he had stated, but the Union military never acted on his idea, and the Doughty shell was never produced for the U.S. Army.[4]

Doughty was not the first to propose the use of poison gas in the Civil War. That honor seems to go to Private Isham Walker of the Confederate army. In 1861, Private Walker wrote to Confederate Secretary of War Lucius Walker suggesting that poison gas be used against the Union defenders of Fort Pickens, at Pensacola, Florida. Walker proposed that the gas be released over the fort through the use of a lighter-than-air balloon that could fly directly over the works. Walker's plan was never acted upon, and the application of chemical warfare from the air would have to wait for future wars.[5]

In April of 1862, Commodore Louis M. Goldsborough sent a letter to Assistant Secretary of the Navy Gustavus V. Fox, stating he had uncovered intelligence concerning a Confederate plot to use chloroform against the crew of the USS *Monitor.* According to Goldsborough, the crew of the CSS *Merrimac* had been provided with grappling hooks and wedges with which to assault the *Monitor*. The grappling hooks were to be used to assist in boarding the Union ironclad, and the wedges were to be used to prevent the turret's revolving. Once the *Monitor* was boarded and its turret incapacitated, the Confederates planned to use chloroform to render the Union sailors insensible and thereby capture the vessel. The plan was never carried out, however, and the *Merrimac* had to be scuttled by its own crew when Union forces captured its port. A Union man also proposed the use of chloroform in the spring of 1862 to render the defenders of the Confederate fortifications at Yorktown, Virginia, and Corinth, Mississippi, incapable of performing their duty. Joseph Lott of Hartford, Connecticut, advocated the use of hand-pump fire engines to spray chloroform at the defenders of Confederate fortifications. The chloroform would not injure the enemy in any way, but it would render them senseless and unable to resist a Union attack.[6] Theoretically, Lott's plan would have worked, but, unlike Doughty's shell, it lacked a reliable form of delivery. Hand-pump fire engines of the day did not have the capacity to spray liquid over any great distance, meaning that the crew would have to come within easy musket range of the enemy in order to dispense the chloroform. It is highly doubtful that Lott's plan would have been feasible under battlefield conditions, as Confederate defenders would surely have shot down any troops approaching their works with a fire engine.

As the conflict progressed, the evolution of trench warfare presented a new set of problems to be overcome by the commanders of the Union and Confederate armies. Frontal attacks against even hastily constructed fieldworks proved to be bloody work, and the casualties sustained in making such assaults prompted some to seek alternative methods of prying an enemy out of their trenches. Forrest Shepherd, a professor of agricultural chemistry at the Western Reserve University, developed a scheme he hoped would break the deadlock in the trenches around Petersburg and Richmond in 1864. Shepherd advocated using a gaseous cloud, composed of hydrochloric and sulfuric acid, that would incapacitate the Confederate troops and render them defenseless to resist a Union attack. Shepherd stated

> that by mingling strong sulfuric acid with strong hydrochloric, or muriatic acid on a broad surface like a shovel or shallow pan, a dense white cloud is at once formed, and being slightly heavier than the atmosphere, rests upon the ground and is high enough to conceal the operator behind it. This may easily be continued by additional sprinkling of the two acids and a light breeze will waft it forward.

Shepherd went on to explain that

> When the cloud strikes a man it sets him to coughing, sneezing, etc., but does not kill him, while it would effectually prevent him from firing a gun, or if he

should fire, to aim at his object. It has occurred to me that Gen. Burnside, with his colored troops might, on a dark night, with a gentle breeze favorable, surprise and capture the strongholds of Petersburg, or Fort Darling, perhaps without loss or shedding of blood.

Shepherd's proposal was flawed in two ways. First, the amount of hydrochloric and sulfuric acid needed to create a cloud capable of covering the distance between the opposing lines and then incapacitating the enemy defenders created a nightmare of both logistics and supply. Second, Shepherd's plan failed to take into account atmospheric conditions. Favorable breezes can instantly turn, and the gaseous cloud Shepherd proposed might have just as easily been blown over Union troops, incapacitating them to resist a Confederate charge. For whatever reason, Shepherd's plan was never acted on by the War Department.

Brigadier General William N. Pendleton, chief of artillery for the Army of Northern Virginia, also proposed the use of chemical weapons during the siege of Petersburg. Pendleton wished to find a way to break the grip of General Ulysses S. Grant's army on the besieged Confederates, and he felt that chemical weapons might just do the trick. Like Doughty, Pendleton planned to use artillery shells as a method of distributing the gas and wished to combine them, in some manner, with stink balls that had been used by the Chinese in 1856. Pendleton wrote to Lieutenant Colonel Briscoe G. Baldwin, chief of ordnance for the Army of Northern Virginia,

I saw in a recent paper a stink-shell, and it seems to me such missiles might be made useful to some extent at least . . . The question is whether the explosion can be combined with suffocating effect of certain offensive gases, or whether apart from explosion such gases may not be emitted from a continuously burning composition as to render the vicinity of each falling shell intolerable. It seems at least worth a trial.

Colonel Baldwin appears to have had little interest or faith in the project, for his response was short and terse. "Stink-balls, none on hand; don't keep them; will make them if ordered."[7] Thus, another proposed application of chemical warfare fell by the wayside during the Civil War.

Captain Edward C. Boynton, while serving on the staff of the U.S. Military Academy at West Point, submitted a plan to construct highly portable chemical weapons intended to be used against enemy ships. Boynton devised a glass hand grenade that would serve as both an incendiary and a toxic gas weapon. As he described to the government:

When Alkarsine is distilled with strong chlorohydric acid, and the product digested in a vessel containing zinc, water, and carbonic acid, a heavy oily

Major General William Pendleton, chief of artillery for the Army of Northern Virginia. Pendleton advised using shells containing chemicals to break the Union siege at Petersburg. (Library of Congress)

> liquid insoluble in water is produced, which takes fire the instant it is brought in contact with the air. If this substance, termed Kacodyl . . . was confined in glass globes or bottles, and dropped in the deck of a vessel, or thrust below, all the horrors of combustion and deadly arsenical inhalations would be realized, beside which the terrors of the Greek fire would be contemptible.[8]

Boynton's device would have combined the effects of a Molotov cocktail with noxious gas, and it would have proved a formidable weapon against Confederate ships. As with the other suggestions made to the War Department, Boynton's proposal met with little or no action, and the Boynton grenades were never developed or produced.

One of the only employments of chemical weapons in the Civil War took place in the siege lines at Petersburg. When Union troops dug a mine underneath the Confederate works, filled it with gunpowder, and detonated it to blow a hole in the rebel defenses, the Battle of the Crater took place.

Though the attacking Union forces were driven back with dreadful losses, the incident made the Confederates wary of further such activities, and efforts were undertaken to prevent them. Colonel William W. Blackford, a Confederate engineer, devised a system to block any future Union tunneling efforts. The Confederates dug tunnels of their own, extending out from several of their key defensive positions. They then bored small holes, approximately 4 inches in diameter, that extended 10–15 feet in the direction of the Union lines. Sentinels were placed in the tunnels to guard against Union mining activity. If enemy miners were detected in the proximity of the small holes, a smoke cartridge was to be used to asphyxiate them. As Captain Blackford explained it,

> In case the enemy struck one of these holes, the guards on duty were provided with cartridges of combustibles, the smoke from which would suffocate a man. These were run into the holes and fired by a fuse, closing their end of the hole tightly, and then, summoning the guard, they were to dig into and take possession of the opposing mine as rapidly as possible, giving another dose of the suffocating smoke from time to time to keep the enemy out of his workings until they could dig into them.[9]

While the Confederates did employ this system, they never had cause to use it in actual battle conditions. The fiasco resulting from the Battle of the Crater had convinced the Union commanders to abandon any further efforts at digging shafts under the Southern positions. The North would use conventional methods to pry Robert E. Lee's army out of its Petersburg and Richmond works, and the Confederates would respond with equally conventional weapons.

It seems appropriate to include here a brief history of the efforts made in the use of biological warfare during the Civil War. Several plots were hatched during the war to spread disease through the Union army, and even to spread infection throughout the civilian populations of various cities. Robert Ruffin Barrow was one of the wealthiest men in Louisiana at the outbreak of the Civil War. Profits from sugar plantations, canals, and steamboat operations had made him a millionaire, and one of the most influential people in the state. On September 11, 1862, Barrow wrote to Confederate congressman Duncan F. Kenner concerning his scheme to spread yellow fever through the ranks of the Union army.

> I have been surprised that nothing has been done to carry the yellow fever into New Orleans. It could be done so easily by sending a man that had already had the disease to some yellow fever town & there procure a fever corpse, wrap the dead body in blankets & put in a metallic coffin. Bring into N.O. Thus started the fever would soon become an epidemic throughout the city.[10]

Barrow's plan was never acted on, and it would have proven to be an absolute failure had Confederate authorities decided to adopt it. Medical science would discover several decades later that yellow fever was transmitted by mosquitoes, and the idea that it could be spread through contact with infected persons or materials they had worn or used was found to be totally erroneous.

Dr. Luke Blackburn of Kentucky had also proposed using clothing from people infected with yellow fever to create an epidemic in Northern cities. According to the testimony of Godfrey J. Hyams, a Confederate double agent, Blackburn obtained trunks filled with clothing used by yellow fever patients in the Bahamas that he intended to send to many major cities in the North. Hyams stated that Blackburn had placed several of the contaminated shirts in a valise that was to be given to President Lincoln from an anonymous admirer.[11] The scheme came to naught and, as previously stated, would not have produced the desired results even if the clothing had been distributed.

Blackburn was alleged to have been involved in another biological scheme that could have been successful. In 1863, he was said to have been involved in a plot to infect clothing with smallpox virus, which would then be sold to Union troops. Whether Blackburn was connected with the scheme or not has never been fully proven, and available evidence is scarce. Many people in the North felt him to be guilty, however, and he was accused of responsibility for the death of at least one Union soldier, Lieutenant Charles W. Randall. An account stated that Randall was a member of the 17th Vermont Infantry, and that

> his health became permanently impaired by smallpox, which it was believed he took from infected clothing, having purchased in Washington some undergarments at a store that afterward came under suspicion as a place of consignment under the infection scheme suggested by Dr. Blackburn of Kentucky. But, whatever the origin, the disease destroyed his blood, and shortly after the war he died of consumption.[12]

While Blackburn's involvement in biological warfare remains in question, no less an authority than William T. Sherman reports a documented case of Confederate attempts to use germ warfare against Union troops. Following the surrender of Vicksburg, the Union army turned its attention to the Confederate forces under General Joseph E. Johnston. As Johnston retreated toward Jackson, Mississippi, he "caused cattle, hogs, and sheep, to be driven into the ponds of water, and there shot down; so that we had to haul their dead and stinking carcasses out to use the water."[13] As the weather was particularly hot, and sources of water for the men and animals were in short supply, Sherman's troops were forced to make use of the contaminated ponds. Luckily, the Union army was in such close pursuit of Johnston's men that

the slaughtered animals did not have time to fully decompose and foul the water past the point of being used. All that was accomplished by the Confederate efforts was to make the water offensive, but not dangerous, to those who
drank it.

Though there were a number of schemes proposed for using chemical and biological weapons in the Civil War, very few were adopted or tested. Science had progressed to the point that some of the inventions would have proved not only feasible but practical on the field of battle, particularly the Doughty shell and the Boynton grenade. But Civil War military commanders were not yet ready to embrace a form of warfare they felt to be barbaric and uncivilized. The use of chemical weapons like these would fall to the generation that would fight in World War I, and the destructive capabilities of such weapons would be witnessed time and time again on the battlefields of Europe.

CHAPTER 8

LIGHT DIVISIONS

The light division traces its roots to ancient times when Greek and Roman soldiers were dispatched from the main body of infantry to act as skirmishers with the enemy and to screen the massed formations of the army from enemy probes. In the eighteenth century, many infantry regiments had a light company composed of smaller, agile men capable of moving quickly and using their own initiative in battle. These men did not fight in the compact, massed ranks of the heavy infantry. Instead, they functioned as skirmishers, fighting ahead of the main battle line to harass the enemy until compelled to fall back to their own forces. Members of light infantry units generally carried lighter muskets and were, in some instances, armed with rifled muskets. The British adopted the practice of grouping light companies together to form light regiments, and this was quickly integrated into the military formations of other nations. During the French and Indian War, Major Robert Rogers formed a light infantry unit commonly called Rogers' Rangers to perform reconnaissance and special operations against the French. Rogers trained his recruits in the art of rapid deployment and to fight deep within enemy lines. Rogers even chose to dress his men in green uniforms that had come to signify light infantry, or riflemen, in European armies. Rogers' Rangers performed exemplary service for the British army during the French and Indian War and came to be relied upon as the chief scouting unit for the Crown's forces in North America. Members of the rangers would serve again during the American Revolution, serving on both sides of the conflict.

The nineteenth century saw the usage of larger and larger armies, as the nations of Europe battled through the Napoleonic era. These larger military formations necessitated the expansion of light infantry units from companies and regiments to brigades and divisions. The British formed a light division in

1803 by bringing together a number of regiments that were already serving as light infantry. Napoléon's army also had large light infantry units, called *voltigeurs* and *chasseurs*. The German army organized their own light infantry units, called *Jäger* troops. Light infantry was considered elite troops in the European armies, and they received specialized training in rapid deployment and skirmishing, as well as the traditional role of heavy infantry. In the British army, this distinction was emphasized on and off the battlefield. British light infantry was expected to march faster than heavy infantry whether it was in combat or marching on the parade ground. The march cadence for heavy infantry was 120 steps per minute, but light infantry was expected to march at an increased rate of 160 steps per minute. Light infantry also used bugles to transmit orders on the battlefield instead of the drums used by heavy infantry. The reason for this was that bugle calls carried further than drum rolls, and a drum was harder to use when moving quickly on a battlefield.

In the United States, there was little attention given to the implementation of light infantry. The country's standing regular army was of small size, and there simply were not enough soldiers to create anything more than the traditional formations. Local militia units were not constrained by the need to perform regular duty and were sometimes quicker to adopt the latest European trends. Many militia units across the country chose to incorporate light infantry tactics into their training. The Zouave uniforms and tactics that had become popular in the French army were incorporated in many local militia companies, both North and South, and many a number of these companies and regiments would enter the war schooled in light infantry tactics. One of the oldest and largest such units was the First Light Division, Maryland Volunteers. The unit traced its roots to 1833, when a number of Baltimore militia regiments were combined into a brigade under the command of Brigadier General George H. Steuart.[1] The brigade was enlarged into a division in 1841, and Steuart continued to command the division until 1861. Six companies of the division, led by General Steuart, took part in the suppression of John Brown's raid at Harpers Ferry, Virginia, in 1859.[2] The coming of the Civil War caused special problems for the Maryland Light Division. Many of the soldiers and most of the officers wished to secede from the Union and join the Southern Confederacy. Maryland remained in the Union, however, prompting General Steuart to disband the division before he and many of his men went south to fight for the gray. Because of this, neither side benefited from the services of a light division in the early days of the war.

When most people think of a light division in the Civil War, the Confederate division of Ambrose P. Hill springs to mind. Hill's unit was commonly referred to as the Light Division, in both the North and South, mainly because of the reputation it had gained for making rapid forced marches in

Lieutenant General Ambrose P. Hill. Though Hill's division was commonly referred to as the "Light Division," it was not organized or trained to fight in that capacity. The nickname was derived from the fact that they had made many rapid marches during the war. (Library of Congress)

numerous campaigns. One veteran of the division stated, "We are lightly armed, lightly fed, but march rapidly and fight frequently."[3] General Hill is the person responsible for naming his division the Light Division, possibly in an effort to establish esprit de corps and instill the idea of speed in his men. To be sure, this division was noted for making quick marches, like the 17-mile trek from Harpers Ferry to Antietam that arrived in the nick of time and saved the Confederate army from destruction. They were quick and hard-hitting, but they were light infantry in name only. Hill's Light Division always fought as heavy infantry and was not trained in the specialized tactics required for units performing the function of light infantry. This division, while courageous and colorful, did not meet the criteria to be considered light infantry.

There was a division of light infantry formed during the Civil War that served in that capacity on the battlefield. This was the Union Light Division, belonging to the Army of the Potomac. In February of 1863, Major General Joseph Hooker, the newly appointed commander of the army, made several changes of organization. Hooker consolidated the cavalry into a cavalry

Major General Joseph Hooker. The Union Light Division was organized by his direction and saw service during the Chancellorsville Campaign. (Library of Congress)

corps. Prior to this, the cavalry of the army had been dispersed throughout the army, with each infantry corps having a suitable complement. The introduction of a unified corps of cavalry made the Army of the Potomac more capable of dealing with their Confederate counterparts. Hooker also did away with the grand division alignment that his predecessor, Ambrose Burnside, had created prior to the battle of Fredericksburg. Instead, Hooker established the corps as the largest military unit in the army. On February 3, 1863, Hooker also created the Light Division. It was his intention that this division act independently from the rest of the army and perform the duties of skirmishing, reconnaissance, and speedy forced marches. Handpicked regiments were assigned to the division because of their reliability on the battlefield. The 31st New York, 6th Maine, 43rd New York, 61st Pennsylvania, and 5th Wisconsin made up the infantry portion of the division, complemented by the 3rd New York Light Battery of artillery.[4] The 61st Pennsylvania was especially suited for the assignment, as six of its ten companies had originally been Zouave units, trained in the tactics of light infantry.

The division was placed under the command of Brigadier General Calvin E. Pratt, a 35-year-old lawyer from Brooklyn who had recruited the 31st

New York at his own expense. Pratt was still suffering the effects of a wound received at the battle of Gaines's Mill the previous summer and did not really want the job. In fact, he wished to tender his resignation from the army altogether. The division was attached to Major General John Sedgwick's VI Corps. Though it was supposed to be an independent command, Sedgwick, a longtime officer, exerted a great deal of control over the unit. He was not convinced of the necessity of such a formation and did not hold with the introduction of new ideas into the army.

The Light Division was assembled in the Belle Plain region, northeast of Falmouth, Virginia, across the Potomac Creek from Fredericksburg, to begin its specialized training. For the next three months, the troops would be schooled in the tactics of light infantry and would learn to march and fight as a specialized, elite unit. General Hooker visited Belle Plain to check on the division's progress frequently, and the troops were even reviewed by President Lincoln. In March of 1863, General Hooker devised a system of corps badges to be worn by his troops to distinguish them from one another on the battlefield and to instill unit pride. Each corps insignia would come in one of three colors. Red designated the first division of the corps, white the second, and blue the third. The symbol for the 6th Corps was the Greek cross, but this corps was given a fourth color of insignia. Green, the traditional color of light infantrymen and riflemen, was selected to be the color for the corps badges of the Light Division.[5]

The elite status of the Light Division was not lost on the soldiers that made up the unit. One member of the 61st Pennsylvania wrote:

> The idea was to form in each corps a division of experienced, sturdy men who would always be ready to move instantly with a battery of artillery, veteran "minute men" constantly supplied with hundreds of rounds of ammunition and eight days' rations. It was understood the best regiments were selected for this service and they were to camp in such places as to render them available for emergencies.[6]

The Light Division was to be a strike force for the corps to which it was attached, and this first experimental division would, as Hooker hoped, pave the way for its adoption throughout the Army of the Potomac.

On April 25, 1863, General Pratt resigned his commission in the army. The nagging effects of his wound was probably one of his reasons, but it is possible that he also resented the manner in which General Sedgwick was treating him and his division. Sedgwick had taken away much of the independence of the Light Division and was using it as if it were a brigade in the division commanded by Brigadier General John Newton. Hiram Burnham, the senior colonel in the Light Division and commander of the

6th Maine, was promoted to take command upon Pratt's departure. Burnham proved to be an efficient and capable commander for the Light Division. A 49-year-old lumberman from Maine, he was sturdy, dependable, and had a commanding presence on the field.[7]

The only engagement the Light Division fought in was the battle of Chancellorsville. General Hooker planned to make a pincer movement against Robert E. Lee's Army of Northern Virginia. The bulk of his army would cross the Rappahannock River and march toward Richmond, forcing Lee to come out of his defensive positions to defend the Confederate capital. Once Hooker had the Confederates out in the open, he would be able to fully utilize his more than two-to-one superiority in manpower. A second force, under General Sedgwick, was left behind to keep an eye on the Confederates around Fredericksburg. When Lee came out of his works to face Hooker, Sedgwick would be in his rear, and the Confederates would be trapped between the two forces.

On April 27, Hooker's army crossed the Rappahannock in the initial phase of the campaign. By April 30, the Federals were concentrated around Chancellorsville Court House, a small hamlet west of Fredericksburg located in a rugged area known as the Wilderness. Everything seemed to be going as planned. But Robert E. Lee did not wait to be trapped in Hooker's pincer movement. Correctly divining the Federal intentions, Lee took the initiative in one of the most audacious actions of the war. Though severely outnumbered, he divided his army, leaving a small portion in Fredericksburg to block Sedgwick, and with the remainder, he marched out to attack Hooker on May 1. On May 2, Lee increased his audacity by once more dividing his army. Intelligence had been obtained that the right flank of the Union army was dangling in the air, unsupported and vulnerable. Lee kept a small screening force in front of Hooker while he sent Lieutenant General Thomas J. "Stonewall" Jackson on a flanking march with his main body. Jackson was able to reach the right wing of the Federal army unimpeded, and he launched a crushing attack that rolled up the flank and threatened to drive Hooker's army from the field. Only darkness prevented the Confederates from attaining a more complete victory. The fighting was resumed on May 3, and after a bloody struggle, the Confederates were successful in placing Hooker completely on the defensive and compelling him to retire from the field and recross the Rappahannock, which he did on May 5.

In the meantime, the Light Division played a prominent role in the fighting taking place at Fredericksburg. On May 3, Sedgwick received orders to break through the Confederate position in his front and march directly to Hooker's support at Chancellorsville. Major General Jubal Early commanded the Confederates in Sedgwick's front. Though outnumbered by the Federals, Early's men held a distinct advantage in position, holding fortified works on and adjacent to Marye's Heights. It was against this very position that General Burnside had almost destroyed the army in a series of futile attacks the preceding December. Sedgwick wanted nothing to do with a frontal attack against this strong position, opting instead to attempt to turn Early's right flank. When this action failed to deliver the desired results, Sedgwick was faced with the unenviable task of storming the Confederate center. Three regiments of the Light Division were chosen to be part of the assault force, along with some regiments from Newton's brigade. The Light Division regiments, the 6th Maine, 31st New York, and 5th Wisconsin, were to act as the spearhead for the attack. The 61st Pennsylvania and 43rd New York would be in support of the initial drive. The men were ordered to fix bayonets but not to load their muskets. Officers wanted a speedy charge up the hill and did not want the men stopping to shoot or reload their weapons. Many of the boys disobeyed the order and loaded their weapons; they just didn't cap them. Colonel Burnham rode to where the spearhead troops were forming and cheerfully called out to them, "Boys, I have got a government contract." When asked what it was a contract for, he responded, "One thousand rebels, potted and salted, and got to have 'em in less than five minutes. Forward! Guide center!" Colonel Thomas S. Allen, commander of the 5th Wisconsin, also gave his men a pep talk before the charge commenced. "Boys, you see those Heights. You have got to take them. You think you cannot do it, but you can and you will. When the signal 'Forward' is given, you will start at the double-quick—you will not fire a gun—and you will not stop until you get the order to halt. You will never get that order."[8]

The signal to advance was then given, and the men of the Light Division moved forward at a run. A gun of the Washington Artillery opened a deadly fire on the advancing Federals, but the Light Division men were moving too rapidly for the shells to be effective. When the troops closed to point-blank range of the stone wall atop Marye's Heights, the Confederate defenders rose to pour a deadly volley of fire into them. Large numbers of Light Division men fell, but the survivors swept forward with a yell, jumping over the wall before the Confederates had time to reload their muskets. The Light Division men closed with the enemy to settle the matter with bayonets and clubbed muskets. In the bitter hand-to-hand combat that ensued, Private George Brown of the 6th Maine was seen to bayonet two men and kill a third with the butt of his musket. Color Sergeant John Gray, also from the 6th Maine, was the first to plant the Federal flag at the top of Marye's Heights, causing raucous cheering from Sedgwick's watching men below. The Confederates were forced to retreat from the impact of the Light Division's assault, and as Sedgwick's supporting regiments entered into the fray, General Early ordered his entire line to withdraw. The entire charge had taken no more than five minutes, the exact time that Colonel Burnham had told the men it must be accomplished in. The cost had been staggering, however; 798 men, fully one-third of the Light Division men making the attack, had been shot down as casualties, but the objective had been taken. The swift-moving, hard-hitting tactics of the light infantry had been successful in capturing the position and breaking the Confederate line.[9]

After carrying the heights, Sedgwick pushed his corps westward toward Chancellorsville. The Light Division was assigned to the left of Sedgwick's line and assisted in repelling a counterattack by the Confederates. The division sustained even more casualties that night when it was attacked while covering Sedgwick's main body as it made a river crossing. In his official report, General Hooker praised the Light Division for its conduct at Marye's Heights, and cited the "gallant conduct of Colonel Burnham" in leading the assault as "worthy of the highest admiration." Nevertheless, the Light Division was disbanded on May 11, 1863. The 31st New York had only enlisted for two years, and its term of enlistment was about to run out. The heavy casualties sustained at Marye's Heights and in the march toward Chancellorsville had greatly reduced the fighting ability of the division, and it was felt that the remaining men were too few to undertake the responsibilities of a light division. The regiments of the Light Division were returned to their former brigades, and the men were forced to trade in their distinctive green Greek crosses for other colors.[10]

The Union's experiment with a light division had lasted only three months. The results on the battlefield had justified the test, as the division exceeded expectations in their performance. Their success also spelled their demise, however. During the Civil War, regiments were generally created from specific areas of the country. All of the men in a particular regiment usually came from the same city or area. The system of replacements, currently used in the military, was not in vogue then. When a regiment suffered extreme losses in an engagement, one of three things generally happened. The regiment would continue to act as an independent unit, though an undersized one. It would send recruiters back to its home area to try to enlist recruits to bring it back up to full strength. Or it would be consolidated with another undersized unit to create a new regiment. The last choice was highly unpopular with the men in the ranks, as individual soldiers developed a fierce loyalty for their own regiments. If Civil War armies had adopted the practice of providing replacement soldiers to compensate for the losses regiments sustained in battle, the Light Division could have been reorganized and retained in their position. As it was, the regiments were too depleted in manpower, especially with the departure of the 31st New York, to continue as a viable light division with the army.

CHAPTER 9

THE BALLOON CORPS

Hot air balloons are the oldest human flight technology and were first successfully used in France by the time the Revolutionary War had come to a close. The first successful flight took place in Annonay, France, on November 21, 1783. The balloon consisted of a large bag, called an envelope, that was capable of holding heated air. A wicker basket, or gondola, was suspended beneath the envelope to carry passengers and a device to burn an open flame that would heat the air going into the envelope. The heated air has a lower density than the colder air around the envelope, causing it to be lighter and rise into the sky. Early balloons had no means of propulsion and had to be tethered to the ground or allowed to float along with prevailing wind currents. By the time of the Civil War, some eight decades later, the technology of lighter-than-air flight had advanced very little, and the airships used by the Union and Confederate balloonists closely resembled those that had been invented in France. The primary difference was the use of an external power plant to create the hydrogen used to inflate the envelope, leaving more room in the gondola for passengers or equipment.

Balloons were first used for military application in France, the place of their birth. During the wars of the French Revolution, Louis-Bernard Guyton de Morveau advocated the use of balloons for military observation of enemy troops on the battlefield. The Committee of Public Safety in Paris was intrigued by Morveau's suggestion and agreed to provide funds for a balloon, a gas plant, and personnel. The balloon was to be made of silk, layered with goldbeater's skin, the membrane of ox intestines, to seal the porosity of the silk in order to retain the gas. Morveau was assigned to General Jourdan, to assist in his campaign against the Austrians. Jourdan was less than enthused about the project but was quickly won over when Morveau ascended with the *Entreprenant* at the battle of Fleurus on June 26, 1794. Morveau transmitted valuable intelligence information by means of hand signals, giving the French a clear advantage in the battle. General Jourdan was a convert, so much so that he ascended himself, in company with Morveau, at the battle of Sombreffe, on July 5, 1794. The *Entreprenant* was destroyed by enemy fire in 1796, but Morveau accompanied Napoléon with the *Intrepide* in his campaign in Egypt in 1797. Napoléon was not a strong supporter of balloon technology, and, following his appointment as First Consul of the Republic, he cut off funding for the project. Military usage of balloons would not be seen in warfare again until the U.S. Civil War.[1]

Ballooning came to the United States in 1793, when Frenchman Jean Pierre Blanchard made an ascension at Philadelphia witnessed by George Washington, his cabinet, and both houses of Congress. During the first half of the nineteenth century, there were a number of American balloonists who made significant advancements in the field. John Wise is known as the father of American ballooning. Born in Lancaster, Pennsylvania, in 1808, he constructed his first balloon at the age of 27 and made his first ascent on May 2, 1835. Wise was responsible for many innovations in ballooning. He invented the rip panel, by which gas could be released from the envelope, allowing the balloon to descend. He also discovered how a torn envelope would gather at the top of the netting, forming a parachute that would safely lower the balloon to earth. Wise was the first to discover the jet stream that blew from west to east, and he delivered the first airmail, in 1859, when he carried letters between two different towns in Indiana.[2]

When the Civil War broke out, the Office of Topographical Engineers contacted Wise, requesting an estimate for the construction of an observation balloon. He responded that such a craft could be built for $850 and that he would be able to complete work on it in two weeks. On July 1, 1861, Wise was appointed as a military balloonist in the Federal army. Wise took his completed balloon to Washington in time to be ordered to Centreville, Virginia, to take part in Major General Irvin McDowell's offensive against the Confederates. Orders were for Wise to inflate his balloon and make for Centreville on the evening of July 19, so that he could be in position to ascend on the field the following day. Delays caused the departure of the balloon to be postponed till the morning of July 21, however. Major Albert J. Meyer had requested and was granted permission to take command of the balloon. Meyer was an officer in the Signal Corps, and since the balloon was to be equipped with a telegraph line, it made sense for him to oversee the project. As Meyer, Wise, and the crew of the balloon made their way toward Centreville, the sounds of the battle taking place at Bull Run could clearly be heard. Trees, telegraph poles, and other obstacles slowed the progress of the balloon and caused Meyer to become highly agitated. He ordered the balloon attached to an escort wagon and started forward at a trot. Near Fairfax Court House the balloon became fouled in the branches of a number of large trees. Wise cautioned Meyer about the potential danger of rushing forward, but the major was all afire with the sounds of battle and refused to heed the warning. He ordered the teamster to take the wagon forward, causing the envelope of the balloon to become torn by the branches. The gas escaped, and Major Meyer was forced to return to Washington with the worthless balloon.

Wise repaired the damage, and on July 24, he ascended from Arlington, Virginia, to observe enemy troop movements around the capital. On July 25, Wise attempted an ascension from Ball's Creek Road for the purpose of reporting on enemy troop positions. There was a strong wind that day, which caught hold of the balloon before Wise could get into the gondola. The wind blew the balloon against telegraph lines, which cut the guide ropes, allowing the craft to sail away toward enemy lines. Troops near Arlington were able to bring the balloon down with several volleys of musket fire before it reached Confederate lines. Wise's balloon was disparaged by the Topographical Engineers, and Wise was unjustly criticized for the failure of the project. Insulted and unappreciated, he went back to Lancaster to take no more part in the war. Before taking his leave from Washington, Wise informed the Topographical Bureau that he would return on 24 hours' notice if his services were ever needed, but no request for his assistance ever came from that sector.[3]

James Allen was another American balloonist who played an important role in the early days of the Civil War. Born in Rhode Island in 1824, Allen was a relative newcomer to ballooning when the war broke out, having made his first ascension only four years before. He and his brother Ezra offered their services to the government shortly after the firing on Fort Sumter, making them the first balloonists to be enrolled in Federal service. Allen arrived in Washington with two of his balloons, and his first ascension was more than a month before Wise. Details are sketchy, but it seems as if Allen was originally enrolled as part of Colonel Ambrose Burnside's Rhode Island Regiment, a member of the Rhode Island Light Artillery Battery attached to Burnside's infantry. Allen made a second ascension on July 9, 1861, before being assigned to Brigadier General Daniel Tyler's division just before the Manassas Campaign. A ground crew of 60 men was provided from Colonel Elmer Ellsworth's 11th New York Zouaves, and the envelopes were inflated at a gas plant in Alexandria on July 14. One of the balloons was so old that it burst as soon as it was fully inflated. The second was to be towed to Falls Church to make contact with General Tyler. Along the way, the balloon was caught by high winds and, despite the efforts of the ground crew, was blown against a telegraph line, where the envelope was punctured. Allen's balloon ended up suffering the same fate as had Wise's, and neither one made it to the field at Manassas.

Allen stated that part of the problem was the inexperience of the ground crew in dealing with balloons. He suggested that permanent transfers be made into the Balloon Corps so that those troops could gain the knowledge and know-how needed to work with the craft. But the Federal government never did act on this piece of advice. For the remainder of its service, the Balloon Corps would be staffed with temporary assignments, and those soldiers would frequently be called back to their respective regiments before they had the opportunity to gain any real on-the-job experience. In their place, a new levee of replacements would be assigned from other regiments, making Allen and his fellow balloonists the only real qualified members of the corps. Allen returned to his home following the Manassas Campaign, until called into service once more in the spring of 1862 at the request of Thaddeus Lowe. Allen would serve under Lowe in the Balloon Corps until that officer resigned, at which time he assumed command of the corps.[4]

A third balloonist who became prominent in the early stages of the war was John LaMountain. As with Allen and Wise, LaMountain applied to serve the Union army as a balloonist in the first days of the war. He submitted two applications but received no response. LaMountain's entrance into balloon service was eventually brought about through the efforts of Major General Benjamin Butler. Butler was in command of the Department of Virginia, with his headquarters located at Fortress Monroe, and he was anxious about Confederate movements along his immediate front. The advantage an observation balloon could provide was evident to Butler, and he wished to add this means of intelligence to his department. LaMountain proved to be just the man for the job. Hailing from Troy, New York, he was as fearless as he was confident, and there were few things that he was not willing to try in the air. Before the war, he had made a balloon trip of some 1,100 miles east from Saint Louis, setting a record for balloon distance travel. By the end of July 1861, LaMountain had arrived at Fortress Monroe with his airship *Atlantic*, and on July 31 he made the first successful observation ascension of a Federal balloon in a battle zone. This was to be the beginning of many firsts credited to LaMountain. He would create the first aircraft carrier when he used the armed transport *Fanny* as a launching base for his balloon to rise above the Chesapeake Bay on August 1, 1861. LaMountain also made the first night ascensions, counting the tent lights in the enemy camps to estimate the size of the Confederate army. This led to the first blackouts in warfare, when Confederate general Pierre G. T. Beauregard ordered that all lights be covered or extinguished when balloons were aloft.[5]

In all, LaMountain made ten ascensions at Fortress Monroe, five of which took place on August 10, 1861. Having used up all the acid and iron necessary to produce the hydrogen gas to inflate his envelope, he obtained Butler's permission to return to Troy to get his larger airship, *Saratoga*, and a specially designed hydrogen generator that operated on decomposed water. Before leaving, however, LaMountain made a proposal to Butler that a large balloon could be built capable of carrying bombs that could "shell, burn, or destroy Norfolk or any other city near our camps." Butler was very interested in the proposal and sent it along to the War Department with his approval. Shortly after LaMountain's departure, General Butler was assigned to a new position, and he neglected to advise his successor, Major General John Wool, about any arrangements he had made with LaMountain. When the aeronaut returned from Troy with his new balloon, he was met with contempt by the new commander of Fortress Monroe, who directed that he report to Secretary of War Simon Cameron for instructions. Cameron ordered LaMountain to join General George B. McClellan's Army of the Potomac, where he was eventually assigned to Major General William B. Franklin's corps. Thaddeus Lowe was already operating with McClellan and had been appointed chief of the newly created Balloon Corps. As LaMountain and Lowe were rivals and bitter enemies, it was questioned whether the two could work together. McClellan instructed General Fitz-John Porter to interview both men and judge if they could function professionally or if the rivalry between them was too great for coordinated action. Porter determined that both men could render effective service to the army, providing LaMountain was allowed to act independently of Lowe in most cases and would be subordinated to the new balloon chief only when absolutely necessary. By October 18, LaMountain was once more aloft and observing the Confederates at Fairfax Station, Manassas, and Centreville. This ascension was made using free flight, as the balloon was allowed to float with the air currents instead of being tethered to the ground. When LaMountain made his descent within Union lines, he was fired upon by troops under the command of Brigadier General Louis Blenker, who were unsure which side the balloon was flying for. Several bullets punctured the envelope, and it was further damaged by the troops once it reached the ground. On November 16, the *Saratoga* was lost when inexperienced ground crew members allowed it to float away in high winds. With the *Atlantic* in a state of disrepair from its many flights at Fortress Monroe, LaMountain was left without a balloon. He tried to get Lowe to release one of the four airships the government had contracted to build for the Balloon Corps, but he was denied. Only two of the balloons had been completed thus far, and they were both employed by Lowe. Without a viable airship, and with little chance of receiving one from Lowe, LaMountain was discharged from the army in February 1862. Before leaving the army, however, he agreed to sell the *Atlantic*, the *Saratoga*, and all of his equipment to the government for the sum of $3,318.14. Thaddeus Lowe was unmoved by the departures of Wise or LaMountain. He stated: "Neither had the least idea

Professor Thaddeus Lowe ascending in a balloon at Fair Oaks, Virginia. (Library of Congress)

of the requirements of military ballooning nor the gift of invention which later made it possible for me to achieve success."[6]

Thaddeus Lowe was the balloonist who would attain the highest distinction during the Civil War. He would be credited with developing the Balloon Corps and would serve as its first commander. Born in Jefferson Mills, New Hampshire, on August 20, 1832, Lowe was a latecomer to the field of ballooning. Like Allen, he had built and piloted his first balloon only four years before the war began. Even so, by 1861, Lowe was one of the most respected balloonists in the United States.

While he had only a grammar school education, Lowe had always been interested in science. In the 1840s, Lowe traveled with a magician whose show included chemical experiments. Lowe later went out on his own on the entertainment circuit, billing himself as "Professor Lowe," a title that stuck with him the remainder of his life. Lowe performed demonstrations of gaseous phenomena, and through this he became interested in ballooning. By 1854 he had determined to make ballooning his life's work. Lowe traveled to France to learn what he could from aeronautical experts then returned to the United States to make a lecture tour to raise funding for his project.

The project that intrigued Lowe most was the possibility of making a trans-Atlantic crossing in a balloon. For this purpose, he built a huge balloon in 1859 named *City of New York*. This behemoth had an envelope capable of holding 725,000 cubic feet of gas. It possessed a lifting power of 22.25 tons. The gondola was spacious enough to accommodate six passengers in addition to food, equipment, and scientific instruments. Suspended from the bottom of the basket was a metal lifeboat with a hand-drive propeller and sails. The *City of New York* was a truly magnificent craft, and Lowe was eager to use it to prove that trans-Atlantic flight was possible. By 1860 he had renamed the balloon, calling it *Great Western*, at the suggestion of Horace Greeley. He took a short test flight from New York to New Jersey, but Professor Joseph Henry of the Smithsonian Institute suggested that Lowe make a long overland flight before attempting any voyage across the ocean. Agreeing that this was sound advice, Lowe prepared his 20,0000-cubic-foot *Enterprise* and left for Cincinnati to make his overland flight. In the early morning hours of April 20, 1861, Lowe made his ascension and began his free flight. He had bought several copies of the local Cincinnati newspaper to take with him, to prove the date he had left when he arrived at his final destination. After sailing over the Cumberland Mountains, the *Enterprise* was caught in a northerly wind, and the craft was blown from its easterly course in a southern direction. When Lowe touched down, he found that he was in Unionville, South Carolina. The firing on Fort Sumter had already taken place, and these South Carolinians took a dim view of this airborne Yankee landing uninvited among them. The day-old copies of the Cincinnati newspaper only served to increase their suspicion, as that particular paper was a well-known abolitionist paper. Lowe was accused of being a Northern spy and was thrown in a local jail. Fortunately, some South Carolina college professors heard of the incident and came to intercede on Lowe's behalf. Freed from his captivity, he made his way back to Cincinnati by rail.[7]

During Lowe's trip north, he witnessed a great deal of war preparation taking place. Lowe decided that it was his duty to postpone his trans-Atlantic flight to offer his services to the Federal government in the impending conflict. On June 6, 1861, Lowe arrived at Washington with his balloon *Enterprise* for the purpose of demonstrating the military possibilities of captive balloons in war. Murat Halstead, a prominent Ohio newspaper editor, provided an introduction to Secretary of Treasury Salmon Chase for Lowe. An exhibition was scheduled, and on June 18, Lowe ascended five hundred feet above the treetops in the *Enterprise*, over the grounds of the Washington

Columbian Armory. The *Enterprise* carried, in addition to Lowe, a telegraph operator and a telegraph. Once aloft, Lowe had the telegrapher send several messages, one of them to President Lincoln:

> Sir. This point of observation commands an area nearly 50 miles in diameter. The city, with its girdle of encampments, presents a superb scene. I have pleasure in sending you this first dispatch ever telegraphed from an aerial station, and in acknowledging indebtedness for your encouragement for the opportunity of demonstrating the availability of the science of aeronautics in the military service of the country. T. S. C. Lowe[8]

Following the demonstration, the *Enterprise* was towed to the White House, where Lincoln inspected the craft from an upstairs window. On June 19, Lowe continued his demonstration for the president and his cabinet. It was reported that Lincoln accompanied Lowe in one of the several ascensions made that day. General Irvin McDowell, in command of the army in and around Washington, had little knowledge of the position or disposition of the 20,000 Confederate troops reported to be in the vicinity of Manassas and Fairfax Court House. He requested that Lowe and his balloon be taken to Falls Church, where ascensions could be made to gain information on the enemy army. Lowe arrived there on June 22 and attempted to make several ascensions. High winds and the dense cover of trees prevented these from taking place, however, and McDowell was denied the information he so sorely needed.

General McDowell advanced to face the Southern forces at Manassas on July 16, 1861. Lowe was instructed to take his balloon to Falls Church to observe and report on the enemy. On July 21, he inflated the *Enterprise* at the Washington Gas Works and, with a ground crew of 20 men, towed the balloon to its assigned position. Before Lowe could get the *Enterprise* to its appointed place, Union and Confederate forces clashed along the banks of Bull Run Creek, and the first major land battle of the Civil War had commenced. The issue was already decided before Lowe could get his craft in the air, and the Union army was in full retreat back to Washington. Lowe was forced to retire to the safety of the capital's defenses, moving his balloon to Fort Corcoran.[9]

Four days after the battle of First Manassas, President Lincoln gave Lowe a letter of introduction to General Winfield Scott, general in chief of the Union army. Scott was a 75-year-old relic of another age, the hero of the War of 1812 and the Mexican-American War, to whom new technology was a source of disdain. Scott refused to grant Lowe an interview, despite the letter from Lincoln, feeling that balloons were nonsense and would contribute nothing to the war. After several failed attempts to gain an audience with Scott, Lowe was personally escorted into the general's presence by President

Lincoln. On August 2, 1861, Lowe received a contract to construct a 25,000-cubic-foot-capacity balloon. He was also employed as a civilian aeronaut at the rate of $5 per day, $10 per day when he performed duty in the air. The latter rate was equivalent to the pay of a colonel in the army. This was the beginning of the Balloon Corps, which Lowe would develop and command for the majority of its existence.

In less than three weeks from the date of receiving the contract, Lowe had completed the new balloon, which he appropriately named *Union*. The airship left Philadelphia for Washington on August 21. On August 29, it made its first ascent to observe Confederate activities. The enemy was found to be constructing fortifications in close proximity to Washington, and Lowe kept the military informed as to their dispositions and movements. On September 24, Lowe was ordered aloft to report on the accuracy of artillery firing from Fort Corcoran against some of these Confederate works. In the first instance of artillery fire being directed by an aerial observer, Lowe telegraphed the accuracy of each shot, allowing the artillerists to correct and pinpoint their fire. This incident, along with the valuable military intelligence gained on previous ascents, led to Lowe being given a contract to build four more balloons, complete with inflating apparatus, on September 25, 1861. The Balloon Corps was now an official part of the U.S. Army.[10]

Lowe was granted a budget of $8,600 to start his new Balloon Corps and, with the balloons he already had, the four additions would mean that the corps would boast seven airships, ranging in size from 15,000 cubic feet to the massive 32,000-cubic-foot *Intrepid*. The smaller balloons were the *Eagle, Constitution*, and *Washington* while the *Union, Excelsior*, and *United States* joined the *Intrepid* in the larger class. The smaller balloons would be manufactured for a cost of approximately $1,000 each, while the larger ones cost up to $1,500. Each was made of double panels of India silk, sewn together to resemble the sections of an orange. On the inside, the panels were oiled to keep them soft and pliable, while the outside was treated with four coats of varnish to keep the gas contained. The envelope was contained by a netting of strong linen cordage, gathered at the bottom and connected to a large wood ring. From the ring was suspended the wicker basket, or gondola, capable of accommodating from one to five men, which was colorfully adorned with stars and stripes.[11]

Lowe was also given a coal barge from the Washington Navy Yard, which he refitted to serve as an aircraft carrier. He had a flat deck placed on the 122-foot hull of the vessel, which was recommissioned the *G. W. Parke Custis*, and had the 20,000-cubic-foot balloon *Washington* moored to the deck. The vessel then sailed up and down the Potomac River, providing naval mobility for the aircraft.[12]

Lowe recruited nine balloonists for his new corps, including James Allen. He did not extend an invitation to John Wise or John LaMountain, however,

The airship *Intrepid* being inflated in the field. (Library of Congress)

as he considered them rivals. With his balloons and balloonists in place, Lowe's next obstacle was how to make his corps more efficient for military use. Up to now, balloons were largely dependent on municipal gas works to fill the envelopes. They would then have to be towed to the place where an ascension was planned. This was a slow and tedious process, and, as had been seen in the Manassas Campaign, it meant that the balloons might not be available when and where they were needed. To combat this, Lowe invented a portable gas generator, consisting of a copper-lined wooden tank where copper filings and sulfuric acid could be mixed to produce hydrogen gas. The generator, mounted on a carriage, was drawn by horses and could move freely with the army. The invention of this portable gas plant meant that Lowe's balloons were now as mobile as any other part of the army, and he could inflate his balloons anywhere they might be needed.

When General McClellan began his Peninsula Campaign in March of 1862, Lowe was given an opportunity to prove the efficiency of his new system. The first ascension of the campaign took place at Yorktown, on April 5, 1862, in the *Intrepid*. Lowe noted that the number of Confederates in the defenses of the city did not match the highly inflated totals presented by Allan Pinkerton's detective agency and advised General McClellan that the force confronting him was much smaller than he had been led to believe.[13] On May 4, Lowe provided McClellan with the first positive intelligence that the Confederates were evacuating Yorktown and retreating up the Peninsula.[14] Following the capture of Yorktown, the Balloon Corps was ordered to take up a position near Mechanicsville, just four miles from Richmond. Lowe and his aeronauts made numerous ascents to observe and report on the activities of the Confederates, in many instances under the hostile fire of Confederate artillery and small arms. On May 30, Lowe reported seeing frenzied activity all along the enemy lines in what looked to him like the buildup for an offensive. His deductions were correct. On May 31, 1862, General Joseph E. Johnston attacked the Federal army at Fair Oaks, and a bloody two-day battle ensued. The Balloon Corps continued to make reconnaissance flights throughout the month of June and performed valuable service during the Seven Days Battles that saw the Federal army withdraw back down the Peninsula to Harrison's Landing. Following the Seven Days Campaign, Lowe was stricken with malaria and was forced to turn command of the corps over to James Allen. Though the corps continued to operate and performed valuable service on other fields of conflict, Lowe did not rejoin it until after the Antietam Campaign, in late September. In the early spring of 1863, the Balloon Corps was placed under the command of Captain Cyrus B. Comstock, chief engineer of the Army of the Potomac. Comstock had little faith in balloons and was openly hostile toward Lowe. Comstock directed a number of insults Lowe's way, including a reduction in his salary so that the balloonist received the same salary as the captain. Lowe protested the treatment received from Comstock, but the military high command refused to become involved in the matter. Still feeling the effects of malaria, and thwarted in his efforts by a superior showing signs of vengeful jealousy, Lowe resigned from the service on May 8, 1863. Most of the aeronauts in the Balloon Corps followed his example. James Allen became commander of what was left of the corps, and he tried to continue its work, but the organizational framework of the unit had been broken, and the Balloon Corps went out of existence about a month later.[15]

During its relatively short existence, the Federal Balloon Corps made more than three thousand ascensions. It provided the Union army with numerous invaluable pieces of intelligence that assisted in the strategy and tactics the Northern commanders used on the battlefield. From portable gas plants to aerial photography and the aerial plotting of artillery fire, it forever changed the manner in which wars would be fought. Though the corps did not survive the war, its trailblazing accomplishments served to blaze the way for aerial combat of the future.

The Confederacy also had a short-lived experiment with ballooning. Feeling the need to counter the advantage balloons gave the Union army on the Peninsula, the Confederates decided to construct airships of their own. The project was met with immediate difficulties, owing to a lack of needed materials and experienced balloonists. The Union blockade prevented the

A Union balloon being inflated. Note the use of the traveling gas plants on the left of the photo. (Library of Congress)

South from obtaining the silk material needed to create balloons like those used by the Federal Balloon Corps, and there was no supply of coke gas to be found in the Richmond area. The Confederates were forced to construct a balloon of cotton material stretched over a wooden frame and inflated with smoke produced from burning oil-soaked pinecones. Captain John R. Bryan was selected to be the aeronaut for the balloon, not because he had any previous ballooning experience, but because he volunteered to a call from General Johnston for a soldier who could correctly estimate the number and character of enemy troops. Bryan, who had been serving in the attorney general's office, wanted to excuse himself when he was informed that the duty would involve piloting balloons, but he decided not to go back on his word. He would become the commander of the Confederate Balloon Service. Bryan made his first ascension during the Peninsula Campaign, south of Richmond. This flight was cut short when the balloon had to be lowered because of heavy enemy fire, prompting Bryan to tender his resignation. General Johnston refused to accept Bryan's notice, however, stating, "You're the only experienced balloonist in the Confederate army!"— despite the fact this was his first ascent.[16]

The Confederacy was able to construct a silk balloon through ingenuity and sacrifice. A call went out to the countryside that the South was in desperate need of silk, and many of the women responded by donating their fancy silk dresses. The balloon was designed by Dr. Edward Cheves of Savannah. The silk was sewn together in a brilliant display of patchwork colors and was varnished with melted rubber. It made several ascents from the Richmond area. A few of these ascents included Colonel Edward Porter Alexander, chief of artillery for the Army of Northern Virginia. Alexander signaled messages about troop strength and positions to the ground by means of semaphore flags. The Confederate silk balloon was eventually captured by Union naval forces as it was being transported by steamer down the James River. The envelope was presented to Lowe, but, having no use for it, he had the material cut up into souvenirs for the members of Congress.[17]

While the Confederacy's efforts to organize a balloon corps were stymied by a lack of materials and experienced balloonists, the ingenuity displayed in attempting to create a counter to Lowe's air service is indeed commendable. The elimination of the Federal Balloon Corps in June of 1863 spelled the end of Southern experiments in the field, as it was no longer deemed necessary to combat this Union advantage. General Pierre G. T. Beauregard did use balloon observation in his defense of Charleston, South Carolina, later in the war, but he employed a private balloonist, hired for the purpose, as the Confederate Balloon Service was no longer in existence.

CHAPTER 10

THE SIGNAL CORPS

To the Signal Corps fell the responsibility of relaying orders, information, and intelligence between the commanders of the Civil War armies. The rapid and accurate transmission of these messages might mean victory on a battlefield and were an integral part of the way Civil War commanders waged war. The ability to communicate between portions of armies the size of which were seen during the war made it necessary to employ faster methods than could be achieved with the courier system that had long been in place. A man on horseback carrying dispatches was too slow, in most instances, to cover the amount of ground between portions of an army on a battlefield. Though couriers were used by both sides throughout the war, technological advances made possible a more instantaneous source of communication and information that became invaluable to Civil War leaders and provided the winning edge on many fields of conflict.

Major Albert J. Meyer is known as the "father" of the U.S. Army Signal Corps. Meyer was an army surgeon with an intense interest in various forms of communication. Meyer had worked as a telegrapher before entering Geneva College at the age of 13. Following graduation, he attended the Buffalo Medical College, from which he received his MD degree in 1851. Meyer's doctoral thesis, *A New Sign Language for Deaf Mutes*, developed concepts he would later use for his invention of aerial telegraphy. While attending medical school, Meyer helped to support himself by working part time for the New York State Telegraph Company.[1]

Meyer set up a private practice in Florida for a few years before applying for a commission as an army assistant surgeon. He entered the service on September 18, 1854, and was posted to duty in Texas. While on this posting, he began to devise a system of signaling over long distances using a single flag or a lantern to convey codes that he had invented. The flag was to be used during daylight hours, and the lantern would be substituted at night. Meyer used a quasi-binary code, similar to Morse code, that was brought to life by waving the flag or lantern back and forth. This method of communication became known as the wig-wag system, or aerial telegraphy.[2] Meyer's wig-wag system should not be confused with semaphore, a two-flag system in which each character is expressed by holding the flags in a unique pattern.

In 1858, the army appointed a board to investigate the possibility of adopting Meyer's signal system for military use. Lieutenant Colonel Robert E. Lee served as chairman of the board, which recommended in 1859 that field tests of Meyer's system be held. That April, tests were held at New York Harbor that proved to be highly successful. The board approved of incorporating the signal system into army operations, and Secretary of War John B. Floyd recommended to Congress that it not only approve the system but also appoint Meyer chief signal officer. Congress approved, granting Meyer a commission as major, and the Signal Corps was born. Meyer was sent to New Mexico for field trials of his system in army operations against the Navajos.[3] Meyer was assisted in this assignment by Second Lieutenant William J. Nicodemus, an officer who would later replace Meyer as chief signal officer. Edward Porter Alexander was also a subordinate of Meyer's who assisted with tests of his system. Alexander would one day organize the Confederate Signal Corps based on Meyer's system. The field test exceeded expectations and impressed a number of officers involved in the campaign. Among these was Major Edward Canby, who would later become a major general in the Union army. Canby became a strong advocate of forming a dedicated Signal Corps, while Meyer believed that the best use of his system would be to train officers throughout the army in its disciplines.[4]

At the outbreak of the war, Meyer returned to Washington to undertake his job as chief signal officer with the newly forming army. The only problem was that an actual Signal Corps had not yet been created, and Meyer found himself as the chief signal officer with no staff or men to direct. His only means of finding signalmen was to persuade officers already assigned to other posts to join him. This was a totally unsatisfactory situation, as most officers felt that they would be squandering opportunities for promotion by joining Meyer. In a proposal to Secretary of War Simon Cameron in August of 1861, Meyer lobbied for the creation of a permanent Signal Corps, requesting seven assistant signal officers, forty warrant officers, and forty signal artificers to serve as line builders and repairmen. Congress failed to approve the plan, and Meyer was left to deal with the situation with the resources he had at hand. That fall, he established training camps for the officers he had been able to induce to join him at Fortress Monroe and Georgetown, Virginia.[5]

Union signal station in Washington, DC. (Library of Congress)

The system that Meyer's officers learned involved the use of seven flags, varying in size from two to six feet square. The size of the flag used depended upon the distance between the signal stations. Different colors were also used. Three of the flags were white with a red block in the center, two were black with white centers, and two were red with white centers. The purpose of the different colors was to enable the signalman to select a flag that could be best seen against the background he was operating in. For instance, a black flag was used when the background was the sky, but white was selected if the signalman was amid trees or other green foliage.[6]

A signal party usually consisted of three men: the signal officer, the flagman, and an orderly to tend the horses. Elevation was an essential element to successful signaling, and the higher a signalman could position himself, the further his messages could be received. In instances where signal stations were temporary or on the move, they would be established in places like the top of a hill or mountain, in a tree, on rooftops, or in the steeple of a church. When signal stations were established in permanent or semipermanent locations, signal towers would generally be constructed of wood. The distance between signal stations was determined by how far away a signal officer could see the flags of another station with a telescope. Stations were rarely more than six miles apart and were usually much closer together on a battlefield.[7]

Flags would be the main instrument used by the Signal Corps during the war. Meyer recognized the need for electrical telegraphy within his corps, and he developed a device called the Beardslee telegraph, which used a dial instead of a key to send Morse code. The Beardslee was a less dependable system than the key currently being used, however, and soon fell into disfavor. The reason Meyer felt a need to design a new system is that the telegraph and telegraph operators were not under the control of the Signal Corps. Meyer had requested that this be done in 1861, but the War Department declined to do so. The telegraph and telegraph operators were overseen by the U.S. Telegraph Corps, a separate entity from the Signal Corps that reported directly to the War Department. In April of 1861, Thomas Scott, an executive with the Pennsylvania Railroad, was summoned to Washington to assist in extending railroad and telegraph lines for a capital whose lines of communication had been cut when the Confederates captured Harpers Ferry, Virginia. Scott was commissioned a colonel in the army and appointed an assistant secretary of war. His first act was to secure the assistance of Andrew Carnegie, another railroad man. He also secured the services of four telegraph operators from the Pennsylvania Railroad. These men would be the first members of a Telegraph Corps that would eventually number more than 1,500.[8]

Scott was the only member actually commissioned by the army, and that was bestowed by the Quartermaster Department in order that he might be able to requisition the supplies and materials he needed. The rest of the members were civilians, hired by the War Department and bound by no military protocol. The Telegraph Corps would remain basically a civilian organization, with only a few commissioned officers, for the duration of the war. Operators in the field would experience the same hardships and dangers as soldiers, but they would not be armed. While employed in laying telegraph wire, serving as operators, or performing other duties, members of the Telegraph Corps suffered a 10 percent casualty rate during the war, roughly equivalent to that sustained by soldiers in the Union army.

The separation of the Signal Corps and the Telegraph Corps was a major source of agitation for Meyer. As the chief signal officer in the army, he felt that military communication should be banded together under his supervision and that all of its members should be in the military. In 1863, when Meyer proposed to do away with his Beardslee device and recruit military telegraph operators into his corps, his relations with the War Department came to a head. Secretary of War Edwin Stanton removed him from his post as chief signal officer and replaced him with Major William J. Nicodemus.[9]

Nicodemus took over an organization that contained approximately 1,200 officers and men. The following year he became embroiled in a dispute with Secretary Stanton when it was revealed that the Signal Corps had broken the enemy code and was able to read their messages. As that fact had not been previously reported to the War Department, Secretary Stanton viewed it to be a breech of security and dismissed Nicodemus from the army in December of 1864. Colonel Benjamin F. Fisher, formerly the chief signal officer of the Army of the Potomac, was chosen as his successor, and Fisher would serve in that capacity until the end of the war.[10]

The U.S. Signal Corps went into full operation during General McClellan's Peninsula Campaign in the spring of 1862. McClellan not only used the trained signalmen for army purposes, he also stationed several of them with the navy to ensure effective cooperation and communication between the two branches of the service. This also allowed him to be able to call for fire support from the navy's big guns in a timely manner when the need arose. At Yorktown, McClellan employed the signalmen as observers, reporting on the position and movements of the enemy. At West Point, following the evacuation of Yorktown, Major General William B. Franklin's command received warning of an impending attack because of the special work of the Signal Corps. During the Seven Days Campaign, information provided by the Signal Corps was indispensable in facilitating McClellan's change of base from the York River to the James, and at Malvern Hill, it was a major factor in securing victory for the Union army. General McClellan was aboard the USS *Galena* when the Confederate attack was launched, and he was apprised of the situation by a flagman who sent messages to the signal officer aboard the *Galena*. The general was able to send back orders for his commanders as well as direct the fire of the big navy guns to where they were most needed on the battlefield. The result was a bloody repulse for the Confederate army.

The Confederate invasion of Maryland would have been a complete surprise had it not been for the watchful eye of a Signal Corps officer, Lieutenant Brinkerhoff N. Miner. From his position on Sugar Loaf Mountain overlooking the Potomac Valley, Miner spotted Confederate forces crossing the Potomac River and relayed the information, giving the Federal army its first indication that Lee's Army of Northern Virginia had invaded the state. Miner stayed at his post, sending messages about the size and composition of the enemy army, until he was finally captured by Confederate troops.[11]

Signalmen took an active role in the battle of Antietam. Stations were set up on the right and left of the Union line to establish easy communication with headquarters and to report on enemy activity. From a vantage point on Elk Mountain, First Lieutenant Joseph Gloskoski spied the movement of General A. P. Hill's division approaching from Harpers Ferry to descend on the flank of Ambrose Burnside's corps. Gloskoski signaled the warning,

Signal station on Elk Mountain, overlooking the Antietam battlefield. (Library of Congress)

"Look out well on your left, the enemy are moving a strong force in that direction," but Burnside was not near his headquarters, and the message did not reach him till after Hill's troops launched a devastating assault that threw the Union troops back.[12]

At Chancellorsville, Brigadier General Daniel Butterfield became concerned that the enemy had broken the Union code and could read their flag messages. Butterfield used this hunch to his advantage by directing Signal Corps flagmen to send messages with bogus information intended to deceive the Confederates. This suspected breech in security led to the common usage of cipher discs, two-disc cryptographic devices that could be easily used to change codes at will.[13]

During the first day of fighting at Gettysburg, Lieutenant Aaron B. Jerome occupied several different locations in the town as he observed and reported on enemy troops movements for Major General Oliver O. Howard. The cupola of the Lutheran Seminary and the steeple of the county courthouse were two of his prime spots. Jerome warned Howard that the Confederates were advancing on his right flank in more than division strength and were only opposed by Federal cavalry, but Howard was already hard pressed and could do little with the advance warning to prevent the eventual crumbling of his line.[14] Signalmen on Little Round Top were responsible for General James Longstreet's roundabout march toward making his attack on the second day of fighting. The Confederates had observed that there were signalmen atop the hill, and Longstreet determined to countermarch his men in order to deceive the Federals as to his intention. The signalmen had indeed spotted Longstreet's column on the march and had reported the information to headquarters. The end result was that Longstreet's countermarching did not deceive the Federals, it just gave General Meade time to move reinforcements from other parts of the field to the threatened area.[15] The signalmen on Little Round Top affected the outcome of the fighting on the final day of battle by influencing the placement of Confederate artillery prior to Pickett's Charge. Edward P. Alexander, Lee's chief of artillery on the field and a signalman himself, was constantly moving his artillery in an effort to keep the cannon out of the sight of the spying messengers on Little Round Top.[16]

In the Overland Campaign, from the battle of the Wilderness to the siege of Petersburg, the Signal Corps provided the army with precious information and timely communication in Grant's march across Virginia. Because of their need to be in highly visible locations, they were often prime targets for enemy sharpshooters who hoped to disrupt enemy communication by eliminating this link in the chain. Despite the danger, these noncombatants continued to man their posts until the war was ended.

The Signal Corps in the West performed the same important duties as their comrades in the East and made numerous contributions to the Union war effort. At Vicksburg, Federal flagmen kept General Grant informed of the movements of General Joe Johnston's forces in his rear and allowed for the fullest coordination of the guns of the Federal fleet to aid in the bombardment of the city.

One of the greatest contributions of the signalmen in the West took place during Sherman's Atlanta Campaign. The Confederate code had been broken before the Federals marched out of Chattanooga to begin the campaign. Signalmen with the Union army were able to decipher and relay Confederate messages as soon as they were sent, giving Sherman a tremendous advantage against General Joseph E. Johnston and his Army of Tennessee. Sherman knew the strength and dispositions of the enemy army, and he received news on their plans as if he was an officer in Johnston's command. For about two months he maneuvered Johnston out of one strong position after another, in large part because he knew exactly where the Confederates were and in what numbers. Then, just before the battle of Kennesaw Mountain, a New York reporter got wind of a rumor that the Federals had broken the Southern code. He filed a story about it in his paper, alerting the Confederates to the breech in their security. Johnston immediately changed his code, and Sherman was once more operating in the dark. The subsequent battle of Kennesaw Mountain resulted in a bloody repulse for the Union army, whose commander no longer was privy to the enemy's information.[17]

One Signal Corps member was awarded the Congressional Medal of Honor for his service during the war. Morgan D. Lane was a private and the orderly of a flag officer attached to the V Corps. On April 6, 1865, during the retreat of the Confederate army from Richmond and Petersburg, Lane was with a party of Union troops who captured some Confederate prisoners at Jetersville. Several members of the crew of the CSS *Nansemond* were among the prisoners, and one of them bore the flag of his old ship. Lane captured the flag, which earned him the medal.[18]

Following the end of the war, the Signal Corps was disbanded in August of 1865. It was revived, by act of Congress, in July of 1866. Albert Meyer was reinstated as chief signal officer with the permanent rank of colonel. In an ironic twist, Meyer was given control over not only his flagmen but also the telegraph service. It had taken the government three years, but they had finally come around to seeing the practical advantage of combining the services.

The Confederate signal service was the first to utilize Meyer's wig-wag system on a battlefield in the Civil War, even though the Confederate government had not yet authorized a signal corps to be raised. Edward Porter Alexander served in the U.S. Army as an officer from his graduation from West Point until the time his home state of Georgia seceded from the Union. He then offered his services to the Confederacy and was commissioned a captain of engineers. President Jefferson Davis remembered that Alexander had previously assisted Meyer in developing his signal system and summoned him to Richmond. Alexander was informed that he was to acquire flags and equipment to put a signal corps in the field on short notice. He was given 10 to 12 men for the duty, and he divided them into small groups to practice sending messages by day and night. When it became evident that a battle was to be fought in the vicinity of Manassas Junction, Alexander was sent to General P. G. T. Beauregard to provide him with signal communications. Alexander set up several signal stations in locations that afforded good views of the proposed field of battle and assigned his signalmen to them. On July 21, the opposing armies did indeed clash on that field, and it was Alexander himself who sent possibly the most significant message of the day. Colonel Nathan "Shanks" Evans had engaged his brigade against a force of Union troops in his front, which was thought to be the Federals' main assault force. It was, in fact, only a feint for the main attack. Alexander spotted the Union main body moving through Sudley Springs and, in the first usage of wig-wag signals on a battlefield, sent Evans the message, "Look out for your left, your position is turned."[19] The message kept Evans's brigade from being swallowed up by the Union advance and allowed the Confederates to redeploy and fight a delaying action that made it possible for other units to be shifted to meet the threat.

Signal officers worked within the Confederate army continuously from Manassas onward. As in the North, however, it took some time for the Confederate government to officially create a formal signal corps. This took place in April of 1862, a year before the Union Signal Corps was officially organized. Alexander was a likely choice for chief signal officer, but the position did not go to him. He had been named chief of ordnance for the Army of Northern Virginia, and he chose to remain in that position. The position of chief signal officer went to Captain William Norris, a lawyer from Maryland. Norris had been serving as a volunteer aide on the staff of Brigadier General John Magruder and had established a signal service for the general on the Peninsula. The Confederate Signal Corps was initially authorized to contain 10 officers of the rank of captain or below and 10 sergeants. A later reorganization promoted Norris to the rank of major and added 10 first lieutenants, 10 second lieutenants, and 20 more sergeants. Furthermore, a signal officer was authorized for the staff of each corps and division commander. Provisions were also made to allow the addition of more personnel as required by circumstances in the field. Though the Confederate Signal Corps was significantly smaller than its Union counterpart, it is estimated that some 1,500 men were enrolled in its service during the course of the war.[20]

The Confederate Signal Corps performed essentially the same duties as Northern signalmen and used basically the same equipment. There was one significant difference between the two, however. The Union Signal Corps was involved in intelligence in performing its duty, but the Confederate corps was also charged to perform acts of espionage. In its dual role as a secret service agency, the Confederate Signal Corps was responsible for covert operations that included maintaining an information network that extended from Richmond into Canada. Because the Confederate Signal Corps was so deeply involved in espionage, a great deal of its activity was conducted in secrecy. Very few records exist concerning the Confederate Signal Corps activities, the result of Confederate authorities burning official files when Richmond fell and a subsequent fire at the home of William Norris that destroyed all of his personal documents.

One would think that, given the covert nature of many of their assignments, the Confederate Signal Corps would have been exceptional at the development of secret codes. Such was not the case. Though they changed their codes frequently, Union signalmen were generally able to decipher Confederate codes quickly and obtain valuable information for their side. Southern signalmen enjoyed the same success in breaking Union codes until the Northern signalmen adopted the cipher disc, which made them almost impossible for the Southern flagmen to crack. In this regard, Confederate signalmen operated at a significant disadvantage for the second half of the war. While Northern signalmen continued to "eavesdrop" on enemy messages, Confederate signalmen were relegated to merely relaying orders and passing along information.

Confederate signalmen performed exceptional service at Charleston, South Carolina, where they kept the garrisons of the forts in the harbor constantly informed of enemy concentrations and movements. Several enemy assaults were thwarted due to the advance notice signalmen provided, which allowed the defenders to prepare appropriately. Signalmen at Vicksburg kept General John C. Pemberton informed on the location and activity of Grant's army, helping to make it possible for the Confederates to resist Union advances for as long as they did.

Stonewall Jackson was a great advocate of the signal system and requested that signal officers be assigned to him early in the war. The friendly fire that wounded Jackson the night after the first day's fighting at Chancellorsville killed a signalman by his side. It was another signalman who caught the wounded general as he fell from his horse.

The Signal Corps of both armies performed invaluable service to their respective causes by providing rapid and accurate communication over long distances. They enabled commanders in the field to more efficiently manage and maneuver their forces and, in several instances, were responsible for providing warnings that averted disaster, such as Alexander's warning to "Shanks" Evans that he was about to be flanked by a superior Union force. In many cases, the part the Signal Corps played in determining the outcome of battles is subtler. Consider the case at Gettysburg where General Longstreet countermarched his forces instead of making an immediate attack because he wanted to stay clear of the spying eyes of the Union signalmen on Little Round Top. One can only speculate what might have been the outcome if he had launched his attack immediately, instead of giving General Meade time to rush reinforcements from other parts of his line to the threatened area.

Though it was disbanded at the end of the war, the military quickly recognized the need for a permanent Signal Corps and reinstituted it in 1866. The corps has seen continuous service since that time and has never failed to provide the quickest and most reliable communication for U.S. armies all over the world.

CHAPTER 11

SNIPERS AND SHARPSHOOTERS

Snipers and sharpshooters are both marksmen, proficient in accurate shooting, generally at long range. The main difference between the two is that sharpshooters usually act in conjunction with other units of an army while snipers usually perform their duty individually or in small teams of snipers that act independently of other troops. The word *sniper* is more of a modern terminology, and while Civil War sharpshooters sometimes acted in the capacity of snipers during the war, they were seldom referred to as such. In most cases, the sniper or sharpshooter uses a weapon specifically designed to deliver maximum accuracy and range. During the Middle Ages, units of marksmen were typically formed from archers having special skill with a bow and arrow. One of the most famous marksmen of all time is probably William Tell, whose renowned skill made him a legend in his own time and a well-recognized name in history. The development of firearms effectively eliminated archers from the armies of Western Europe, but the musket was not really suited to marksmanship or accuracy, given that it was smoothbore and fired a round ball slightly smaller than the diameter of the barrel. A round fired from a musket tended to bounce against the sides of the barrel and exit the muzzle at differing angles. This meant that precise shooting was all but impossible and necessitated that men armed with muskets be massed together to fire at enemy targets. The concept of rifling the inside of a barrel, or cutting spiral groves that would cause the bullet to spin in a rotation that would improve accuracy, was developed in Germany in the late 1400s, but it did not find its way into common usage until the nineteenth century. The reason for this is that black powder had a tendency to foul the rifling grooves. In 1847, Claude Minié invented a conical bullet with a hollowed base, intended to expand when fired to catch the rifling inside a musket barrel. This improvement greatly increased both the velocity and accuracy of the bullet, making the widespread use of rifled firearms possible. Muskets previously accurate only at a range of 50 yards could now fire with deadly precision at a distance of 300 yards or more. Armies had been employing rifles for several decades previous to Minié's invention, such as the green-jacketed sharpshooters of the British army who were employed during the Napoleonic Wars. The time taken to load and fire a rifle made them much slower than a musket, however, limiting both their effectiveness and usage. Minié's new bullet was easy to load and fire and could be done as quickly as with a smoothbore, making rifled muskets practicable for universal issue for the first time.

Minié's bullet, called the minié ball, was quickly embraced in the United States by the arms-making industry and by the U.S. military. All new army weapons were manufactured with rifling, and great numbers of existing smoothbores were reconditioned to add rifling to their bores.

At the outbreak of the war, both sides realized the battlefield advantages to be derived from having units of highly trained marksmen in the ranks. Sharpshooters, able to kill the enemy at long range, would provide not only a tactical but also a psychological edge in combat. Accordingly, men having particular skill in shooting were recruited for special units from the very commencement of hostilities. The most famous sharpshooter unit to be formed during the war was undoubtedly Berdan's Sharpshooters, organized under the direction of Colonel Hiram Berdan. An engineer and inventor who had amassed a considerable fortune through the development of a gold amalgamation machine, a reaper, and a mechanical bakery, Berdan was also acknowledged to be one of the finest marksmen in the country and had invented a new type of rifle and a center-fire primer.[1]

In the summer of 1861, Berdan suggested to the government that a regiment of sharpshooters be raised from among the best marksmen in the Northern states. His plan was accepted, and Berdan was given a colonel's commission to command the new regiment. Recruitment posters were distributed throughout the North, stating, "no man be accepted who cannot, at 200 yards, put 10 consecutive shots in a target, the average distance not to exceed five inches from the center of the bull's-eye." The potential candidates were allowed to use their own weapons and would be paid the sum of $60 for their rifle if they were successful in qualifying. Secretary of War Simon Cameron gave Berdan 90 days to raise his regiment, which was recruited from the middle of June to the middle of September. Ten full companies of qualifying men were recruited from New York, Vermont, New Hampshire, Michigan, and Wisconsin in the time allotted. There were enough men desiring entrance into this elite service that it was determined to raise a second regiment, and eight additional companies from Pennsylvania, Maine, New Hampshire, Vermont, Minnesota, and Michigan were also recruited.[2]

Hiram Berdan. One of the finest marksmen in the country and commander of the 1st U.S. Sharpshooters Regiment. (Library of Congress)

During the third week in September, the sharpshooters were ordered to report to Washington, where a camp of instruction was established. They were officially designated as the 1st and 2nd Regiments U.S. Sharpshooters. The recruits were drilled daily, until they attained a reputation as one of the most disciplined units in the army. Special attention was given to their training as skirmishers, which would be their primary duty when they eventually marched for the front. Significant time was also spent on the firing range, where the skill each man already possessed was honed to a fine edge. Spectators from Washington would often turn out to witness and marvel at their shooting practice, which was many times conducted at a distance of 600 yards. The men of Companies C, E, and F of the 1st Sharpshooters were all armed with personal rifles, being of the sporting or target match variety.[3] These rifles varied widely. Each was handmade by a master gunsmith, crafted to perform exceptionally in competitive shooting matches or for hunting. The calibers were generally smaller than military muskets, and they were usually shorter than their military counterparts. Half-stock models were preferable to the full-stock varieties, and most examples featured

Sketches of Berdan's Sharpshooters as they appeared in *Harper's Weekly*, October 5, 1861.

heavy, octagonal barrels. Many came equipped with set triggers, and some had false muzzles to protect the bore and rifling when loading the piece. Weights varied between 14 and 30 pounds, with a few bench-rest target rifles tipping the scales at an incredible 50 pounds. These weapons were excellent choices for use against fixed positions, while the armies were in stationary position. They were not desirable for skirmishing, however, as they were too heavy and too slow to load for the rapidly changing positions of battle formations and the need for fast and sustained fire.

Weapons were not the only distinctive feature associated with Berdan's Sharpshooters. Their uniforms made them easy to pick out in camp or on the battlefield and signified their elite status within the army. Dark green coats and kepis with a black plume set off by blue trousers (later replaced by green trousers that matched the coats) with leather leggings were in sharp contrast to the blue uniforms worn by the rest of the army. Their knapsacks were cowhide covered with horsehair. On their kepis, the standard bugle infantry insignia was replaced with "U.S.S.S." enclosed in a wreath.[4]

The volunteers of Berdan's units had been promised to be issued the finest long-range weapons available, if they did not wish to bring their own, but Colonel Berdan encountered difficulty living up to this promise. The War Department saw no need to supply these marksmen with special weapons. Instead, it proposed to issue the sharpshooters the standard Springfield Rifled Musket, the same long arm being issued to all other infantrymen being mustered into the service. Berdan favored the Sharps breech-loading rifle, invented by Christian Sharps in 1848. The Sharps Rifle was a drop box, .52-caliber, single-shot weapon, renowned for its long-range accuracy. Being a breech-loader, it was also capable of being fired four times as quickly as the Springfield muzzle-loaders, an important advantage for troops who would be performing extensive skirmish duty. Brigadier General James Ripley, chief of ordnance, and Colonel Thomas Scott, assistant secretary of war, both opposed the purchase of Sharps rifles for Berdan's Sharpshooters, and it eventually took the intercession of President Lincoln to secure special weapons for the marksmen.[5]

Before their order for Sharps could be delivered, the sharpshooters were issued Colt Revolving Rifles. The Colt employed a five-shot cylinder of .56 caliber and provided the bearer with rapid-fire capability. While they did not have the range or accuracy of the Sharps, the Colt was still superior to a standard-issue Springfield. One important failing was the fact that they were prone to multiple discharges, a dangerous situation that arose when the firing of one cartridge sparked the rest of the cylinders and caused them all to fire simultaneously. Berdan's troops would begin the Peninsula Campaign armed with the Colt rifles as well as with the personal arms of Companies C, E, and F. In April of 1862, the first six hundred Sharps rifles arrived at Fortress Monroe for the men of the 1st U.S. Sharpshooters. By May 24, the entire contract of two thousand rifles had been delivered, and those sharpshooters using government-issued weapons finally had the rifles they would make famous during the war.[6]

During the siege of Yorktown, Berdan's marksmen proved especially useful in dealing with enemy artillerymen inside the city's defenses. In one instance, a few sharpshooters disabled a Confederate cannon by shooting down its entire crew from long distance. They kept the piece out of action by shooting down every enemy soldier attempting to get the gun back into the fight. Another large cannon was destroyed by carefully placed shots at sandbags surrounding the piece. The bags were pierced in such a way as to allow sand to spill into the bore of the gun. When the Confederates tried to fire the cannon, it exploded, destroying the piece and causing casualties among its crew. Berdan's men performed conspicuous service during the Seven Days Battles. At Mechanicsburg, Gaines's Mill, Bottom's Bridge, and Malvern Hill, they had the opportunity to show both friend and foe alike what they could do with their new Sharps rifles. On the battlefield of Antietam, the sharpshooters punished the Confederates with their rapid, well-aimed fire. They all but wiped out the enemy regiment facing them, and they did more damage than any other Union unit on their part of the field. Their fighting abilities were on display at Fredericksburg and at Chancellorsville, but their constant skirmishing in over a year of fighting was starting to take its toll. Casualty rates were high. The regiments now were well below half their effective strength. What they lacked in numbers was made up for with grit and determination. At Gettysburg, Berdan led four companies of his sharpshooters out from Major General Dan Sickles's line on July 2 on a reconnaissance mission to find out what the Confederates were up to at the southern end of Seminary Ridge. There were only one hundred men in all four companies, a quarter of the number they were mustered in with. They were accompanied by two hundred men of the 3rd Maine Infantry as they marched over the ground toward Pitzer's Woods. The Federals soon stumbled into the Confederate skirmishers of Brigadier General Cadmus Wilcox's brigade, and a firefight broke out. In their front were the 10th and 11th Alabama Infantry Regiments, with a force far superior to Berdan's. Nevertheless, the sharpshooters opened with such a deadly fire that the Southern units were stopped cold. Wilcox reported that there were two full Union regiments in his front and called for assistance. The arrival of Confederate reinforcements, combined with the fact that the sharpshooters were running out of ammunition, finally compelled Berdan to order a withdrawal. The reconnaissance had been successful in developing the position of the Confederates, and it led to General Sickles's fateful decision to advance his corps forward from its assigned position to a line running along the Emmitsburg Road.

After Gettysburg, the 1st and 2nd U.S. Sharpshooter Regiments fought in Grant's Overland Campaign of 1864, where their ranks were further thinned. During the siege of Petersburg, both regiments were under two hundred men, and the sharpshooters were a mere shadow of their former selves, but they still performed invaluable service against the enemy occupying the fortifications barring their way to Richmond and Petersburg. In February of 1865, what was left of the two regiments were mustered out of the service, and the units that had become a legend were no more. Over the course of the war,

California Joe. One of the most famous members of Berdan's Sharpshooters, Joe's shooting abilities made him a celebrity in the army. (Library of Congress)

2,570 men had been enrolled in the ranks of the 1st and 2nd U.S. Sharpshooters. Of this total, nearly 300 had been killed and more than 1,000 were wounded, meaning that they had suffered more than 50 percent casualties.[7]

Berdan's troops were unique in the eastern Union army, being the only units of sharpshooters banded together into full regiments. Most other sharpshooter companies in the East were attached to regiments of regular infantry, to act as skirmishing specialists within their regiments. The 1st New York Sharpshooters was intended to be a full regiment, but it was unable to secure the full complement of men needed. Major W. S. Rowland, one of Berdan's officers, had received authority to raise a regiment of marksmen from New York and Pennsylvania in October of 1862, but he was able to recruit only four companies. These were organized into a battalion and attached to Colonel Alfred Gibbs's provisional brigade at Suffolk, Virginia, where they participated in the siege of Suffolk and Major General John Dix's Peninsula Campaign from April to June of 1863. They were then transferred to the Army of the Potomac in time to take part in the pursuit of General Lee's army from Gettysburg, before participating in all the major engagements of the Overland Campaign and the siege of Petersburg. The 16th Michigan Infantry boasted three companies of sharpshooters within their ranks: Brady's Sharpshooters, Dygert's Independent Company of Sharpshooters, and Hall's Independent Battalion of Sharpshooters. The 16th Michigan was down to only 263 men at the battle of Gettysburg. They were part of Colonel Strong Vincent's brigade charged with holding the all-important heights at Little Round Top. While the 20th Maine earned eternal glory on the left of Vincent's line, the 16th Michigan held Vincent's right, on top of the hill. The Michigan men fought off repeated attacks by the 4th and 5th Texas Regiments and were rallied to hold firm by Colonel Vincent just prior to his receiving a mortal wound. Fighting from behind rocks and trees, the Michigan troops did hold, in large measure due to the marksmanship of their sharpshooter members.[8]

On the left flank of Vincent's line, Colonel Joshua Chamberlain's 20th Maine Regiment received fire support from a detachment of the 2nd U.S. Sharpshooters.

The 1st Regiment Michigan Sharpshooters was recruited from April through October of 1863. It was formed by Captain John Piper, an officer serving in another sharpshooter regiment in the Western Theater, Birge's Western Sharpshooters. Though their unit designation stated that they were a regiment, there were only six companies in the 1st Michigan, meaning that they were just slightly above battalion strength. The Michigan sharpshooters saw action against Major General John Hunt Morgan's Confederate cavalry in Indiana and performed guard duty at Camp Douglas before being attached to the Army of the Potomac in time to take part in Grant's Overland Campaign of 1864. They fought in every major engagement of that campaign and took an active part in the siege of Petersburg. Following the surrender of Lee's army at Appomattox Court House, the unit marched in the Grand Review in Washington prior to being mustered out of the service in July 1865. Despite their relatively short period of time in the field, the 1st Michigan Sharpshooters suffered heavy attrition in their ranks, losing 362 men dead by all causes.[9] The 64th Illinois Infantry was commonly referred to as Yates's Sharpshooters, in honor of Richard Yates, governor of the state, but the nickname was misleading. The regiment served as regular infantry, was not armed with long-range rifles, and was not specially recruited for use as sharpshooters.

The 1st Massachusetts Sharpshooters Company, also known as the Andrews Sharpshooters, was attached to the 15th Massachusetts Infantry Regiment in Major General Winfield S. Hancock's 2nd Corps, and the 2nd Massachusetts Sharpshooters Company was assigned to the 22nd Massachusetts Infantry and dueled with Confederate sharpshooters at Devil's Den on July 2 at Gettysburg. Virtually every Northern state having regiments in the Army of the Potomac had companies of sharpshooters embedded in their organizations in the field.

In the West, efforts were undertaken to raise a regiment of sharpshooters that would emulate the 1st and 2nd U.S. Sharpshooters. Major General John

C. Frémont, commander of the Department of the West, made the creation of a sharpshooter regiment a pet project, and in August of 1861 he authorized John Ward Birge to raise a regiment at Benton Barracks in Saint Louis. Birge, like Berdan, was a civilian, not a military man. In fact, he was an eye doctor from Saint Louis, but, also like Berdan, he was well known for his shooting abilities. In a letter to the newly commissioned officer, General Frémont outlined the qualifications he expected the recruits for the regiment to meet.

> To Col. J. W. Birge, St Louis. Sir, You are hereby authorized to raise a regiment of Riflemen to be under your command and to serve for three years or during the war, unless sooner discharged in accordance with the late act of Congress. The men of your regiment must have produced satisfactory evidence of their ability to hit a target at two hundred yards, no three shots to measure more than ten inches. Your Regiment will rendezvous in this city to which place transportation will be furnished to all recruits and subsistence on their arrival. Recruiting officers will be provided with transportation when traveling in connection with their duties. You will report the progress of your organization to the Head Quarters which will be complete in six weeks.[10]

Men for the regiment were recruited from every loyal state within Frémont's department, with Missouri, Illinois, and Ohio being most heavily represented. Designated Birge's Western Sharpshooters, the regiment was mustered into Federal service on November 23, 1861. Frémont had envisioned a uniform for his elite regiment that distinguished it in the field in the manner Berdan's troops enjoyed. What he envisioned was a standard dark blue Union frock coat, piped with green instead of the normal sky blue that signified infantry. Gray pants with a green stripe down the seam would complete the look, topped off by a distinctive gray sugar-loaf hat—a tall, tapering top hat—to which three squirrel tails were to be attached in recognition of their shooting abilities. Frémont's plans did not materialize as he wished, and the regiment would eventually be issued standard Union infantry uniforms, but sugar-loaf hats remained, making it easy to identify members of the regiment in camp and on the battlefield. Sadly, the hats had also disappeared from their uniform by July of 1862.

Frémont awarded a contract to Horace Dimick, a Saint Louis gunsmith, to provide one thousand plains rifles for the regiment. These were to be hand-made, half-stock long rifles, fitted for bayonets. Dimick had only 150 rifles that were suitable at the time he signed the contract and was forced to secure the rest of the weapons needed from other gunsmiths. The contract price was $25 per rifle, and it was stipulated that a bullet mold, ball screw, and wiper would be provided with each weapon. Owing to the fact that Dimick had to scour the country in search of the thousand rifles needed, there was much diversity in the arms finally issued to Birge's men.[11]

In December of 1861, the regiment was ordered into the field to deal with roving bands of Confederate irregulars and guerilla fighters. From December 14 to 28, it was constantly engaged with forces of Major General Sterling Price's army, culminating with the battle of Mount Zion. The Western Sharpshooters did scouting duty in Missouri in January of 1862 before being transferred in February to General Ulysses S. Grant's army, operating against Fort Henry in Tennessee. The sharpshooters arrived too late to take any part in capturing the fort, but they accompanied Grant's forces in the subsequent campaign against Fort Donelson, where they performed exceptional service in silencing a Confederate battery and keeping it out of action for the entire three days of the battle. The sharpshooters carried whistles that were used to communicate their movements to one another. One reporter who witnessed them in action thought that they moved through the forest like Indians and "wanted no better fun than to creep through the underbrush and pick off the Rebels."[12]

At the battle of Shiloh, the sharpshooters were attached to Major General William H. L. Wallace's division. On the first day of the fighting, the regiment took part in the fearful fighting that took place on the part of the Union line known as the Hornet's Nest. Eleven different Confederate charges were repulsed here before the Southerners massed 62 pieces of artillery to bombard the position. The subsequent charge by Confederate infantry was successful in breaking the line and capturing all of the troops unable to retreat.[13]

Following Shiloh, the designation of the regiment was changed to the 14th Missouri Infantry, Western Sharpshooters. Despite their reclassification, which would be changed again in November of 1862 to the 66th Illinois Infantry, the unit was commonly referred to as simply the Western Sharpshooters for the duration of the war. The regiment participated in the Corinth Campaign, skirmishing daily with the enemy until that city was captured. It fought at Iuka and the second battle of Corinth. Most of 1863 was spent in operations engaging enemy scouts and guerillas before the regiment was attached to General William T. Sherman's army prior to the opening of the Atlanta Campaign. During the latter part of 1863, many members of the regiment rearmed themselves with 16-shot Henry Repeating Rifles. The cost for each rifle was $40, or more than three times the monthly pay of a soldier in the ranks, but more than 250 of the sharpshooters made the investment to acquire the reliable, rapid-firing weapons.[14]

The Western Sharpshooters distinguished themselves in the opening battle by driving a portion of Major General Joe Wheeler's cavalry, along with a brigade of infantry, away from Snake Spring Gap and holding the position until Sherman could effect a flanking march around the Confederate defensive fortifications. The regiment was under fire for 120 days during the campaign and lost 255 men killed and wounded. At the Battle of Atlanta, the Western

Sharpshooters were hotly engaged and added new laurels to their fame. The regiment then took part in Sherman's March to the Sea. On December 9, 1864, the sharpshooters captured a two-gun battery that had opened on them along with seven members of the crew. At Eden Cross Roads, they defeated and drove off a detachment of Georgia militia, nearly a thousand strong, who were fighting from behind breastworks. After the capture of Savannah, the sharpshooters took part in Sherman's campaign through the Carolinas, and they fought their last battle of the war at Bentonville, North Carolina, March 19–21, 1865. With the surrender of General Joseph E. Johnston's army, the war was effectively over for these midwestern marksmen. They participated in the Grand Review, held in Washington on May 24, 1865, before being finally mustered out on July 7. During the course of the war, the Western Sharpshooters suffered 227 fatalities, from all causes.[15] The regiment had earned a glorious reputation during its nearly four years of service as an elite group of fighting men. In the years after the war, many of its members acknowledged this distinction by writing "W.S.S." after their signatures.

As in the East, there were numerous companies of sharpshooters embedded in regular infantry regiments of the western armies. Just like their eastern counterparts, these companies performed the duties of skirmishers and provided long-range fire support for the regiments they were part of.

The use of sharpshooters and snipers was not confined to the Union army. They were well represented in the ranks of the Confederate armies, both East and West, where they performed the same service as skirmishers and long-range specialists as their Northern foes. Confederate troops were generally accredited as being better overall marksmen than the average shopkeeper or laborer of the North, because of their more rural way of life, which included hunting and shooting. Despite this fact, the South was slow to come to the realization that units of long-range marksmen should be included in the ranks of their armies. While there were sharpshooter companies embedded in regiments, just as in the North, there were no large units composed solely of marksmen. The accomplishments of units like Berdan's and Birge's Sharpshooters convinced many high-ranking Confederate officers that the South was operating at a disadvantage by not having similar organizations. Accordingly, in April of 1863, the Confederate Congress passed legislation authorizing the raising of sharpshooter battalions, specifying that these units be not less than three companies, not more than six companies. The troops were to be selected for their shooting abilities and armed with special long-range rifles.

The system of raising sharpshooter battalions in the South differed greatly from that which was employed in the North. Instead of calling for volunteers and holding qualifying shooting matches, the Confederates put together units with men gleaned from existing regiments already in the field. Men who had been serving with their friends and neighbors in the field for a year were often reluctant to leave the regiments they now took pride in to join these new marksman organizations. In many cases, officers of existing regiments were opposed to losing their best marksmen, as well, and found ways to keep these soldiers right where they were. As a result, many of the sharpshooter battalions raised in the South were a mixture of crack shots and average infantrymen from the line. Given the fact that the average Confederate infantryman was still generally a better shot and marksman than his average Northern counterpart, Confederate sharpshooter units operated at a high level of efficiency, but they did not attain the level of excellence that would have been probable if their selection process had mirrored that used in the North.

Most Southern sharpshooter units also lacked the level of training given to units like Berdan's. Target practice, while extensive in the North, was almost unheard of in the South. Most Confederate commanders felt that shooting at targets was a waste of powder and lead. The favored weapon of Confederate sharpshooters was the British Whitworth, a single-shot, muzzle-loading rifle designed by Sir Joseph Whitworth in 1854. At first glance, the Whitworth looked like the British standard-issue 1853 Enfield. The primary difference between the two was that the barrel of the Whitworth had a .451 bore, of hexagonal shape, with a 1-in-20 twist to its rifling. In comparison to the 1-in-78 rifling in standard Enfields, the Whitworth produced a much tighter spiral to its bullets, allowing them to be accurate at far greater distances. The specially designed bullet was longer and thinner than a standard round, and was also hexagonal in shape, to maximize its rotation and distance. Whitworths were accurate to a distance of two thousand yards, or more than a mile, and when equipped with telescopic sights were the state-of-the-art weapon for sharpshooters and snipers. The only problem with the Whitworth was its price. Costing more than four times as much as an Enfield, the Whitworth Rifle was a luxury the Confederacy could barely afford. Instead of arming sharpshooter units exclusively with this weapon, most carried Enfields or sporting target rifles, with a smattering of Whitworth Rifles shared by the members and used when targets of opportunity presented themselves. Only about 250 Whitworth Rifles were purchased by the Confederate government during the war, but the incredible accuracy achieved with them when in the hands of a competent marksman made them one of the most highly regarded weapons of the conflict.

The 17th Alabama Sharpshooters and the 9th Missouri Sharpshooters were the first of the Confederate sharpshooter battalions to be raised and take the field. Both were mustered in to Confederate service by the end of April 1862, a matter of weeks following the passage of the act authorizing their creation. The 17th Alabama was raised by Lieutenant Colonel Benjamin C. Yancey and consisted of two companies raised from within the ranks of the 19th and 39th Alabama Infantry Regiments. The Alabama marksmen served primarily in the brigade of Brigadier General Zachariah C. Deas, taking part in the battles of Stones River, Chickamauga, and the battles around Chattanooga. They saw extensive service in the Atlanta Campaign, by which time their ranks had been severely thinned. By August of 1864, the unit ceased to exist on the rolls of the Confederate army, and those few members still remaining were probably returned to their original regiments.[16]

The 9th Missouri Sharpshooters was raised by Major Lebbeus Pindall and was formed at Fort Smith, Arkansas. A large number of its members came from the ranks of the Missouri State Guard. The unit saw its first action on December 7, 1862, when it fought with distinction at the battle of Prairie Grove. At the battle of Helena, on July 4, 1863, they led the Confederate charge on the Union's fortified positions. The 9th Missouri Sharpshooters played an active role in repulsing General Nathaniel P. Banks's Red River Campaign, and they fought valiantly at the battle of Pleasant Hill. On April 30, 1864, they were engaged in the battle of Jenkins Ferry. For most of the remainder of the war, the unit was engaged in garrison duty, guarding Confederate-held portions of southern Arkansas and northern Louisiana. They were surrendered on June 2, 1865, as part of General Edmund Kirby Smith's Trans-Mississippi Department.

The 14th Battalion Louisiana Sharpshooters was raised through the selection of two hundred men from the 11th Louisiana Infantry when that unit was disbanded. The battalion was formed on August 21, 1862, under the command of Major John E. Austin. On October 8, 1862, the Louisiana Sharpshooters saw their first combat in the battle of Perryville, where they received praise for their gallant conduct. At Stones River, on December 31, 1862, the battalion covered the retreat of the Louisiana brigade after its unsuccessful attack on the Union lines. In May of 1863 the unit was transferred to Mississippi, to reinforce General Joe Johnston's army forming at Jackson to assist the beleaguered forces at Vicksburg. It subsequently took part in the engagements at Jackson until that place was evacuated on July 25. Joining the Army of Tennessee, the 14th Louisiana Sharpshooters fought conspicuously at Chickamauga, where they captured 2 cannon and 86 Union prisoners. They took part in the battles around Chattanooga before the commencement of the Atlanta Campaign in the spring of 1864. Frequent skirmishing during the Atlanta Campaign decimated the already thin ranks of the battalion, and by May 24, at the battle of Pumpkin Vine Creek, only 45 men were present for duty. Of these, 15 fell as casualties. After the fall of Atlanta, the battalion accompanied General John Bell Hood on his invasion of Tennessee. The unit's strength had evaporated to only 24 members by this time, and while they fought bravely at the battle of Nashville in December of

1864, their numbers constituted only a rifle platoon, not a battalion. In February of 1865, the remaining members of the 14th Louisiana Sharpshooters were consolidated with the survivors of three other Louisiana regiments to form Company H of the Chalmette Regiment, and the sharpshooters officially disappeared from the rolls of the Confederate army.[17]

By 1863 the Confederate high command recognized the errors it had made in forming the sharpshooter battalions for the army. Officers like Major Generals Patrick Cleburne and Robert Rhodes were taking steps to ensure that the efficiency of sharpshooter units within their sphere of influence were brought up to the standard of elite units. Whether it was because of his previous military service in the British army or due to a belief that Civil War battles would increasingly be fought from behind fieldworks and fortifications, Cleburne recognized that sharpshooter companies with extensive marksmanship training would be essential on the battlefield. Cleburne gained the support of his officers and men for the project, and orders went out for each regimental commander to submit the names of the five best marksmen in their unit. These men were then tested on the firing range, and the best among them were selected to form the battalion. The men were then extensively trained in skirmish tactics and for use as flankers. They were also trained to be used for the specific duty of silencing enemy artillery.[18]

In Virginia, General Robert Rhodes formed a sharpshooter battalion within his brigade in similar fashion. Rhodes assigned Major Eugene Blackford, of the 5th Alabama Infantry, to raise and command the battalion. The nucleus of the unit was a sharpshooter company currently serving with the 5th Alabama that Blackford had already recruited. To this core was added the finest marksmen in the brigade, and the battalion spent the winter of 1862–63 constantly training in skirmish tactics and improving their marksmanship. Regrettably, the Confederate army did not adopt the models Cleburne and Rhodes presented until 1863 and 1864, thus losing a tactical advantage that might have been gained on many hard-fought fields of battle.

An example of the slowness with which the Confederate high command fully embraced the role of sharpshooters with the army can be seen by examining the Army of Northern Virginia during the Gettysburg Campaign. Before embarking on the invasion of Pennsylvania, orders went out that each regiment must provide one skirmisher out of every six soldiers to form ad hoc sharpshooter battalions. Calls for volunteers were also made. These troops, with little or no real training as sharpshooters, performed the duties of sharpshooters during the battle of Gettysburg. In spite of their lack of training, they accredited themselves admirably during that battle, and they made things hot for the Federals on numerous occasions. At the end of the campaign, these sharpshooters were returned to their former units, however, instead of continuing in the service as elite marksmen.[19]

In 1864, the Army of Northern Virginia finally got around to establishing permanent sharpshooter battalions that were indeed elite fighting units. This time, orders went out to the regimental commanders to select three or four men from each company who displayed not only superior shooting abilities but who also exhibited the finest qualities of courage and steadiness on the battlefield. Commanders of the sharpshooter battalions then screened the candidates to fill the battalion with the absolute best from the soldiers who had been selected. The situation had changed dramatically since the army had first formed sharpshooter battalions in 1862 in that the soldiers were no longer reluctant to leave their old regiments. Part of this change of heart was due to the fact that sharpshooter service was now seen as elite duty, even if it was extremely hazardous. The main reason for the change in opinion, however, came from the privileges being granted to sharpshooters. Sharpshooters were exempt from all regimental or camp duty and were excused from picket duty except in the face of the enemy. This distinction set the sharpshooter apart from the average infantryman in the ranks. Also, their work as skirmishers ensured that they would usually be the first to engage the enemy and, as such, the first to reap the spoils of enemy goods when the Federals were defeated and driven back from a position or campsite.[20]

While it took some time for the Confederates to create truly elite sharpshooter units within the Southern army, several of the most significant shooting events of the war were attributed to Confederate marksmen. Major General William H. Lytle was mortally wounded at long range by a Confederate sharpshooter while leading a charge during the battle of Chickamauga. Major General John Sedgwick, commander of the VI Corps in the Army of the Potomac, was felled by a sharpshooter's bullet at Spotsylvania Court House on May 9, 1864. In Sedgwick's case, the general had just chided his nervous staff officers that the enemy infantry was so far away that they "couldn't hit an elephant at this distance." Within a matter of seconds, he was struck in the head with a bullet fired from within the Confederate lines, some eight hundred yards away. Several Confederate sharpshooters took credit for making the shot, and there is no definitive evidence to credit or discredit any one of them from being the marksman. Accounts vary, but the shooting of Major General John Reynolds on the first day of fighting at Gettysburg may have been the work of a Confederate sharpshooter. It is an unresolved question that has been argued since the time of the battle.

Some snipers and sharpshooters attained great personal fame during the war, to the point of becoming national celebrities. Private Truman Head of the 1st U.S. Sharpshooters Regiment was one of these. Known as California Joe (not to be confused with the western scout with Custer at the Little Big Horn), Head displayed remarkable feats of shooting prowess that soon made him a favorite with the press. His exploits in the field were well documented, and his fame rivaled that of Colonel Berdan himself. The most notable Confederate sniper of the war was Jack Hinson, a partisan sniper from Stewart County, Tennessee. Hinson, a farmer, had been neutral at the outbreak of the war, but his allegiance quickly changed when his two sons were executed in 1862 by Federal troops on suspicion of being bushwhackers and their heads were cut off and placed on the gate posts to Hinson's home. The grieving father sought vengeance on the Union army and undertook a one-man campaign to exact it. Using a custom-made .50-caliber Kentucky Long Rifle, Hinson went on a killing spree that lasted more than two years and saw him take the lives of more than one hundred Union soldiers. His Kentucky Long Rifle was notched 36 times, marking about a third of his victims. As most of his sniper activity was conducted at very long range, these notches possibly commemorated especially difficult shots. The Union army made a full-scale effort to apprehend Hinson, committing portions of four regiments to chase down and capture him, but Hinson evaded all attempts and continued to wage war on the Union until the end of the conflict.[21] He even served as a scout for General Nathan Bedford Forrest during his attack on the Federal supply base at Johnsonville, Tennessee, in November of 1864. Hinson was at the same time the most hated, feared, and celebrated sharpshooter and sniper to emerge from the Civil War—an ironic fate for a farmer who just wanted to be left alone to tend his crops.

CHAPTER 12

THE AMBULANCE CORPS

At the outset of the Civil War, most people on both sides thought that the conflict would be short-lived and relatively bloodless. One Congressman boasted that he would be able to wipe up all the blood spilled in the struggle with his handkerchief. U.S. war history had not prepared the people for the level of carnage and suffering that would be visited upon the land. In the Revolutionary War, 4,435 soldiers had been killed or died of illness. The War of 1812 produced but 2,260 deaths. The Mexican-American War had been the costliest of all U.S. wars, but total deaths to the national forces were still only 13,283. The country would be staggered by four years of fighting that would produce more deaths in a single battle than had been lost in the entire Mexican-American War. Civil War deaths, from all causes, would total an estimated 624,511 men. Almost as many men died in this war as in all the other wars the United States has fought in combined. Another 475,881 soldiers were wounded in the war, making total casualties of just over one million men. The nation, on the whole, was not prepared for bloodletting on this scale and was numbed by the magnitude of the casualty lists that came in from every major battle in what seemed a nightmare of death and destruction. The medical departments of both armies were particularly hard-pressed to provide care to the wounded on the battlefields, awash in a sea of blood and misery with few trained medical personnel and fewer resources to draw upon. In battles such as Spotsylvania Court House, Antietam, Shiloh, Chickamauga, the Wilderness, Stones River, and Gettysburg, where casualties were numbered in the tens of thousands, the medical service found itself hopelessly unable to keep pace with the overwhelming need at hand. Doctors quickly hardened themselves to the harsh reality that they would be limited in their ability to save lives. The Civil War is known as the first modern war because of the technological advancements of weapons, transportation, and communication employed, but medical science was lagging far behind and had advanced little since the Dark Ages.

One of the main problems faced by both armies was the removal of wounded soldiers from the battlefield to receive medical care. In the North, battlefield evacuation was hampered by the fact that there was no special corps to administer the distribution of ambulances. The small number of ambulances in the Union army was under the control of the Quartermaster Corps. They were small, two-wheeled carts pulled by one horse and were extremely uncomfortable for the wounded who occupied them, giving a hard and bumpy ride to their passengers. Inadequate as they were, these ambulances were often unavailable to service the wounded. In many instances, they were commandeered to serve as personal supply wagons by officers or used for military purposes.[1]

After the early battles, most wounded were left to their own devices, or to the charity of comrades, to make their way to the field hospitals to seek medical aid. Those too badly wounded to be able to walk were left to await the arrival of stretcher bearers. The stretcher bearers were also under the control of the Quartermaster Department and were usually regimental cooks or musicians who had no medical training.[2] The system of removing wounded from the battlefield was so bad that William Hammond, surgeon general for the Army of the Potomac, wrote that "600 wounded still remain on the battlefield" eight days after the fighting at Second Manassas had concluded.[3] These horrible conditions had led to the death of many Union soldiers who might otherwise have survived if they had been able to receive medical attention in a timely manner. The deficiencies of the medical service were quickly recognized, and efforts were undertaken to remedy the situation. This reorganization would result in Second Manassas being the last battle where Union wounded did not have access to reliable and efficient removal from the battlefield. A new system of care for the wounded had been instituted, resulting in the birth of the Ambulance Corps.

Military commanders had given little attention to the expanded needs of the medical service. This changed with the appointment of General George McClellan to command of the Army of the Potomac. Dr. Charles S. Tripler was appointed to be the first medical director of the army on August 12, 1861. Tripler began his responsibilities by developing a vast reorganization of the medical service with the army. He advocated the enlistment of regimental surgeons to accompany the troops into the field and the creation of a system of general hospitals where the wounded could be taken to receive proper care.[4] Accordingly, orders were issued in May of 1862 that each regiment must recruit one surgeon and one assistant surgeon before that unit could be activated for service in the field.

On April 25, 1862, Dr. William A. Hammond was appointed to the post of surgeon general by Abraham Lincoln. Hammond had served as an army surgeon from 1849 to 1860, when he resigned to accept a position at the University of Maryland. When the war broke out, he again offered his services to the army and was assigned to Brigadier General William S. Rosecrans's forces in West Virginia. While there, he met Jonathan Letterman, with whom he worked on the design of a new ambulance that was better suited for transportation of the wounded. When Clement Finley was dismissed from his post as surgeon general by Secretary Stanton, Lincoln appointed Hammond to the vacancy, against Stanton's advice.

Hammond assumed his office and immediately began instituting wide, sweeping reforms for the military medical service. He established an army medical school and a permanent general hospital in Washington, placed all ambulances, medical supplies, and hospital construction under the control of the surgeon general, and set up a system of better record keeping for the wounded. He also made it more attractive for doctors to serve in the army by raising their rank and pay.[5]

Hammond knew that before any of his improvements to the medical service could be brought to bear, the wounded must first be evacuated from the battlefields. This meant that the formation of an ambulance corps was a top priority among the surgeon general's list of reforms. Hammond turned to Jonathan Letterman to supervise the development and implementation of the Ambulance Corps for the Army of the Potomac on July 4, 1862. Letterman had graduated from Jefferson Medical College in 1849 and was immediately commissioned as an assistant surgeon in the U.S. Army. He had continued in that capacity until meeting Hammond in West Virginia. When General McClellan came east to assume command of the Union forces at Washington, Letterman came with him. By virtue of Hammond's appointment, Letterman would now become the chief medical officer for the Army of the Potomac.

Letterman, like Hammond, initiated a vast number of reforms upon taking his post. He started by removing regimental control over ambulances. According to his system, each army corps containing two divisions or more would have its own Ambulance Corps commanded by a captain. Each corps would be divided into divisions led by lieutenants. The divisions would travel together and, in certain circumstances, would be combined to form a corps train. Letterman's rule of thumb was that there should be an ambulance for every 150 soldiers. Each corps would have a reserve medicine wagon, and each brigade would have a wagon filled with essential medical supplies.[6] Field hospitals would be established for each division of the army and would be located just beyond the range of enemy artillery. The wounded would be transported by ambulance to these hospitals to receive medical care until they

Jonathan Letterman, the creator of the Union Ambulance Corps. (U.S. Army Medical Department Museum)

could safely be transferred to general hospitals removed from the battle zone. Letterman's arrangement also provided for the first use of triage on the battlefield. Triage is a system used to classify wounded men by priority of treatment. Letterman's triage guidelines used a three-tier priority rating. First priority were those soldiers having serious but survivable wounds. Second priority were soldiers having less serious wounds. Those thought to have fatal or mortal wounds were given the lowest priority and would be evacuated from the battlefield last.

Each ambulance was to be equipped with a locked box under the driver's seat containing six two-pound cans of beef and pork, three different sizes of camp kettles, six tin plates, six tin tumblers, six tablespoons, one lantern and candle, one leather bucket, and three bed sacks. When fighting was imminent, ten pounds of hard tack would be added to the box. Ambulance attendants were trained in rudimentary first aid, a huge improvement over the untrained cooks and musicians that had previously been performing the duty.[7] On August 2, 1862, General McClellan issued orders establishing the

Letterman and a group of his officers. The improvements made in removing the wounded from the battlefield under Letterman's plan saved thousands of Union lives during the war. (Library of Congress)

Ambulance Corps for the Army of the Potomac following Letterman's framework. In little more than a month, care for wounded in that army would be appreciably improved, and all of Letterman's reforms would be justified.

The light, uncomfortable two-wheeled ambulances that had previously been used were phased out in favor of larger, better-constructed four-wheel models. The favored ambulance quickly became the Rucker Ambulance, invented by Brigadier General D. H. Rucker. His design incorporated two movable platforms inside the ambulance that could be positioned to accommodate four prone or six sitting wounded men. Two stretchers were hung from the roof of the ambulance, and two more were on the floor. Louvers were cut into the sides of the ambulance to allow fresh air to ventilate the compartment, which was suspended on platform springs to provide a less jarring ride for the occupants. The two front wheels were somewhat smaller than the rear, also contributing to a softer, less bumpy ride.

By September of 1862 the Ambulance Corps was beginning to take shape, and many of Letterman's reforms were in place. It would take a few more months for the corps to be in total compliance with Letterman's directives, but the framework of his plan was operational and ready to be tested on the field of battle. The Ambulance Corps would face its baptism of fire in the bloodiest day of the entire war, at the battle of Antietam, in the Maryland fields just outside of Sharpsburg. This single day of fighting, the costliest in U.S. military history, would witness approximately 23,000 total casualties, of which 12,469 would be Union soldiers. Of these, 9,416 would be listed on the records as wounded.[8] The number of actual wounded on the field was probably well over 10,000, accounting for those whose wounds proved mortal and were listed among the dead instead of the wounded. Letterman's system would be put to the test under extreme conditions far beyond those imagined when the Ambulance Corps was brought into existence, and it would perform superbly.

Ambulance crews worked efficiently throughout the battle, many times sending stretcher bearers into the midst of heated engagements to remove wounded from the field. Unlike the situation following the battle of Second Manassas, where wounded remained on the field for more than a week after the fighting had ended, Letterman was able to report that all Federal wounded had been evacuated to hospitals within 24 hours of the conclusion of hostilities at Antietam. In fact, one member of the Ambulance Corps stated that "Most of our badly wounded were brought into the hospitals by dark," only a few hours after the battle.[9] "The removal of so large a body of wounded was no small task," Letterman later wrote. "The journey to Frederick in ambulances was tedious and tiresome, and often painful to wounded men. It was necessary that they should halt at Middletown for food, and to take rest." One of the primary reasons for a rest stop was so "the ambulance horses should not be broken-down by the constant labor required of them."[10]

Letterman's plan had successfully saved thousands of Union lives by providing timely evacuation to hospitals where they could receive proper care. It also had a military effect not foreseen during its planning and implementation. In the past, their comrades often helped wounded soldiers to the rear in search of medical attention. This practice naturally weakened a line of battle, where numerous casualties were being taken by able-bodied soldiers vacating their places in the formation. Letterman's system for efficiently removing the wounded drastically cut down on the need for comrades to leave the line, keeping more soldiers at the front, where they could fight the enemy.

By the time the battle of Fredericksburg was fought, in December of 1862, the Letterman system had been fully incorporated in the Army of the Potomac. It would shine at Chancellorsville, in May of 1863, when the Ambulance Corps operated with a speed and efficiency that cleared the wounded Union soldiers from the field with unbelievable rapidity. Dr. Charles O'Leary, medical director for Major General John Sedgwick's VI Corps, left a glimpse of just how well Letterman's system worked in practice when

Union ambulances removing the wounded from the field of Fredericksburg. (Library of Congress)

Sedgwick's troops charged the Confederate defenders on Marye's Heights. O'Leary stated that "The charge was made at 1 p.m ... the heights were taken, and in less than half an hour we had over eight hundred wounded. Two hours after the engagement, such was the celerity and system with which the ambulances worked, the whole number of wounded were within the hospitals under the care of nurses."[11]

Commanders in other theaters of the war had been observing the success of the Letterman system and were making changes within their own medical service. General Ulysses S. Grant was convinced by the spring of 1863, and he ordered that his Army of the Tennessee adopt it on March 30. The Federal government was slow to acknowledge Letterman's accomplishments and embrace the Ambulance Corps, but finally, on March 11, 1864, an act of Congress finally authorized the uniform system of ambulance service throughout the military. The Ambulance Corps, which had been in existence for almost two years, was at last recognized as an integral part of the army.[12]

The corps displayed its training and discipline to the fullest during the battle of Gettysburg. Nearly 14,000 Union soldiers were wounded during the three days of battle that took place from July 1 to 3, 1863, but by the early morning hours of July 4, the corps was able to report that not one wounded man was still on the battlefield.[13]

When General Grant began his Overland Campaign in the spring of 1864, the Ambulance Corps prepared itself for what would be several of the bloodiest months of the war. From May through July, Grant's army engaged in almost daily combat with the enemy. At the Wilderness, Spotsylvania Court House, and Cold Harbor, there were more than 51,000 wounded Federal troops to be transported, and the Ambulance Corps proved itself equal to the imposing task. This was possible because of the sheer size to which it had grown. In 1861, there was usually one ambulance for every thousand soldiers. By 1864, the Fifth Corps could report that it had 160 ambulances for its 17,000 men, or about one ambulance for every hundred men. From the battle of the Wilderness to June 30, when the armies were locked in siege operations at Petersburg, Captain William F. Drum, a medical officer in the Fifth Corps, reported that the 160 ambulances had transported some eight thousand wounded soldiers.[14]

Ironically, neither of the men responsible for the creation of the Ambulance Corps would maintain their post till the end of the war. William Hammond had not been the choice of Secretary Stanton, with whom he had a stormy relationship throughout his tenure as surgeon general. In September of 1863, Stanton sent Hammond on a lengthy tour of the South, to effectively remove him from office. He then appointed Joseph Barnes, a friend and his personal physician, to the post of acting surgeon general. Hammond demanded to be reinstated in his position, and when that was not forthcoming, he requested a court martial. Stanton agreed and then hand selected a board of officers to preside over the proceedings. In a mock trial that was a travesty of justice, several witnesses were brought forward to tell half-truths, innuendos, and flat-out fabrications that impugned Hammond's reputation and demeaned his service. The court found him guilty of "irregularities" in the purchase of medical furniture, and he was dismissed on August 14, 1864.[15]

Letterman continued in the service for only a few months following Hammond's dismissal. After serving briefly as an inspector of hospitals in the Department of the Susquehanna, he resigned from the army in December of 1864. He moved to San Francisco, California, where he served for five years as coroner for the city.[16] The Ambulance Corps would continue to do admirable service through the end of the war, but it would do so without the guiding hand of either man that had been responsible for its creation. The system that Hammond and Letterman had put in place had moved the medical service from the Middle Ages into the Industrial Revolution. It had accounted for many thousands of lives saved and had contributed greatly to diminishing the suffering of the wounded by ensuring them timely medical treatment. The Union Ambulance Corps would serve as a model for military medical departments around the world, and its system of operation would be employed into World War I, where motor vehicles replaced the horse-drawn carts of the Civil War.

A Union ambulance train waiting to go into action. (Library of Congress)

The Confederate army adopted a medical corps that was structured the same as the U.S. Army, but from the very beginning of hostilities, the Southerners operated at a severe disadvantage. The Confederacy found itself short on all medical supplies, particularly surgical instruments. Medicine, and other medical supplies, had to be obtained from sources outside the Confederacy, usually by means of blockade-runners who smuggled the precious cargo from Europe. David C. DeLeon was appointed the first surgeon general of the Confederacy. With little experience in military matters, DeLeon found himself overwhelmed by his responsibilities. His inferior planning for the wounded at the battle of First Manassas led to his dismissal by President Davis. Samuel Preston Moore was selected as his successor, and Moore moved quickly to implement medical standards into the military. He had been an army surgeon since 1835 and was well acquainted with the special needs and operations of the military. One of his first steps was to put in place a review system to evaluate doctors currently serving as surgeons and assistant surgeons with the army. Many of them had been pressed into service in the early days of the war, despite the fact that they were not qualified to hold the positions. Moore weeded these inadequate officers out of the service and replaced them with competent surgeons.[17]

The South was so short on medical supplies and facilities that the military initially employed a policy of furloughing wounded soldiers to go to the homes of family or friends to recover from their injuries. For the first year of the war, army surgeons were expected to provide their own medical supplies and instruments. In 1862 the government took over responsibility for providing these items, and each regiment was issued a medical kit containing essential material needed for the care of the wounded.[18]

Beyond taking steps to ensure that Confederate surgeons were fully qualified to perform their duties, Dr. Moore initiated several other policies that had far-reaching effect. He established the *Confederate States Medical and Surgical Journal*, which was designed as a manual to instruct surgeons using descriptions and drawings of operations. He also founded the Association of Army and Navy Surgeons of the Confederate States of America and included dentists into the organization. This meant that for the first time in U.S. history, soldiers and sailors would have access to dental care. Moore led the way in developing new drugs, to supplement the few medicines that could be smuggled through the blockade, by using the South's indigenous plants to create substitutes. One of his greatest contributions came from the design of a barracks-style hospital layout. These were single-story, pavilion-type structures built like an army barracks complex. His system was highly functional and is still in use today. These hospitals were built throughout the South to serve as general hospitals for the Confederate sick and wounded.

The most famous of these was Chimborazo Hospital, in Richmond. This massive facility, located on Chimborazo Hill, overlooking the Confederate capital, would contain 150 hospital buildings, each being 100 feet long, 30 feet wide, and one story tall. Surgeon James B. McCaw was in charge of the complex, which included five icehouses, a Russian bath, a bakery, herds of cattle and goats, and a canal boat used for trading to obtain needed medical supplies. So far as it was possible, men from the same state were housed together in the hospital wards and were ministered to by surgeons from their home state. From 1862 to 1865, Chimborazo Hospital was the largest medical facility in the world, treating some 76,000 patients during that time. Of these, approximately 17,000 were wounded. The hospital did an admirable job of restoring soldiers to good health, having a death rate of just over 9 percent—very low when compared to other hospitals of the time. When Richmond was evacuated by the Confederate army on April 3, 1865, Union forces under the command of Major General Godfrey Weitzel took possession of Chimborazo. Weitzel placed the medical staff and patients under his protection and issued passes for the doctors to pass through army lines freely. He also offered to place Doctor McCaw in the general service of the United States so that he might requisition supplies and medicines for the hospital the same as any other medical director in the Union army. McCaw declined Weitzel's generous offer because General Lee's army had not yet surrendered and he felt it would be a traitorous act to place himself under the command of the enemy.[19]

Regrettably, the Confederate army did not have a Jonathan Letterman, and it did not have a unified ambulance corps during the Civil War. This was more the result of shortages of material than of personnel. The South had far fewer ambulances than were available in the North. Though they tried to do the best they could with the resources at hand, the Confederate ambulance service operated throughout the war under the organizational system that had been present in the Union army prior to Letterman's system being accepted. Generally, each Confederate regiment possessed an ambulance to serve the soldiers in that regiment. Not being under a central authority, Confederate ambulances were often used for purposes other than bearing wounded, just as had been practiced in the Union army before they were removed from the control of the Quartermaster Department.

One noted Southern ambulance organization of the war is the Richmond Ambulance Corps. When the war first broke out, a number of prominent citizens of Richmond formed a committee to serve the medical needs of the soldiers. John Dooley was chosen captain of the organization, though none of the members were enrolled in the Confederate army nor received any pay for their services. The Richmond Ambulance Corps served during all of the major engagements of the Army of Northern Virginia through the war, and it was not disbanded until Lee's surrender at Appomattox Court House on April 9, 1865. Several of its members went into the army as soldiers, while others hired substitutes to take their place so they could continue their work. Most were exempt from military service for one reason or another. The Richmond Ambulance Corps counted some 50 members during its existence and, as one former Confederate soldier put it, deserved "the gratitude of all surviving veterans."[20]

Barring the availability of necessary ambulances, one Confederate doctor sought to improve the care of wounded Southern soldiers through an innovative method that would find further implementation in later wars. Samuel H. Stout was a surgeon for the 3rd Tennessee Infantry before being placed in charge of a general hospital in Nashville. When Union forces captured that city, Stout relocated to Chattanooga, where he was soon made medical director of hospitals for the Army of Tennessee. Stout established a system of movable hospitals that would serve as pioneer for the MASH units of the Korean War. He selected locations in towns that were close to the front to allow easy access to battlefield wounded and were along railroad lines for easy transportation. In the event that enemy forces threatened to overrun a hospital, Stout's system provided for mobilization that would evacuate the sick and wounded to a preselected "safe" location. The medical staff would pack up bedding, food, and medical supplies and follow to the new site. Stout's system of moveable hospitals was used repeatedly during the Chickamauga and Atlanta Campaigns, as hospitals for the Army of Tennessee were constantly relocated to keep them out of the reach of the ever-advancing Union army. During his tenure as medical director, Stout supervised the location and construction of twenty-three hospitals in Alabama, four in Florida, fifty in Georgia, three in Mississippi, twenty-one in North Carolina, two in Tennessee, and thirty-nine in Virginia.[21] Stout attempted to follow General John Bell Hood into Tennessee during that officer's invasion of the state in the fall of 1864, but problems with the deteriorating transportation and supply systems of the Confederacy prevented him from doing so.

CHAPTER 13

PARTISAN RANGERS

Partisan rangers are special fighting units that make war on the enemy using irregular tactics in occupied areas. Their objectives are to disrupt enemy communications and supply lines, ambush enemy columns, provide intelligence regarding the movements and dispositions of enemy forces, and compel the use of large numbers of troops to guard against their raids that would otherwise have been available for service at the front. They are one of two basic groups that engage in irregular warfare, the other being guerillas. The difference between the two is that guerillas are generally loosely organized units made up of civilians and operating independently of any higher military authority. Partisan rangers are usually enrolled in the army as soldiers and operate under a chain of command to accomplish specific military objectives. Confusion arises due to the fact that many Southern units called themselves partisan rangers when they were, in fact, guerilla organizations, operating on their own accord for personal animosity or profit.

In an effort to harass Union forces operating in Confederate territory, the South enacted the Partisan Ranger Act on April 21, 1862. This law granted President Davis the authority to commission officers to raise companies, battalions, and regiments of partisan rangers for Confederate service. These troops would be regularly enrolled in the Confederate army and would be provided the same pay, equipment, and supplies as all other Southern troops. One great difference was the fact that these troops would be able to profit greatly from their military activities. All arms, ammunition, and supplies captured by them were to be turned over to the Quartermaster Department. They would then be paid a fair market value for these items, to be distributed by shares among the men. In this way, partisan rangers were rewarded by the same sort of "prize" system in use by the Union and Confederate navies. The ability to

Colonel John Singleton Mosby, commander of the most successful partisan ranger unit in the war. (Library of Congress)

profit from spoils of war was a great incentive for many soldiers to join the partisan rangers.

The most famous partisan ranger unit to emerge from the war was Mosby's Rangers, named for their leader, John Singleton Mosby. Mosby was diminutive in appearance, but he was possessed of fierce determination, unbounded energy, and a courageous nature that more than made up for his slight size. The target of bullies as a boy, he never ran away from a fight, even though he rarely won. While attending the University of Virginia, he was bullied by the local tavern keeper's son, George Turpin, a large and imposing young man. An altercation developed between the two, at which time Mosby produced a pistol and shot Turpin in the neck, killing him. He was arrested and brought to trial, where he was found guilty of unlawful shooting, a misdemeanor offense punishable by a year in prison and a $500 fine.[1]

Mosby served a small portion of his sentence before being granted a pardon by the governor of Virginia. While in jail, he had become friends with the prosecutor in his case, William Robertson, and had expressed a desire to study law. Mosby studied for months before taking and passing the Virginia bar exam. In 1857 he settled in Bristol, Virginia, to set up his private practice. When war broke out, Mosby was against secession, but when Virginia left the Union he enlisted as a private in a local cavalry unit, the Washington Mounted Rifles, that would become a part of the 1st Virginia Cavalry Regiment. He fought at First Manassas, and his subsequent service was such that he was promoted to the rank of first lieutenant and transferred to Jeb Stuart for service as a scout. He was captured during Stuart's celebrated ride around McClellan's army during the Peninsula Campaign and sent to Washington pending exchange. While there, he collected several valuable pieces of information, which he imparted to General Lee upon his release, that were highly beneficial in the planning of the Second Manassas Campaign.[2]

Mosby had been lobbying Stuart to allow him to create an independent cavalry command of partisan rangers in Northern Virginia, and his request was granted in December of 1862 when he was authorized to raise the 43rd Battalion Virginia Cavalry. The area he would operate in was primarily located in Fauquier and Loudon Counties, though missions would sometimes carry him beyond this region. Most of his recruits were men living within his area of operations, residents who could easily blend in with the local populace and who had intimate knowledge of their surroundings. They would dress in civilian clothes when not on a raid and disperse among the local population. When called for a mission by Mosby, they would dress for the occasion in some sort of uniform. The uniform each man wore was according to his own particular taste and style. " 'Something gray' was the one requisite of our dress," wrote one of the rangers in later years.[3]

Mosby did not issue swords to his men. He felt them to be useless weapons in a battle. He ordered each of his troopers to be armed with two .44-caliber Colt army revolvers, worn in belt holsters. Many of his troopers carried additional revolvers in the tops of their boots. James Munson, one of the rangers in Mosby's command, stated that their commander stressed accuracy in close engagements, which, when combined with a surprise attack, would generally give victory to the partisan force.

> Revolvers in the hands of Mosby's men were as effective in surprise engagements as a whole line of light ordnance in the hands of the enemy. This was largely because Mosby admonished his men never to fire a shot until the eyes of the other fellow were visible. It was no uncommon thing for our men to gallop by a tree at full tilt, and put three bullets in its trunk in succession. This sort of shooting left the enemy with a good many empty saddles after an engagement.[4]

Mosby achieved his first great exploit of the war on March 9, 1863, when he led 29 men into Fairfax Court House on a raid. Fairfax was occupied by

Colonel Mosby and a group of his rangers. Mosby is seated in the second row with his legs crossed. (*The Photographic History of the Civil War in Ten Volumes: Volume Four, The Cavalry*, Review of Reviews Co., New York, 1911, p. 171)

thousands of Federal soldiers and served as headquarters for Brigadier General Edwin H. Stoughton. Mosby's men made their way through Union lines undetected and rode to Stoughton's headquarters, where they found the general asleep in bed. Mosby spanked the officer on the back, rudely awakening him from his slumber. When Stoughton demanded to know the meaning of this outrage, he was asked if he had ever heard of Mosby. "Yes, have you caught him?" the general replied. Mosby introduced himself and informed Stoughton that he was his prisoner. He then ran a bluff by informing the general that "Stuart's cavalry has possession of the Court House; be quick and dress." The rangers then escorted the general out of town, along with 2 captains, 30 enlisted men, and 58 captured horses. The entire operation had been conducted without firing a shot, and when its results were made public, Mosby was at once catapulted into national prominence.[5]

As many as 1,900 men would serve with Mosby during the war, though he never had more than a couple hundred at any one time, and these were usually separated into different commands to strike multiple targets at the same time. This strategy kept the Federals constantly on the alert and forced them to use large numbers of troops to protect their lines of communication and supply. This was Mosby's objective. He stated that a "small force moving with celerity and threatening many points on a line can neutralize a hundred times its own number. The line must be stronger at every point than the attacking force, else it is broken."[6]

On February 17, 1864, the Partisan Ranger Act was repealed under pressure from Robert E. Lee and other high-ranking Confederate officers. The actions of many of these units had become an embarrassment to the Confederate government, and their lawless activities were felt to be damaging to the Southern cause. Officers and men of the partisan units were ordered to report for regular service, and their organizations were officially disbanded. Two units in the field at that time were exempted from this law, one of them being Mosby's Rangers. Mosby's troopers had a reputation for exercising military discipline in the field and for operating within the bounds of military law. The other unit granted exemption was McNeill's Rangers, which will be discussed later in this chapter.

On August 13, 1864, Mosby's Rangers pulled off one of their most spectacular accomplishments of the war. With approximately 330 men, the largest force he would ever lead at one time in the war, Mosby, now a lieutenant colonel, made a raid on the supply lines of Major General Phil Sheridan. The rangers intercepted Sheridan's wagon train near Berryville, Virginia. After driving off the train's cavalry and infantry escort, Mosby's men descended on their prize. About a hundred wagons, loaded with badly needed supplies for Sheridan's troops, were put to the torch. The rangers captured 208 prisoners, 500 mules, 36 horses, and 200 head of cattle. The capture of this supply train dealt a crippling blow to Sheridan, who was forced to fall back to his former position.[7]

A celebrated event known as the Greenback Raid took place on October 14, 1864. Mosby's band derailed a train on the Baltimore & Ohio Railroad near Kearneysville. The raid was successful in capturing and destroying a U.S. military train consisting of a locomotive and 10 cars. Twenty prisoners and 15 horses were also captured. Among the prisoners were two army paymasters, carrying $168,000 in currency to pay Federal troops. The money was divided between the rangers, with each man getting about $2,000. Mosby declined to take a portion of the money himself.[8]

A sad event took place in November of 1864 when Mosby ordered the execution of seven Union prisoners belonging to the command of Brigadier General George Armstrong Custer. This act was in retaliation for an earlier incident in which seven of Mosby's men had been hung or shot. On September 23, 1864, six rangers had been captured during an attack on Union cavalry at Front Royal, Virginia. By the orders or consent of General Custer, all six were executed. Four were shot to death and two were hanged. A Federal trooper scrawled a note that was hung around the neck of one of the hanged men. It stated, "This will be the fate of Mosby and all of his men." Another member of Mosby's command had been hanged by order of

Brigadier General William Powell. Mosby wrote to General Lee of his intention to execute seven Federal prisoners in retaliation for this atrocity, and he received the endorsement not only of Lee, but of the Confederate War Department as well. On November 6, at Rectortown, Virginia, Mosby made good on his threat of retaliation. The rangers had captured 27 men belonging to Custer's command, and these were assembled for a lottery. A hat containing 27 pieces of paper, 7 of them being numbered, was passed among the prisoners to draw lots. Those drawing the marked slips were to be executed. One of the condemned was a drummer boy, and when it was brought to Mosby's attention he ordered that another lottery be held to replace him. The seven men were then taken away for their execution. Along the way, one of the prisoners noticed that an officer of Mosby's command, just returning from a raid, wore a piece of Masonic regalia on his uniform. The prisoner was also a Freemason, and he gave the secret Masonic distress signal. The Confederate officer, Captain R. P. Montjoy, recognized the sign and substituted one of his recently captured prisoners for the condemned man. When the rangers arrived at the place where the executions were to be carried out, three of the condemned men were hanged. Two more were shot in the head but miraculously survived. The remaining two escaped, much to the relief of those assigned to perform the executions.[9] On November 11, Mosby sent a message to General Sheridan explaining his actions and asking that both sides resumed treating prisoners humanely. He pointed out to Sheridan that his troops captured far more of his men than they lost to the Federals. The Union high command agreed, and for the rest of the war captured members of Mosby's command were treated as prisoners of war.[10]

Mosby and his command participated in nearly three dozen raids and engagements during the course of the war. The exploits of his rangers accounted for more than 1,200 Federal soldiers killed, wounded, or captured, including a general. More than this, their actions immobilized an inordinate number of Union troops to guard against his forays. "General Grant at one point reported that seventeen thousand of his men were engaged in keeping Mosby from attacking his weak points, and thus away from active service on the firing line."[11] With a force barely reaching the size of three full companies, Mosby's Rangers were able to confuse, harass, and immobilize enemy armies nearly a hundred times their own size. It is little wonder that this command emerged from the war as one of the most famous on either side.

McNeill's Rangers was the other partisan ranger unit that was allowed to continue after the repeal of the Partisan Ranger Act. John Hanson McNeill was born and raised in western Virginia. In 1848, he and his family moved to Missouri, where McNeill made a living in the cattle business. When the war broke out, he raised a company of men for the Missouri State Guard and fought in several engagements before being captured by the Federals.

McNeill escaped and made his way east to Richmond, where he gained permission to raise a unit of partisan rangers in the South Branch Valley where he had been born and raised. Captain McNeill was directed to report to Colonel John D. Imboden, and on September 5, 1862, that officer gave McNeill written authorization to recruit his volunteers.[12]

McNeill enrolled more than two hundred troopers during the course of the war, but he never had more than one hundred men in his command at any given time. Despite their small number, McNeill's Rangers caused havoc for the Union forces in western Virginia, West Virginia, and Maryland that was greatly disproportionate to their own size. Their operations included raids on Federal camps and wagon trains, but their main focus was the disruption of the Baltimore & Ohio Railroad.

The first important action for McNeill's Rangers was on January 2, 1863, when they accompanied a raid into Hardy County commanded by Brigadier General William E. Jones. The rangers scouted in advance of Jones's force and covered his withdrawal. McNeill's men were credited with capturing 33 Union soldiers, 46 horses, and 5 wagons during the raid.[13] On February 16, 1863, McNeill's Rangers attacked a Union supply train near Romney, West Virginia. The rangers only had 23 men, and the supply train was guarded by 150 Union infantry and cavalry, but McNeill's men emerged victorious. Their wild rebel yell so frightened the guard that McNeill's men were able to take 72 of them as prisoners. They also captured 106 horses and 27 wagons filled with supplies.[14]

McNeill devised a plan to destroy the Cheat River Bridge, an important span on the B&O Railroad, and submitted it to higher authorities. His plan called for a swift-moving force of six hundred men to make a surprise attack on the bridge. The attack on the bridge was approved, but McNeill's plan was expanded into a large-scale operation involving the commands of both John Imboden and William E. Jones and encompassed other targets over and above the Cheat River Bridge. McNeill's Rangers were assigned the mission of destroying the B&O Railroad bridge at Oakland, Maryland. The large numbers of Confederates involved in the operation warned the Federals, and the Cheat River Bridge was not destroyed. McNeill's portion of the mission was a huge success, however, as the rangers destroyed the bridge assigned to them and returned with 57 Union prisoners.[15]

On September 11, 1863, McNeill's Rangers participated in an attack on a force of three hundred Federals near Moorefield, West Virginia. A surprise assault was launched at dawn, when many of the Federals were still in their tents. In the short fight that ensued, about 30 Union soldiers were killed or wounded too badly to be moved. Another 146 were captured, along with 9 wagons, 2 ambulances, and 46 horses. The loss to McNeill's command was three wounded.[16]

Piedmont, West Virginia, was a frequent target for raids by McNeill's Rangers. The reason for this was that there were located in Piedmont several machine shops that were crucial for the operation of the B&O Railroad. On one such raid Captain McNeill reported that his rangers had "burned some seven large buildings filled with the finest machinery, engines, and railroad cars; burned nine railroad engines, some seventy-five or eighty burthen cars, two trains of cars heavily laden with commissary stores, and sent six engines with full head of steam toward New Creek. Captured the mail and mail train and 104 prisoners on the train."[17]

McNeill's Rangers were a constant source of irritation to the Union army in their theater of operations for the entire war, but John McNeill would not lead them in all of their successful raids. His service to the Confederate cause would culminate on October 3, 1864, in an attack on a Union supply train at Mount Jackson, Virginia. The rangers numbered 60 men, and the train was guarded by approximately 100. As was his custom, McNeill launched his assault at dawn, and the rangers rode into the camp of surprised and frightened Federals without much trouble. The Union troops were offering light resistance, and 60 of their number were taken prisoner, in addition to those killed by the rangers. The raid proved to be a disaster for the rangers, however, as Captain McNeill fell from his horse, mortally wounded. It was reported that the shot came accidentally from one of his own men. McNeill called his son, Jesse, to his side and instructed him to take command of the unit. Jesse and other rangers got McNeill back into the saddle and took him back to Hardy County, where he died on November 10, 1864.[18]

Young Jesse did an admirable job as commander of the rangers. Under his direction the unit pulled off its most dangerous raid and one of the most notable exploits of the war. In the early morning hours of February 21, 1865, McNeill's Rangers rode into Cumberland, Maryland, for a very special mission. Cumberland was a Federal-held city and was garrisoned by several thousand Union troops. McNeill's Rangers numbered only 63 men. The reason for the raid was to fulfill a threat John McNeill had made before his death to avenge a wrong done to his family. McNeill's wife and children had been arrested by Brigadier General Benjamin Kelley in 1862 and had been confined for a while at Camp Chase. The elder McNeill had vowed to get even with Kelley one day by riding into Cumberland and kidnapping him from his headquarters. Jesse sought to fulfill the vow before the war was ended.

The rangers made their way to Cumberland in a blinding snowstorm. They divided into parties, with one going to the Revere House Hotel and another to the Barnum House Hotel. General Kelley roomed at the Barnum House and Major General George Crook was a guest at the Revere House. Both generals were asleep when the raiders entered their rooms, but each was quickly awakened and apprised of the fact that they had fallen into the hands of the

Confederates. The generals dressed and were then led out to the street, where they were mounted. The rangers successfully bluffed challenges by the Union pickets on their way out of Cumberland and were several miles away from the city when they heard a cannon shot sound the alarm for the garrison. After eluding the Federal pursuit sent to catch them, the rangers delivered their captives to Confederate authorities in Richmond. When Colonel Mosby heard of the exploit, he was reminded of his mission to capture General Stoughton at Fairfax. Laughingly, Mosby stated, "You boys have beaten me badly. The only way I can equal this will be to go into Washington and bring out Lincoln."[19]

Brigadier General John Hunt Morgan led another famous partisan ranger unit in the war. Morgan's cavalry would gain everlasting fame during an 1863 raid that covered one thousand miles, from Tennessee to southern Ohio. His raiders would also be credited with achieving the deepest penetration northward of any Confederate unit during the war.[20] While this raid captured the imagination of the people of the South and caused considerable concern for the North, its end result was a complete failure for the Confederate cause. To begin with, Morgan had undertaken his raid in violation of orders from his superior. General Braxton Bragg had explicitly instructed him not to cross the Ohio River and enter Northern states, but Morgan, seeking glory, disregarded his orders and pushed northward anyway. During his raid, which lasted from June 11 till July 26, Morgan's men captured and paroled some 6,000 Federal troops, mostly militia, destroyed 34 bridges, and disrupted the railroad at 60 locations. In Ohio alone, his raid caused such concern as to necessitate the calling up of 49,357 militia troops to man 587 local companies.[21]

On July 19, 1863, a force of Union cavalry, supported by naval gunboats, trapped Morgan's Raiders at Buffington Island, West Virginia. In the ensuing fight, 750 of Morgan's men were captured, but the general made good his escape with some 400 followers. Barred from crossing into West Virginia, Morgan's remaining raiders rode into southern Ohio, pursued by Union cavalry. At Salineville, on July 26, his force was finally overtaken. In the resulting battle, Morgan's Raiders ceased to exist as a military unit. Twenty-three of the remaining raiders had been killed and nearly 300 more taken prisoner. General Morgan was captured himself later that day. Morgan and several of his officers were taken to the Ohio Penitentiary, in Columbus, and held there till November 27, when Morgan and six of his officers escaped.

Following his return to Confederate service, he was placed in command of the Trans-Allegheny Department, embracing East Tennessee and southwestern Virginia, on August 22, 1864. At this time, he was being quietly investigated for charges of criminal banditry by Confederate officials. Morgan organized a raid aimed at Knoxville, Tennessee, which would be his last operation of the war. On September 4, his force was surprised by Union cavalry at Greenville, Tennessee, and Morgan was shot and killed.[22]

Other notable leaders of partisan groups were Turner Ashby, whose Black Horse Cavalry terrorized Union forces in Virginia during the early stages of the war. Ashby was the most famous cavalry leader on either side during the first year of the conflict, but his service was cut short when he was killed on June 6, 1862, near Harrisonburg, Virginia. Captain John "Dixie" Dickinson commanded a unit of partisan rangers in Florida. Though his exploits were on a grand scale, the distance between his command and the major centers of media kept them largely unreported and unknown. Captain Dickinson is credited with commanding the only unit of cavalry to sink an enemy gunboat in U.S. history, when his force sank the USS *Columbine*. Quantrill's Raiders were another famous partisan force to emerge from the Civil War. Under the command of Colonel William Quantrill, this band operated in Kansas and Missouri, raiding Union supply lines and terrorizing the pro-Northern citizens of Kansas. They were responsible for the infamous raid on Lawrence, Kansas, in which the town was burned and 150 to 200 of the male residents were killed. Quantrill's Raiders were more of a guerilla force than partisan rangers, however. Though Quantrill had been granted a commission in the Confederate army, it was later revoked due to stories of the lawless nature of his raids. Despite this, Quantrill continued to lead his guerilla force in the field, settling old grudge matches, until he was shot in a Union ambush on May 10, 1865. He would die as a result of those wounds on June 6.

CHAPTER 14

SCOUTS AND SPIES

Scouts and spies have been a part of the military as long as wars have been fought. The mission of both is to gain information about the enemy that can be used by military commanders in the field. The main difference is that spies usually operate independently of military control, while scouts are part of an army who operate well to the front or flanks of that army, providing information of a more immediate nature. In many cases, scouts performed their duty dressed in the uniform of the enemy, placing them in a most precarious situation. They could be shot by their own troops, who justifiably thought them to be enemy soldiers. If captured, they would be shot as spies, according to the rules of war. Archibald Rowland Jr., a scout who won the Congressional Medal of Honor during the war, described the danger.

> With each day of service in the ranks of the scouts danger became more imminent; the chances of meeting again some party of Confederates with whom previous lies and explanations would not tally with present movements. Also, in the Federal army there were sure to be Southern spies whose business it was to report descriptions of the scouts, and, if possible, their movements; within the Confederate lines; recognition because of these descriptions might take place at any moment. That meant death by noose, or, at best, to be shot down in a last-stand fight ... And then there was the danger of meeting death at the hands of their own men. It happened not once, but many times, that, discovered and hard pressed by the enemy, the scouts in their gray uniforms rode for their lives for the safety of the Union lines, only to be met by the murderous volley of their own mistaken pickets.[1]

Faced with such dangers, what compelled soldiers to volunteer for scout service? Rowland stated that reasons varied, but "there was the money, good gold—no less. They were paid in proportion to the value of the information they brought in and the services they performed; expense money was portioned out with a prodigal hand from the Secret Service chest. They were the Aristocracy of the Army! But most of all they risked their necks because it was exciting."[2]

One of the early scouting organizations of the war were the Jessie Scouts. In the early days of the conflict, Major General John C. Frémont put together a company of scouts and spies who dressed in Confederate uniforms to infiltrate Southern-held territory and gather information. They were named the Jessie Scouts in honor of Frémont's wife, Jessie Benton Frémont. Charles C. Carpenter was given command of the unit, owing to the fact that he had been performing scouting and spying work for General Frémont prior to the raising of the company.[3] Carpenter was described by one Union officer as being "admirably adapted for the dangerous services in which he engages. During the times that General Frémont was in command, he several times performed such services as clearly indicated that he adds shrewdness to the reckless courage which he undoubtedly possesses."[4] Carpenter is reported to have infiltrated the Confederate defenses at Forts Henry and Donelson. His shrewd nature was put to use in ventures outside the realm of scouting, however, and he soon gained a reputation of being a swindler. Regardless of this, he and the other Jessie Scouts accompanied Frémont east in early 1862 when the general was placed in command of the Mountain Department, encompassing portions of Virginia, Tennessee, and Kentucky. Carpenter would later be arrested by order of General John Schofield for his nefarious actions. In the meantime, the scouts performed many missions during Stonewall Jackson's Valley Campaign, spying on Confederate movements and gathering information useful to the Federals.

When Frémont resigned his commission in the end of June 1862, the Jessie Scouts in the East came under the command of Brigadier General Robert Milroy. They served under Milroy until Brigadier General William W. Averell took command of the Fourth Separate Brigade, made up of several of the West Virginia regiments formerly in Milroy's command. The scouts then served under Averell until Major General Phil Sheridan was given overall command in the Shenandoah Valley, in 1864. Sheridan directed Averell to send him his longest-serving scouts, and these Jessie Scouts became the core for what would become Sheridan's Scout Battalion.

General Sheridan authorized the raising of a full battalion of scouts, numbering four hundred men, and selected Major Henry Harrison Young of the 2nd Rhode Island Infantry to command them. Sheridan established the number of scouts to be a battalion strength in order to confuse enemy spies and get the enemy looking over their shoulders, as Young commanded no more than 60 Jessie Scouts while under Sheridan's command. Sheridan charged Young and his scouts with two vital missions. They were to gather

A group of Union scouts and guides posing for the camera. (Library of Congress)

information on the enemy, as the scouts had always done, but they were also to act as an antiguerilla force to track down and eliminate partisan forces such as Mosby's Rangers. The Jessie Scouts, under Major Young, provided valuable information about the Confederates that enabled General Sheridan to win the third battle of Winchester on September 15, 1864. The battle of Cedar Creek could have been very different because of the Jessie Scouts. Information was brought into the Union camp by two of them that General Jubal Early's army was preparing to attack in the morning. General Sheridan was not with the army, being instead at Washington in conference with General Halleck, so the scouts made their report to General Crook. Crook dismissed the information, stating that he had sent out a reconnaissance detail that had found no Confederates. Early's army was there; Crook's detail had not gone far enough to find them. The following morning the Confederates completely surprised the Union army in their camp and nearly dealt a crushing blow to Sheridan's force, setting up that general's spectacular ride to the battlefield to snatch victory from the jaws of defeat. How different the outcome might have been if the warning of the Jessie Scouts had been heeded.[5]

Information they provided was also critical in the decisive Union victory at Waynesboro, Virginia, on March 2, 1865. During Lee's retreat toward Appomattox, Jessie Scouts are credited with intercepting trains carrying supplies for the Army of Northern Virginia when one of the scouts showed the engineers a captured message from General Lee and led them down the tracks, where they were captured by cavalry under George Armstrong

Custer. While the Jessie Scouts had little luck in locating or curtailing the activities of Mosby's Rangers, their greatest accomplishment was the capture of Major Harry Gilmore, commander of the 1st Maryland Cavalry. Gilmore's cavalry had made raids into Union-held territory, and as such, he became a target for the antiguerilla operations of the Jessie Scouts. Young received information as to where Gilmore was staying in Hardy County, West Virginia, and a handful of scouts were sent to capture him.[6]

Another well-known unit of scouts operating with the Army of the Potomac was Blazer's Scouts. This unit traces its beginnings to Colonel Carr B. White, a brigade commander in the VIII Corps operating in West Virginia. On September 5, 1863, White issued orders to create the "Independent Scouts," calling for three officers, sixteen noncommissioned officers, and one hundred men to fill out the company. White advised that "At least half the company will be expected to scout all the time. Its headquarters will be in the woods. None but experienced woodsmen and good shots will be accepted."[7]

Captain John Spencer was appointed to be the first commander of the Independent Scouts, but he served only a short time before resigning from the position. Command then fell to the unit's two lieutenants, Richard Blazer and Harrison Otis.[8]

Lieutenant Blazer was a very meticulous officer. He spent several days before his unit's first mission familiarizing himself with the region he was to operate in. When satisfied that he was sufficiently familiar, he ordered his men to light torches one night and led them on a march through the hills. They did not stop till midnight, and they were once again on the march before dawn. After proceeding a short distance, Blazer ordered the men to stop and check their rifles. He then led them to the bivouac site of a group of Southern partisans known as Thurmond's Rangers. The scouts launched a sudden attack against the camp, taking the enemy completely by surprise. Blazer's men captured 13 prisoners, along with 13 horses and 22 head of livestock, while sustaining no casualties themselves.[9]

Over the next few months, Blazer's Scouts were employed in antiguerilla activities, as well as serving as an advanced guard for Colonel White's brigade when it was on the move. In February of 1864, General Crook became commander of the division the scouts served in, and their status in the army changed. Crook wished to expand both the size and focus of the scouts, and, accordingly, he issued an order that

> The regimental commanders of this division will select one man from each company ... to be organized into a body of Scouts, one man from each regiment so selected to be a Non-Commissioned Officer ... All these scouts when acting together will be under the command of Commissioned officers ... Officers will

be particular to select such persons only as are possessed of strong moral courage, personal bravery, and particularly adept for this kind of service ... The men selected who are not already mounted will mount themselves in the country by taking animals from disloyal persons in the proper manner ... providing, however, that sufficient stock is left these people to attend crops with.[10]

Lieutenant Blazer was given command of this force, which contained several members of his old unit. The Blazer Scouts operated in the area around Charleston, West Virginia, performing missions against local partisans.

When General Sheridan moved his command to the Shenandoah Valley in 1864, he found that his efforts were greatly harassed by the partisan bands operating within the region. Mosby's Rangers were particularly notable for their destructive raids, which at times paralyzed the movement of the entire army. Because of this, General Sheridan decided that he needed to organize a scouting force whose sole mission would be the targeting and destruction of Mosby's Rangers. He spoke to General Crook on the matter, knowing that Crook had experienced success within his division in employing scouts, and asked if there was an officer he could suggest to lead such a unit. Crook immediately recommended Lieutenant Blazer as the best man for the job, stating he was perfect for that kind of work.[11]

Sheridan accepted Crook's recommendation, and Blazer's Scouts became the primary scouting unit for the entire army, not just Crook's division. General Sheridan intended for his scouts to be provided the best equipment available for their mission against Mosby's Rangers. Accordingly, he sent a message to Washington stating, "I have one hundred hand picked men who will take the contract to clean out Mosby's gang. I want one hundred Spencer repeating rifles for them. Send them to me if they can be found in Washington."[12] The Spencers were found, and soon Blazer's men were issued firepower that would make them a serious threat to any partisan band in the region. Richard Blazer was promoted to captain, and he began the specialized instruction his men would need to complete their mission.

Blazer taught his scouts to move with celerity and adapt to changing situations. He instructed them to never make camp until late at night and to break camp before daylight every morning. Instead of operating in the field for long periods of time, his scouts would go on missions lasting only a few days when reliable information was presented to them. Most importantly, he taught his scouts to treat the Southern people humanely and kindly. This was in great contrast to the methods usually employed by Union soldiers operating in the region. Over time, this philosophy ingratiated Blazer and his men to the Southern citizens. Because of this, residents rarely fled or gave warning when his troopers rode into an area, because they did not fear his presence. In many ways, Blazer and his scouts managed to blend in with their surroundings so that they could perform their missions unnoticed. Mosby himself once joked that Blazer had become so popular with the locals that they might make him a "naturalized Confederate citizen."[13] In this way, Blazer's Scouts were able to capture numerous partisans who had not been forewarned of the presence of the enemy.

On September 3, 1864, Blazer's Scouts fought an engagement with Mosby's Rangers at Myer's Ford, Virginia. The scouts had received information that as many as 150 of Mosby's men were there, and Blazer's men proceeded to this ford on the Shenandoah River with great caution, expecting a possible ambush. When they arrived, they found Mosby's men resting on the west side of the river. Blazer attacked and scattered the force but, fearing reinforcements, called off the pursuit and headed back toward the river. In his official report he stated,

> I came upon Mosby's guerillas, 200 strong, at this place, and after a sharp fight of thirty minutes we succeeded in routing him, driving them three miles, over fences and through corn fields. They fought with a will, but the seven-shooters proved too much for them. My loss is 1 killed and four wounded, 1 severely; his is, 1 commissioned officer and 6 privates killed, and 1 commissioned officer and 4 privates wounded. I have 6 prisoners.[14]

The defeat at Myer's Ford, along with an ambush of ranger forces under Captain Montjoy, enraged Mosby, and he concluded that this Federal threat must be dealt with once and for all. He assigned Major Adolphus Richards, with two companies of rangers, to "wipe Blazer out! Go through him!"[15] Mosby told Richards, "You let the Yankees whip you, I'll get hoop skirts for you! I'll send you into the first Yankee regiment we come across."[16]

On November 19, 1864, Richards rode out in search of Blazer. The rangers soon got word that Blazer's men were at Kabletown, West Virginia, and they hurriedly rode in that direction. Upon reaching Kabletown, Richards discovered that Blazer's men had recently left. Richards began searching for Blazer, who was, at the same time, searching for the rangers. Early the next day, the two forces came together. Blazer had 62 men in his command, and Richards had at least 110, maybe more. Richards's men closed on the scouts, who lost a third of their men in the initial attack. The Spencer repeating rifles they carried were not suited to close combat as were the Colt revolvers used by the rangers. Blazer's Scouts were completely routed and fled in the direction of Myerstown, West Virginia, where Captain Blazer himself was overtaken and captured. In his report of the incident, General Sheridan stated that Mosby's men had "killed 16, wounded 6, and scattered the command. Twenty-nine have come in; eleven are still missing."[17] With their commander captured and approximately half their numbers casualties, Blazer's Scouts ceased to exist as a military unit. Scouting missions would still be conducted within the army, but this band of elite soldiers had vanished into the pages of history.

Units of scouts such as those already described were the exception rather than the rule. Scouting was usually done by individual volunteers within a particular unit on an ad hoc basis. For many, it was an opportunity to gain recognition or glory. For others, it was a chance for adventure and gain. John Singleton Mosby began his brilliant career as a partisan ranger by serving as a volunteer scout for Jeb Stuart's cavalry. A great many scouts, on both sides, performed similar service, returning to the ranks once their particular mission was accomplished, and scouting only when circumstances required it. In this world of deception and disguise, the names of many of these brave volunteers have been lost forever.

Scouts were not the only means by which armies obtained information about enemy plans or movements. Civilian and military spies were used extensively by both sides during the course of the war. In the early days of the conflict, the Federal government contracted Allan Pinkerton and his detective agency to perform the work of espionage. Reports from Pinkerton's operatives were discovered to be exaggerated and unreliable, however, and other sources had to be found.

In July of 1861, Lafayette Baker approached General Winfield Scott with a plan to go to Richmond to spy on Confederate activities. He had once lived in Richmond, and he proposed to mask his activities by posing as a photographer wishing to take pictures of the Confederate generals. Scott approved the plan and sent Baker on his way. On July 11, however, Baker was arrested by Union soldiers and charged with being a Confederate spy. General Scott interceded in the affair before Baker was placed before a firing squad, and he was released to make his way south. Upon reaching Confederate lines, he was arrested under suspicion of being a Union spy. Baker professed his loyalty to the Confederate cause, and in interviews with Jefferson Davis and General P. G. T. Beauregard, he gave bogus information about Union troop positions and movements that convinced his captors to release him. He was then free to roam through the camps of the Confederate army, where he gathered valuable information. During his return to Washington, he was once more arrested by Confederate troops at Fredericksburg and condemned to be executed. He managed to use a small knife he had concealed in his shoe to free two bars in his cell and made good his escape. Upon reaching Washington, Baker reported his findings about the Confederate army to General Scott, who was so pleased with the information that he made him a captain and placed him in charge of his intelligence network. When Secretary of War Edwin Stanton heard of Baker's exploits, he recruited him to take Pinkerton's place as head of the Union Intelligence Service.[18]

Baker was placed in charge of the National Detective Police, an undercover spy organization responsible for uncovering enemy operatives. In this capacity, he employed the services of numerous spies in his own network. One of his greatest successes was the arrest of the Confederate spy Belle Boyd. In true J. Edgar Hoover fashion, Baker spied on everyone. He was eventually caught tapping into the telegraph line of Secretary Stanton, which led to his dismissal.

Despite the existence of the Union Intelligence Service, much espionage was carried out on an individual basis by commanders in the field who set up their own spy networks. The absence of a truly centralized system for gathering and evaluating information was a weakness of Union spying during the war, though the individual services of civilian spies such as Elizabeth Van Lew, who provided Union forces with valuable information regarding the dispositions and movements of Confederate troops in Richmond, were invaluable.

Baker's peer in the Confederate service was Thomas Jordan. Jordan was a West Point graduate in the class of 1840 who had served in the war against the Seminoles and the Mexican-American War during his antebellum service. A native Virginian, Jordan's sympathies were with the South in the days leading up to the Civil War. As such, he took steps to ensure that the South would be well informed by establishing a secret network of spies in Washington as early as 1860. His operatives included Rose Greenhow, whose information would later be largely responsible for the Confederate victory at First Manassas. When Jordan resigned from the army to join the Confederate forces, Greenhow was left in charge of the network he had established. He could not have made a better choice. Greenhow's late husband had been a State Department official, and she was thus connected to some of the most important and influential people in Washington. Secretary of State William Seward and Senators Henry Wilson and Joseph Lane were among her admirers and prime sources for information. Greenhow provided intelligence on everything from the organization of the Federal army to where President Lincoln's guards were placed at the White House. Greenhow and Jordan had set up a courier system by which the information could be transmitted in a timely fashion in ciphered code. Messages from the Confederate high command requesting specific information from her were sent by this same courier system with ease.[19] Greenhow was eventually arrested and confined in the Old Capital Prison before being sent south.

Security during the Civil War was extremely lax for both the Union and the Confederacy, making spying a relatively easy pursuit for those of an adventurous nature. To be sure, those captured in the act of espionage faced dire consequences, but the odds of successfully completing their missions were usually with them. The accomplishments of many spies such as Pauline Cushman, Nancy Hart, Antonia Ford, and Emma Edmonds have been widely reported and are a part of our nation's history. Hundreds, and possibly thousands, of other spies performed the work of espionage undetected and unreported as they sought to give their side an edge on the battlefield. From the famous and the unknown, leaders on both sides gained valuable intelligence that allowed them to make informed decisions as to their own strategy and tactics.

CHAPTER 15

THE MARINES

The U.S. Marine Corps traces its roots to the British Maritime Regiment of Foot that was organized in the seventeenth century during the Franco-Dutch War. The purpose of the force was to conduct shipboard security, conduct ship-to-ship fighting, and to assist in landing parties. Early British marine units were temporary organizations, formed only during times of war. In 1755, the Corps of Royal Marines was authorized by the Admiralty, and from that time forward, they were a permanent part of the British Navy.

On November 10, 1775, the first U.S. Marines came into existence when the Second Continental Congress authorized the raising of two battalions. Captain Samuel Nicholas was the first commissioned officer of the U.S. Marines and is considered as the first commandant of the corps. In 1776, Captain Nicholas led his men in their first amphibious raid, in the Bahamas. Over the course of the war, Nicholas and his marines performed a variety of services for the fledgling Continental Navy. The Treaty of Paris, in April of 1783, which ended the Revolutionary War, also ended the need for the marines, however, and the unit was dissolved.

The Marine Corps was formally reestablished in July of 1798 and has continued in constant service since that time. Marines took part in numerous naval actions during the War of 1812, and marine units fought in the battles of Bladensburg and New Orleans. In the years after the War of 1812, marines protected U.S. interests around the world. They also took an active part in the wars fought against the Seminole Indians in Florida. When the Mexican-American War broke out, marines were responsible for seizing Mexican seaports along the Gulf and Pacific coasts. A battalion of marines was with General Winfield Scott's army and fought conspicuously at the battle of Chapultepec, or the Halls of Montezuma, as it is referred to in the Marine

Corps anthem. One of the most memorable engagements of the marines in the years before the Civil War was when a detachment accompanied Robert E. Lee to Harpers Ferry to put down John Brown's raid in 1859.[1]

At the beginning of the Civil War, the Marine Corps was drastically under-sized for the task at hand. To further complicate matters, a large number of existing officers and men resigned when their states seceded to offer their services to the Confederacy. The 1,892 officers and men in the corps before the war began would be drastically reduced by these Southern defections. Especially hard hit was the officer corps. While only a couple field officers resigned, half of the captains, two-thirds of the first lieutenants, and half of the second lieutenants tendered their resignations to fight for the Confederacy.[2] In 1861, Congress authorized the U.S. Marine Corps to enlarge to 93 officers and 3,074 enlisted men. President Lincoln felt this number to be too low, and ordered it to be increased by 1,000 additional men. Lincoln's addition of manpower was indeed optimistic. The marines had a longer term of enlistment and offered no bounties for potential recruits until 1864, factors that kept them constantly beneath their authorized strength. The head of the corps was Commandant Colonel John Harris. At the beginning of the war, Harris determined that responsibilities of the corps would be limited to guard-ing ships and forts. Simply put, the limited manpower of the Marine Corps meant that it would not have the means to engage in any activities outside the responsibilities it had previously been performing. Given the loss of expe-rienced personnel that took place when the Southern members of the corps left to offer their services to the Confederacy, Harris's decision seemed appro-priate. Though this war would involve the use of amphibious troops on numerous occasions, in almost all cases, these troops would come from the army and not the marines.

The regulation dress uniform for the Marine Corps was a double-breasted frock coat of dark blue color, with a skirt extending three-fourths of the dis-tance from the top of the thigh to the bend of the knee. Brass buttons had an "M" to designate Marine Corps. Pants were to be sky blue. Caps were to be of black cloth for officers and black felt for enlisted men. The top and bands were fine glazed black leather, with a visor bound around the edges. Boots were of the ankle pattern that was being issued to the infantry. The undress uniform was a blue frock for winter and a white coat for summer for officers. Enlisted men were permitted to wear a fatigue sack coat during warm weather.[3]

Commandant Harris may have wished for the members of his corps to stay clear of land battles for the present, but circumstances forced him to alter his plan when Secretary of War Simon Cameron requested on July 14, 1861, that a battalion of marines be raised to accompany Brigadier General Irvin McDowell's army on its upcoming campaign to capture Richmond. Major

U.S. Marines in full uniform. (Library of Congress)

John G. Reynolds was selected by Secretary of the Navy Gideon Welles to command the battalion. Reynolds, a 38-year veteran of the corps, had seen combat in the Mexican-American War, taking part in the marine assault at Chapultepec Castle during the battle for Mexico City. Most of his company commanders were also veterans of the Mexican-American War or had seen combat elsewhere during the course of their service. The same could not be said of the junior and noncommissioned officers and men who would be making up the battalion. All of the second lieutenants in the battalion had been in the service for two months or less, and none of them had previously seen action. Only one of the twelve noncommissioned officers had ever been under fire before. Of the 324 privates in the ranks, only 7 had been in the service prior to the bombardment of Fort Sumter in April, and 90 percent of them had enlisted since June. As a whole, they were green and untried and relatively untrained. Given the fact that the limited amount of training furnished them would have been consistent with their intended duties aboard ships, they were totally unprepared to take part in an overland campaign as an infantry unit.[4]

The battalion was assigned to the division commanded by Colonel Andrew Porter. Despite their reputation as fighting men, these marines did not make a favorable impression on their new commander. Porter stated, "The marines were recruits, but through the constant exertions of their officers had been brought to present a fine military appearance, without being able to render much active service. They were therefore attached to the battery as its permanent support."[5] The battery Porter referred to was Captain Charles Griffin's West Point Battery of six guns, officially designated Battery D, 5th U.S. Artillery.

On the morning of July 21, 1861, the Marine Battalion was up at 2:00 a.m., along with the rest of McDowell's army, as the Union forces prepared to initiate the first great battle of the war. Later that morning, the battalion followed Griffin's battery to Dogan's Ridge, where the cannon unlimbered and began shelling the enemy. It was here that the marines suffered their first casualties of the war when three of their number were killed by cannon fire. Just before 2:00 p.m., Griffin was directed by Major William Barry, McDowell's chief of artillery, to relocate his guns to Henry House Hill, approximately one thousand yards forward. Barry informed Griffin that the 11th New York Zouaves would provide infantry support for his battery along with the marines. The Zouaves were nowhere in sight, however, and Griffin argued against advancing before they had arrived, but Barry insisted that the cannon must go in first. The infantry would follow as soon as possible. Under protest, Griffin limbered up his guns and went forward. Griffin's guns would be joined in the advance by the five-gun battery of Captain James Ricketts on his right. When Griffin reached the top of the hill, he deployed a two-gun section, under the command of Lieutenant Henry Hasbrouck, to the right of Ricketts's guns in order to cover the entire field of fire. The marines arrived on the double-quick shortly after the deployment of the guns and positioned themselves between Hasbrouck and Ricketts. The 11th New York took up a station to the rear and right of the guns.[6]

The Union artillery was engaged in battery fire with Confederate guns, and the marines did their best to keep out of the way of shells being sent their way by the enemy, but more casualties were sustained. It was at this time that a body of troops emerged from the woods in Griffin's front. The battery commander was positive that they were the enemy and ordered his guns loaded with canister to open on them. At this moment, Major Barry arrived on the scene and ordered Griffin not to fire. Barry insisted that the troops in Griffin's front were Union soldiers, part of the artillery support. Griffin argued that they were Confederate troops, but Barry insisted and ordered the Union guns pointed away from the oncoming regiment. The troops were indeed Confederate. They were the 33rd Virginia Infantry, and they halted about 70 yards from Griffin's position, raised their muskets, and fired a volley that devastated the artillerymen. The Virginians pressed forward, reloading as they came, while Griffin called to the 11th New York to save his guns. The New Yorkers had trouble of their own. They had just fended off an attack by the 1st Virginia Cavalry and were disorganized and somewhat demoralized. The steady advance of the 33rd Virginia, firing as they came, was more than the New Yorkers could stand. They broke and ran for the rear.[7]

The marines endured the shock of the first Virginia volley and began to return fire on the oncoming enemy. They were taking casualties but held firm in the face of the advancing foe. Officers both encouraged and threatened their men, waving their swords in the air, admonishing them to hold their positions and contest every foot of ground. Then the New Yorkers broke on their right. The rush of beaten Zouaves through their ranks had an unhealthy effect on the morale of the marines, and the panic spread throughout their ranks. Soon, they were running too, abandoning the guns to the victorious enemy.[8] Most histories of the marines at Manassas end here, with their stampede from the field. The battalion was routed, but there is much more to the story that deserves to be told.

When the battalion reached the rear, Major Reynolds was successful in rallying his men. When several of the other regiments that had been driven from the fight reorganized to make another charge, the marines were among them. The 14th Brooklyn Infantry led the charge, followed by Reynolds and his men. As the attacking columns neared the position held by General Thomas J. Jackson's brigade, the 4th and 27th Virginia Infantry Regiments opened fire on them. The 14th Brooklyn anticipated the volley and fell to the ground just before it was fired. The marines, in line just behind them, took the full impact of the volley, which staggered them momentarily. Along with the 14th Brooklyn, the marines now pressed the attack but were repulsed and driven back down the hill. They once more rallied and took a position behind an embankment at the foot of the hill. From this point, they took part in yet another charge on the hill, but they were forced to retreat again when the Union forces were attacked on their flank by Confederate reinforcements. Reynolds rallied his men once more. By this time, there were only about two hundred marines remaining in the ranks. Reynolds got his men ready to make another charge, but the situation on the battlefield had deteriorated into chaos and confusion. Hordes of Union soldiers were running for their lives, trying to escape the onslaught of the onrushing Confederates. They were all headed for the Sudley-Newmarket Road, the main avenue of retreat from the field. Reynolds positioned his men to act as a rear guard, to protect this road, near the Stone House. The marines held their position resolutely, despite the frightened stampede taking place all around them, until they were relieved by the 71st New York State Militia, at which time they marched from the field in a disciplined manner.[9]

As can be seen from the historical record, the marines did break and run from the attack that captured Griffin's and Rickett's guns on Henry House Hill, but they did not long stay out of the fight. The battalion rallied and charged several more times, with undaunted courage, despite the confusion caused by retreating troops all around them. In their first taste of combat these inexperienced marines did no worse than most other Union regiments on the field that day. In fact, they performed better than the majority of the volunteer regiments, who had gone through their trial by fire and discovered war was not the romantic and glorious adventure they thought it would be.

The fighting at Manassas was a rare instance for the Marine Corps during the Civil War. For the most part, the corps performed the duties outlined for it by Commandant Harris at the beginning of the conflict. Marines saw shipboard service and did garrison duty at marine posts and installations. The experience of Corporal John Mackie, the first marine to win the Congressional Medal of Honor during the war, is indicative of the service of the majority of marines during the conflict.

Mackie had enlisted in the Marine Corps in August of 1861 and had been promoted to the rank of corporal in 1862. May 15 of that year saw him serving as a member of a marine detachment aboard the USS *Galena*, an ironclad warship serving on the James River. The *Galena*, along with four other warships, steamed up the James in an effort to test the Confederate defenses of Richmond. Marines aboard the ship served as sharpshooters, protecting the vessel from enemy infantry along the banks of the river. The naval flotilla ran into trouble as it neared Richmond. As it rounded a bend upstream from Dutch Gap, it ran afoul of obstructions placed in the water and came under fire of the heavy guns of Fort Darling, atop Drewry's Bluff. The Confederate artillery was briefly silenced by the fire from the Union ships, but when gun crews from the recently scuttled *Merrimac* arrived to reinforce the garrison, the fire from the fort redoubled in ferocity. The *Galena* was severely punished by the plunging fire from the fort, and her deck was soon so slippery from a film of human blood that it was almost impossible to walk. The numerous hits created a cloud of smoke around the vessel that gave the impression to observers that the *Galena* was on fire. When an enemy shell struck the 100-pounder Parrott, killing its entire crew, Mackie sprang into action. Calling on several marine comrades to follow him, Mackie rushed to the gun. The bodies of the dead and dying were removed, the splinters swept away, and, under Mackie's direction, the gun was put back in the fight. Despite the fact that none of the marines had been trained as artillerists, the gun crew did excellent service, even landing a shell inside a casemate in Fort Darling that did terrific damage to the works. Mackie and his marines kept the gun firing all through the fight, until the captain of the *Galena* ordered his ship to retire back down the river.[10] Marines provided similar service aboard ships the length of the Atlantic and Gulf coasts, as well as with warships operating on the inland waters of the continent. Though often unheralded, their contributions to the naval war were significant, and they contributed mightily to the success of the naval blockade and to the Union offensives along the Mississippi, Tennessee, and Cumberland Rivers.

The U.S. Marines would have other opportunities to serve as ground forces during the war. On April 25, 1862, a detachment of marines from Rear Admiral David Farragut's fleet landed in New Orleans to take possession of the city. The mayor of New Orleans balked at surrendering, stating that only the commanding general of the Confederate forces had the authority to do so, but the Southern forces were already evacuating the city, and Major General Mansfield Lovell informed the mayor that the responsibility for surrendering New Orleans rested in his hands. Though the issue was not formally resolved until General Ben Butler's army arrived on May 1 to occupy the city, New Orleans was really in Union hands from the time the marines had landed.

In the late summer of 1863, marines took part in an amphibious operation in the port of Charleston intended to capture Fort Sumter. Rear Admiral John Dahlgren had been trying to put together a joint operation between the army and navy, and he wanted the marines to play a part. The marine commander, Major Jacob Zeilin, rejected the idea, stating that his men were too raw and untrained to undertake the mission. When Zeilin became ill, he was replaced by Lieutenant Colonel George Reynolds, an officer far more willing to commit his troops to battle. The Confederate abandonment of Battery Wagner on Morris Island presented the Union forces with a rare opportunity to make a strike against Fort Sumter. In an all-navy operation, Admiral Dahlgren ordered five hundred men to make a night amphibious assault on the fort on the evening of September 8. Marines would make up a large portion of this detachment.

Everything went wrong from the beginning. Faulty reconnaissance failed to reveal that the rubble caused by Union bombardment would require the landing party to use ladders to climb above it. The Confederates had previously broken the Union code, and they read Dahlgren's wig-wag messages as they were being sent and were thus apprised of the coming attack. All of the fort's big guns, as well as those of all the surrounding forts, were trained on the seaward approach the attackers must use in reaching Sumter. The 500 men were loaded aboard 25 small boats. As soon as they were cast off from a tug that had been pulling them, the small boats became widely separated by the tide. A Confederate sentry spotted the tiny flotilla and fired a signal rocket to alert the garrison of the fort. Within seconds, all the Confederate guns in the harbor were belching iron at the bobbing vessels. Only 11 of the little boats made it through the hail of fire to land at Fort Sumter. The rest were either sunk or got lost in the darkness and confusion. The battle lasted for a mere 20 minutes, with the landing party taking heavy casualties at the hands of the fort's defenders. One hundred and five survivors, a great many of them marines, were forced to surrender. Twenty-one of those marines would later die as prisoners at Andersonville, Georgia.[11]

By the end of 1864 the Union fleet had almost sealed off the Confederacy from the outside world by means of its blockade. The only Southern port still open to blockade-runners was that of Wilmington, North Carolina, protected at the entrance of the Cape Fear River by the massive earthwork fortification, Fort Fisher. The capture of Wilmington had long been a top priority of the navy, but it was a job that could not be accomplished without support from the army. Up to this point, the army had been reluctant to participate in a joint operation against Wilmington because of other, more pressing issues in the various theaters of operation. By the end of 1864, however, Ulysses S. Grant came to see the closing of the port of Wilmington as being strategically important in his quest to wrest Robert E. Lee's Confederate army out of its entrenchments in and around Richmond and Petersburg. Grant agreed to provide an army land force to accompany the navy, and an expedition was undertaken in December of 1864 to silence Fort Fisher and capture Wilmington. The December expedition ended in failure, but a second attempt was planned for January of 1865. Major General Alfred Terry would command the 8,500 soldiers in the army contingent, and Rear Admiral David D. Porter commanded the fleet of some 50 warships.

The attack took place on January 15. Terry and Porter had decided that it would be a joint mission between the two arms of the service. The army would attack the north or land face of Fort Fisher. A landing force made up of 1,600 sailors and 400 marines would simultaneously assault the northeast or sea face of the fort. The sailors, armed with cutlasses and pistols, were to deliver the main attack in their sector. They were formed in three lines, by battalions. In their rear were the marines, under the command of Captain Lucien Dawson. The mission of the marines was "to form in the rear and cover the sailors" with rifles as they delivered their attack. Once the sailors had scaled the walls of the fort, Dawson's Marines were to "follow after, and when they gain the edge of the parapet they will lie flat and pick off the enemy in the works."

The army began its attack on the land face before the naval units were fully prepared before the sea face. The naval commander, Lieutenant Commander Randolph Breese, ordered his lines of sailors to advance by the flank along the beach, hoping to get them into formation under the protective covering fire of the marines. The movement marched the sailors out of range of the marines' supporting fire, however, and the three lines became jumbled together in a large and confused mass. In this condition, they rushed forward toward the fort with a yell and closed to within 40 yards of the parapets. The Confederate defenders then opened with artillery and musket fire, stopping the advance cold. Clustered together as they were, the sailors provided an excellent target for the enemy gunners and infantrymen, and casualties began to mount heavily. It was too much for the sailors to endure; "the whole line commenced doubling up and flying, everybody for themselves." Dawson and his marines did what they could to provide covering fire for the sailors, and once they had broken, the marines formed a rear guard to protect the fleeing mass and defend against an attack. The naval assault had been a complete failure, but the marines had done their best to carry out their part of the mission.[12]

The attack was not without benefit to the Union cause. The Confederate defenders had concentrated their efforts against the naval force, which allowed Terry's army troops to gain a foothold on the traverses of the land face. Though there were still a couple hours of hard fighting in front of them, the piercing of the fort's defenses by the army signaled doom for the Confederate defenders within. The marines had taken an active, if inauspicious, part in capturing Fort Fisher and closing the last remaining port of the Confederacy to the outside world.

The Confederate States Marine Corps was established on March 16, 1861, by an act of the Confederate Congress. The corps was to be modeled after the U.S. Marines and was authorized to raise 46 officers and 944 enlisted men. Lloyd J. Beall was named colonel commandant of the Confederate Marine Corps, and he faced many of the same problems as his Northern counterpart. Chief of these was the fact that the Confederate Marine Corps was never able to recruit enough men to reach the number authorized by congress. It is estimated by historians that the number of marines in Confederate service never exceeded six hundred. A camp of instruction was established at Drewry's Bluff, just outside of Richmond, named Camp Beall, for the commandant.[13] A number of officers and men would receive their training at this camp as the corps prepared for its mission of guarding naval stations at Richmond, Charleston, Wilmington, Savannah, Mobile, Charlotte, and elsewhere, as well as serving aboard a number of the larger ships in the Confederate navy. In May of 1861, the Confederate Congress expanded the number of men authorized to be raised by the marines, but it was a futile gesture, as the original quota was never reached. The Confederate Marine Corps did have an advantage of not having to start from scratch. As previously noted, a large number of officers and men from the U.S. Marine Corps had resigned when the Civil War broke out to offer their services to the Confederacy. Beall would have a strong nucleus of trained marines to build his corps around, and though they were undersized, they would prove to be a disciplined and efficient organization. Beall himself was not a former marine. Instead, he had been a paymaster in the army. He was an able administrator, though, and worked hard to ensure the corps was supplied with everything it needed to do its job.

The Confederate Marine uniform was essentially the same as the dress uniform of the Confederate army, a cadet gray, double-breasted coat with a high collar, which was marked to indicate rank of the officers. Seven brass buttons were on either side of the coat, and these were surplus from the U.S. Marine Corps taken when Southern naval posts were captured. A crimson sash and sky blue pants completed the uniform. White canvas trousers were worn during the summer.[14]

The Confederate Marines saw their first naval action at Hampton Roads, Virginia, on March 8, 1862, aboard the ironclad CSS *Virginia*, where they provided rifle support against enemy infantry on the shore and helped to man the guns of the ironclad. More than 50 marines are listed among the crew members of the *Virginia*, under the command of Captain Julius Ernest.[15] The marines took an active role in the sinking of the USS *Cumberland* and the near destruction of the USS *Congress*. On the following day, when the *Virginia* steamed out to finish off the *Congress*, it was met by the Union iron-clad *Monitor*, and the two metal monsters joined in the first battle between iron ships in maritime history. For three hours, the opposing ships blazed away at one another without either being able to gain a clear advantage or do any significant damage to the enemy. The battle ended in a stalemate, but the Confederate Marines had taken part in an event that would forever change the navies of the world.

Some Confederate Marines served with the Naval Artillery Battery attached to General Joe Johnston's army at Centreville, Virginia. Others formed part of the garrison force at Fort Darling, on Drewry's Bluff, guarding the James River approach to Richmond. These troops played a conspicuous part in the battle on May 15, 1862, in which John Mackie won his Congressional Medal of Honor. On April 24, 1862, Confederate Marines serving on board the CSS *McRae* took part in the fighting at Forts Jackson and Saint Philip on the Mississippi River. The *McRae* engaged four different Union warships, including the USS *Iroquois*, which had a complement of U.S. Marines aboard. It was the first time in the war where the marines of both sides fought against one another.

Confederate Marines were charged with several special missions during the war. A detachment in Charleston was trained to attempt the capture of Union ironclads blockading the harbor. They were to board the ships at night, drop sulfur, gunpowder, and wet blankets down the smoke stacks, and wait for the gassed crew to emerge from the holds to be shot down. The operation was cancelled when fire from land batteries forced the Union blockaders to leave their posts, eliminating the threat. Another marine special detachment took part in the capture of the USS *Underwriter*, at New Bern, North Carolina, on February 2, 1864. The Confederate boarding party rowed to their target in small boats and captured the *Underwriter* in hand-to-hand fighting with her crew. Since the Union warship did not have steam up, she could not be moved quickly, and, fearing that a Federal response was forthcoming, the vessel was ordered to be burned. Commander John T. Wood of the Confederate navy was in command of the operation, and he gave great praise to the marines involved. "Though their duties were more arduous than those of the others, they were always prompt and ready for the performance of all they were called upon to do. As a body they would be a credit to any organization, and I will be glad to be associated with them on duty at any time."[16]

On June 3, 1864, a detachment of marines formed part of the 130-man force led by Lieutenant Thomas Pelot to capture the USS *Water Witch*, off Ossabaw Island, Georgia. In the early morning darkness, Pelot guided his small boats to within 29 yards of his target before being discovered by the enemy. The boarding party was on the *Water Witch* before her crew could be gotten to quarters, and a hand-to-hand fight ensued in which the Confederates took control of the ship. Unlike the *Underwriter*, the *Water Witch* had fire in her boilers and was ready to sail. Pelot had been killed in the fighting, and Lieutenant Joseph Price assumed command of the mission. He ordered the ship to be sailed up the Vernon River, above the obstructions guarding Savannah, where it was turned over to the Confederate navy. The *Water Witch* became part of the Southern fleet and served the remainder of the war flying the stars and bars.[17]

A detachment of Confederate Marines defended the port city of Wilmington during the two Union expeditions against Fort Fisher. These marines, under the command of Captain A. C. Van Benthuysen, formed part of the garrison force at Battery Buchanan, an ellipse-shaped earthen fortification at the tip of Confederate Point, that was to serve as a rallying point and stronghold should Fort Fisher be captured. The fort contained four large-caliber coastal guns, which were manned by the marines. Van Benthuysen's detachment fought in both the December 1864 and January 1865 engagements at Fort Fisher, and many of them were taken prisoner when the fort fell on January 15.[18]

Confederate Marines took part in the final phases of the war in Virginia as part of Tucker's Naval Brigade, attached to Lee's Army of Northern Virginia. Commodore John R. Tucker commanded the Naval Brigade, also referred to as the Marine Brigade, at Drewry's Bluff at the time Richmond was evacuated on April 3, 1865. In their haste to evacuate the Confederate capital, the army failed to inform Tucker of the plans to withdraw, and the naval commander first learned of the move when he saw smoke from war material that was being set to the torch. Tucker marched his command, which contained a size-able contingent of Confederate Marines, away from Drewry's Bluff, in search of Lee's army. Upon making contact, he was assigned to Major General Custis Lee's division of Lieutenant General Richard Ewell's corps. On April 6, Ewell's corps was attacked by vastly superior Union forces at the battle of Sayler's Creek. Tucker's men fought valiantly, repulsing the first attack on their line. Unaware of the numerical advantage held by the Federals,

Tucker ordered his brigade, only about four hundred strong, forward in a counterattack. The charge decimated the 37th Massachusetts Infantry and roughly handled the 2nd Rhode Island Infantry, whom they engaged in close combat. Tucker's men fought with such ferocity that Union commanders estimated the size of the enemy force in their front to be two thousand men. But while the Marine Brigade was making a heroic stand, other portions of Ewell's corps were not faring so well. Union forces had captured 7,700 of Ewell's troops, including the commanding general and both of his division commanders. As the Union forces tightened their grip around the Marine Brigade, Tucker learned of the plight of the rest of the army, and a dialog was opened, which led to him surrendering the remainder of his brigade. The marines had fought well, and while the battle of Sayler's Creek was a debacle for most of Lee's army, Tucker and his men had earned glory and respect on that field.[19]

Civil War marines were not the island-storming amphibious troops that they are commonly thought of being today. Their size prevented them from taking any appreciable part in the land battles that raged throughout the nation during those four bloody years of conflict. The entire U.S. Marine Corps constituted only about an average brigade in size, and it was hard pressed with that many men to perform all of the shipboard and guard duties assigned to it. There simply were not enough marines to permit an active and sustained role in land fighting. On the Southern side, the Confederate Marine Corps was a fraction of the size of their Union counterpart. The total number of marines in the service amounted to slightly over half a normal regimental strength. Though they had far fewer ships to serve upon, the Confederate Marines felt the same lack of manpower prevalent in the North, and their activities were similarly restrained as a consequence. Nevertheless, marines on both sides distinguished themselves during the war and added laurels to their already rich history of valor, tradition, and sacrifice. Their elite status would grow as their numbers increased in the following decades, and they would earn the motto of "First to Fight" on scores of beaches throughout the Pacific.

Chapter 16

SAPPERS AND MINERS

Sappers and miners are combat engineers whose specialized duty it is to dig trenches, under cover of small arms or artillery fire, to advance a besieging army toward a fixed enemy fortification. They also dig tunnels, extending beyond the foremost trenches, or "saps," up to and under the fortifications so that charges of explosives might be used to blow up the enemy defenses. When saps are being dug, they are usually done in a zigzag pattern so as to avoid enemy enfilade fire as much as possible. As the saps move forward, positions are usually constructed for the placement of artillery, to harass the enemy and further protect the sappers as they move forward with their saps. The object is for the sappers to continuously move the artillery of the attacking army forward until it occupies a position from which it can breech the walls of the enemy fortification. The work of mining was typically undertaken when the walls of an enemy fortification were too strong to be breeched by artillery fire. By planting explosives under the walls of an enemy work, it was hoped that a hole could be blown in the fortification through which an infantry charge could be mounted against the enemy.

Sapping and mining were done by the same troops, and both activities were extremely hazardous. While sapping, the soldiers were constantly under fire from enemy small arms and artillery and were prime targets for marksmen and sharpshooters. As the saps neared the enemy works, they would commonly be exposed to hand-thrown grenades, as well. Mining was even more dangerous. The diggers worked under the constant threat of the tunnel they were digging caving in on them. Enemy defenders would also countermine, in an effort to uncover and kill the miners before they could complete their mission and place a charge. They would also attempt to create cave-ins to bury the miners alive. Working with the black powder charges was also risky and apt to cause premature explosions that could kill the diggers. Sappers and miners have seen service with every U.S. army since the time of the Revolution, when they were employed by George Washington at Yorktown against British defenses.

During the Civil War, the work of sapping and mining was primarily a Union activity. This was because the war aim of the North was to conquer the South and force it back into the Union. As such, Union troops usually assumed the role of the aggressor, placing Confederate forces on the defensive. Confederate forts protected numerous strategic points throughout the South, and the Union armies were obliged to capture them. In many instances, these forts were taken solely by artillery fire or by a combination of artillery and infantry. Confederate coastal fortifications were the most common examples of this, as most were reduced by naval bombardment, without the need for sappers and miners. Inland forts were quite another story. In several campaigns of the war the special services of sappers and miners would be would be put to the test.

It is amazing to think that the U.S. Army had only one battalion of engineers at the outbreak of the war, and that number was not increased after the commencement of hostilities. The U.S. Volunteers raised a complete regiment of engineers. Michigan raised the 1st Michigan Regiment Engineers and Mechanics, as well as Howland's company of engineers. Missouri formed the 1st Missouri Engineers Regiment, Balz's Company Sappers and Miners, and Wolster's Independent Company Sappers and Miners. Kentucky organized Patterson's Independent Company of Engineers and Mechanics. Pennsylvania formed Wrigley's Independent Company Engineers. The state of New York organized four full regiments of engineers, the 1st, 2nd, 15th, and 50th New York Engineer Regiments. The U.S. Colored Troops raised the largest number of engineer regiments, however, forming the 1st, 2nd, 3rd, 4th, and 5th U.S.C.T. Engineer Regiments.[1] This meant that during the course of the war, there were twelve full regiments of engineers (excluding a regiment of pontoniers, which was also part of the engineers), along with a battalion and six independent companies. Each regiment was authorized to raise 12 companies of 150 men each, for an effective strength of 1,800 men per regiment. If at full strength, this meant that there were more than 23,000 who served in the engineers during the war. Of this total, only Balz's and Wolster's companies from Missouri had been formed as dedicated sappers and miners, or 300 of the 23,000-man total. Other engineers would have to be pressed into service as sappers and miners during the campaigns of the war, along with a great many regular soldiers from the ranks who had received no special training in engineering.

To be sure, a great many officers, on both sides, had received their education at West Point, which was the only engineering school in the nation.

Commissary Department of the 50th New York Engineers. (National Archives)

A number of the leading generals in the war, including Robert E. Lee, had graduated from the academy with commissions in the Corps of Engineers. As such, most of the officers that had received their military education at West Point were fully capable to oversee engineering operations. These officers would put their academy training to use in many practical applications, using manual labor from troops in the ranks to accomplish needed engineering projects.

The first opportunity for engineers to use sapping and mining skills in the Civil War took place deep in the South, during one of the shortest siege operations on record. Brigadier General Thomas W. Sherman commanded an army expeditionary force aimed at Fort Pulaski, Georgia, on Cockspur Island, at the mouth of the Savannah River. The capture of this fort would effectively close the port of Savannah, freeing Union blockading ships for service elsewhere. Sherman would have approximately 10,000 troops under his command, including Companies A and D of the 1st New York Engineers.

Brigadier General Quincy A. Gilmore, a West Point graduate, was appointed to serve as Sherman's chief engineer, and on November 29, 1861, he was ordered to proceed to Tybee Island, just south of Fort Pulaski, to determine if that island could be used in operations against the Confederate stronghold and if he felt it practicable to reduce and capture the fort. Tybee Island was a mud marsh island, with only a few ridges of firm ground, but Gilmore felt the Union forces could use it as a base of operations. So far as Fort Pulaski was concerned, he was sure the fort could be reduced by the use of heavy mortars and rifled cannon. As a result of his report, the 46th New York Infantry was sent to take control of Tybee Island in early December. In

February, this regiment was joined by the 7th Connecticut Infantry and the two companies of New York Engineers, all under the command of Colonel Alfred Terry.[2]

Work began in preparation for siege operations, as supplies and heavy ordnance were landed by the navy. These materials would have to be moved two and a half miles along the beach from the landing point to their intended position of placement, the entire route under the effective range of the guns of Fort Pulaski. Gilmore and his engineers devised an ingenious plan to accomplish this work without exposing themselves to the deadly fire of the fort's big guns. The work of digging the entrenched positions for the big guns was all done at night, with the greatest care to noise and light discipline. Their efforts were screened through the use of deception. The distribution of brushwood and bushes in front of the five advanced battery positions they were constructing was kept constantly the same, so as to obstruct any discernible changes in the landscape from the view of the fort. Work was completed little by little, each night, with the element of surprise being the paramount concern of the engineers. Only after the concealment of the positions had reached a point where parapets could be constructed in front of them was the effort at secrecy abandoned. By that time, five full batteries of heavy Federal guns were in place, and it was too late for the garrison in Fort Pulaski to do anything about it.[3]

Fort Pulaski was a five-sided brick fort, with walls eleven feet thick. Colonel Charles H. Olmstead commanded a garrison of 385 men and 48 guns of heavy caliber. The fort was constructed to hold as many as 140 cannon, but only about a third of that number were in place. Olmstead and his superiors thought the fort to be impregnable, because the heavy smoothbore cannon necessary to accomplish the destruction of the fort's walls only had a range of half a mile, and Tybee Island was further away than that. Gilmore had not proposed to use smoothbore artillery, however. He had advised using the newly developed rifled artillery, having a much longer range and a more accurate fire.

From February 21 to April 9, work on the construction of the Federal gun emplacements had taken place. On April 10, they were finally completed, and the order to fire was given. The mortars were instructed to direct their fire to the inside of the fort, while the rifled artillery was ordered to fire directly at the walls of the fort where the south and southeast faces joined. General Sherman sent an officer, under a flag of truce, to demand the fort's surrender, but Colonel Olmstead declined. At 8:00 a.m., the first shell was fired, and by 1:00 p.m., the effects of the bombardment started to become telling. By the time the bombardment was called off for the night, a large breach in the wall of the fort was clearly visible. Firing resumed on April 11, shortly after daybreak, and within a few hours the breach in the walls was expanded to the point that it was large enough for an infantry assault to pass through. Preparations were made for a storming force, but at 2:00 p.m., a white flag was seen flying from the fort, and the Confederate banner was hauled down. From the time the siege was initiated, it had taken less than two days to reduce the fort and close off the mouth of the Savannah River. The work of the engineers had been a critical component in the success of the operation. They had advanced the pits for the batteries without observation by the enemy's artillery, two of which were large Blakely rifled cannon that could easily reach their position.[4]

The 1st Michigan Engineers and Mechanics Regiment formed part of Major General Henry Halleck's army as it inched toward Corinth, Mississippi, following the battle of Shiloh. Though Halleck's army held a two-to-one advantage over the Confederate forces under General P. G. T. Beauregard, it took him from April 29 till May 25, 1862, to cover the 22 miles that separated Shiloh from Corinth. Advancing only a couple miles at a time, at a tedious and overly cautious pace, Halleck would end the march each day with plenty of daylight remaining for his engineers to go to work. Their job was to dig trenches and defensive works running forward, toward the enemy, behind which the Federals could rest in relative safety. In this manner, the 1st Michigan Engineers and Mechanics honeycombed the Mississippi country-side as Halleck's 120,000-man army went forward with the speed of a turtle. By May 25, the Federals had reached Corinth, and the engineers went to work constructing a new line of trenches and works. All their labors went for naught. General Beauregard, knowing that his 65,000-man army could not hold the town against Halleck's overwhelming force, made plans to evacuate Corinth. Halleck opened a bombardment on the town and maneuvered for position, with his engineers leading the way by digging the trenches and approaches. Beauregard made a show of force, as he prepared to secretly slip away with his army. Trains coming into town were represented as bearing reinforcements, but were, in fact, transporting the Confederates to Tupelo, Mississippi. By the night of May 29, Beauregard's entire army had been evacuated, and the Federals awoke the following day to find the town aban-doned. The Michigan engineers had done their duty throughout the campaign of digging saps toward the enemy, but the Confederates didn't accommodate them by staying around to fight.[5]

In the East, General George McClellan, an engineering officer himself, organized the Army of the Potomac with a special view to engineering ser-vice. Brigadier General John G. Barnard was appointed chief engineer officer for the army, and a large force of engineers would be collected together under his command. The Engineers Battalion of the regular army, under the com-mand of Captain James C. Duane, was attached to the Army of the Potomac. To it were added the 15th New York Engineers, under the command of Colonel J. McLeod Murphy, and the 50th New York Engineers, under the command of Colonel Charles B. Stuart. The result was the creation of the Engineer Brigade, placed under the immediate command of Lieutenant Colonel Barton S. Alexander of the Corps of Engineers. On April 4, 1862, the Engineer Brigade arrived at Yorktown, Virginia, and prepared to take an active part in General McClellan's siege of Major General John B. Magruder's defensive works. The 15th and 50th New York pitched in to build roads and bridges to facilitate the movement of the army. They also constructed a large number of gabions, large cylindrical wickerwork baskets that were filled with soil or sand to be used to create walls around artillery emplacements and trench saps. McClellan's army would need these movable barricades to help establish its position in front of the Southern works.

The Confederate defenses were 12 miles long, running in a southwesterly direction from Yorktown to the James River, and had been constructed by the Confederate Corps of Engineers using the manual labor of one thousand slaves.[6] The Warwick River flowed in front of the Confederate line, and the defenses had been built to take full advantage of this natural obstacle. Five dams had been built to flood the marshy ground along the banks of the river. The only viable approaches to the Southern works were the narrow causeways across the breasts of these dams. Artillery emplacements were positioned to cover the causeways over each dam, allowing the defenders to concentrate superior numbers and firepower at the point of attack. The Confederate defenders, who were severely outnumbered, would be able to offset this disadvantage by forcing the Federals to advance over these narrow funnels of ground, where there was not enough ground for even a company front. The works themselves were the expanded and enhanced British works that had been dug during the Revolution. Measuring 15 feet thick, they were fronted by ditches 10 feet deep and 15 feet wide.[7]

Most of the Engineer Brigade was employed in duties other than digging trenches and sapping toward the enemy works. The manual labor to accomplish these objectives came largely from the ranks of the Army of the Potomac, as troops performed fatigue duty, under the direction of officers with engineering backgrounds, when they were not detailed for skirmishing or guard duty. Confederate skirmishers frequently disrupted the work through skirmishing forays, but the trenches and saps inched forward toward the rebel works with menacing regularity. By April 30, General Joseph E. Johnston sent a letter to Robert E. Lee, then serving as President Davis's military advisor, stating, "We are engaged in a species of warfare at which we can never win. It is plain that General McClellan will adhere to the system adopted by him last summer, and depend for success upon artillery and engineering. We can compete with him in neither."[8]

Johnston had seen enough. As the Union army moved steadily forward behind the earthen trenches and saps, feeling their way toward his own lines, a course of action was decided upon. Remaining at Yorktown would place the Confederate army at the mercy of superior Union artillery once McClellan's lines had been sufficiently prepared. These big siege guns would be able to blast the defenders out of their position, where they would then be faced by the superior numbers of the Federal army on open ground. Not willing to risk such an encounter, the Confederates decided to abandon Yorktown. At nightfall on May 3, Johnston began pulling his troops out of their lines and heading them north, toward Richmond. The evacuation was covered by an artillery bombardment. At daylight on May 4, the Confederates were gone, and the U.S. flag flew over Yorktown.[9] Just as at Corinth, the Confederates did not wait around to fight against the trenches and saps being constructed in their front. The mere fact that they were being constructed was enough to convince General Johnston to relinquish his strong position and withdraw.

A number of engineers accompanied General Ulysses S. Grant's Army of the Tennessee during the Vicksburg Campaign. A battalion of the 1st Missouri Engineers, commonly called the Engineer Regiment of the West, were joined by Patterson's Independent Company of Engineers and Mechanics from Kentucky. After two Union attempts to take the Confederate works by storm ended in bloody repulses, Grant determined to settle into an extended siege of the Southern works. The Great Redoubt, or 3rd Louisiana Redan, located in the center of the Confederate line, was the most formidable work in all of Vicksburg's defenses. Built to protect the Jackson Road entrance into the city, it was manned by the 3rd Louisiana Infantry and a strong battery of artillery. On May 23, 1863, it was decided that a sap be run from the Union lines toward this enemy stronghold, one of several such approaches to be constructed along the 12 miles of works that defended Vicksburg. Two fatigue details of 150 men each were assembled. One detail was to work at night, beginning the sap under the relative cover of darkness. Relays of men would be sent out at five-foot intervals, armed with picks and shovels. Their job was to start a trench that would connect to the worker five feet from them and be of sufficient depth to allow some measure of concealment from enemy sharpshooters. The next day, the second detachment would take over, digging the newly constructed sap deeper to allow troops to move forward in relative safety. The whole process would be repeated that night, when the first detachment extended the sap closer to the enemy. In this manner, the sap was carried forward until June 22, when the head of the sap reached the outer ditch surrounding the Great Redoubt. An order had gone out a few days before this for all soldiers having practical experience as coal miners to report to the chief engineer. From these men, 36 were chosen for the work of digging a mine into the Confederate bastion. The miners were divided into two shifts of 18 men each. One shift worked at night and one during the day. Each shift was further divided into three reliefs. Each relief was to work an hour at a time, with two men picking, two men shoveling the loosened earth into grain sacks, and the remaining two men carrying the sack back to the ditch of the fort. By this means, the miners were able to dig a gallery four feet wide and five feet tall at a right angle into the fort. The work was completed so quickly that by June 25, the shaft had been dug 45 feet into the works, and two smaller galleries had been dug at 45-degree angles, extending 15 feet from the main gallery. Eight hundred pounds of gunpowder were placed in the main gallery, and seven hundred pounds were placed in each of the lateral galleries. Fuses were run back from the charges before much of the excavated soil was replaced in the mine. On the afternoon of June 25 the charges were detonated, and as one observer stated,

> At the appointed moment it appeared as though the whole fort and connecting outworks commenced an upward movement, gradually breaking into fragments and growing less bulky in appearance, until it looked like an immense fountain of finely pulverized earth, mingled with flashes of fire and clouds of smoke, through which could occasionally be caught a glimpse of some dark objects— men gun carriages, shelters, etc.

The Confederates regrouped quickly after the shock of this explosion and rallied to prevent Union troops from breaking their line. On July 1, another mine was completed, and the resulting explosion all but destroyed the fort, but the Confederates were able to once more hold their line. In the meantime, the main sap had been expanded to the extent that it would allow an assaulting party to advance to the very edge of the enemy works in columns of fours, and preparations were made for an assault. This charge proved to be unnecessary when Lieutenant General John C. Pemberton surrendered his army on the Fourth of July.[10] Normal infantrymen had performed the lion's share of the work of digging the saps at Vicksburg, aided by the special talents of coal miners in digging the galleries into the fort. Though their efforts had not been decisive in determining the outcome of the campaign, their constant threat had been a prime consideration in Pemberton's decision to surrender his command, before the saps could be fully brought to bear.

Coal miners from Pennsylvania were responsible for digging the most famous mine to be constructed during the war. After fighting a bloody series of battles across the Virginia countryside in the summer of 1864, Ulysses S. Grant and the Army of the Potomac stalled in front of Richmond and Petersburg. After making futile assaults on the Confederate works, Grant settled in to conduct siege operations, just as he had at Vicksburg. It was at this juncture that Lieutenant Colonel Henry Pleasants, commander of the 48th Pennsylvania Infantry, came forward with a suggestion. Pleasants had been a mining engineer in civilian life, and most of the men in his regiment had

Members of the 1st U.S. Engineers at Petersburg. (Library of Congress)

been miners in Schuylkill County.[11] Pleasants proposed digging a long mine
shaft underneath the Confederate lines and placing it under Elliott's Salient,
as it was called, in the middle of Lieutenant General James Longstreet's
First Corps line. General Ambrose Burnside, commander of the IX Corps,
approved of the plan. Generals Meade and Grant added their endorsements,
despite the fact that neither officer believed any good would come of it.
Pleasants and his men began digging on June 25. No assistance came from
any quarter, and all work was completed by the four hundred troops in the
48th Pennsylvania. Pleasants was unable to acquire even the most basic tools
and equipment and was forced to improvise with materials at hand. Standard
army picks were straightened to make them more like mining picks. Old
cracker boxes were fitted with skids to serve as wheelbarrows to remove the
earth to be excavated. Lumber for shoring up the shaft came from a bridge
Pleasants's men tore down, as well as from an abandoned Confederate saw-
mill. An instrument was needed for Pleasants to triangulate the exact distance
to the Confederate works. Though one was available at army headquarters,
Pleasants was denied access to it and was forced to obtain an old-fashioned
theodolite from Washington.

Despite the obstacles and lack of support, the men of the 48th Pennsylvania
set to work on the mine with resolve and conviction. They dug a tunnel 3 feet
wide and 4½ feet high for a distance of 511 feet, until they had reached a
point directly under Elliott's Salient. From there, a perpendicular gallery, 75
feet long, was dug. Pleasants devised an ingenious method for providing fresh
air for his work crews while they toiled deep in the mine. By means of a

Sketch of Colonel Pleasants placing the powder charge in the Petersburg mine as appeared in August 20, 1864, *Harper's Weekly*. (Library of Congress)

canvas duct and a wooden duct he used fire in the tunnel to suck the old air out to the mouth of the shaft. This created a draft that sucked fresh air into the tunnel. By July 25, the magazines were complete and ready for the placement of powder charges. Though Pleasants had requested 14,000 pounds of powder, he was given only 8,000 pounds, which he had placed in the magazines. Fuses were set, and the tunnel was filled back in with earth so the explosion would go upward instead of blowing back out the shaft. The early morning of July 30 was set as the time for detonation of the powder, as preparations to coordinate an infantry assault were made.[12]

General Burnside had previously selected a division of U.S. Colored Troops under the command of Brigadier General Edward Ferrero to spearhead the assault, supported by his two white divisions. These troops had trained behind Union lines for weeks in preparation for making the charge. At the last moment, General Meade ordered a change in the plan. Concerned that the attack might fail, and that the black troops would therefore be slaughtered, Meade felt there would be political repercussions in Washington. He therefore ordered one of the white divisions make the charge. Burnside protested this change, but Grant supported Meade's decision, and Burnside was forced to substitute troops who were not given time to

Explosions destroy defensive works of the Confederate fort at Petersburg in the Battle of the Crater, July 30, 1864. (Library of Congress)

familiarize themselves with the ground, much less practice for their important assignment. At 4:44 a.m., the charges were exploded, and a massive cloud of earth, men, and guns was lifted skyward. When the dust settled, a huge crater, 170 feet long, more than 100 feet wide, and 30 feet deep, occupied the spot in the Confederate line that had been Elliott's Salient. The blast momentarily stunned the assaulting white troops, and when they started moving forward they made right for the crater. Instead of passing to the right and left of the hole, as the black troops had been trained to do, the white soldiers went straight into the depression. When they tried to emerge on the opposite side, Confederates on either side of the crater fired into their rear, causing them to seek shelter back in the crater. Supporting troops, including Ferrero's division, were thrown into confusion, as a mass of humanity huddled amid the debris in the bottom of the crater. Confederate forces were quick to respond, and the Union troops found themselves ringed by deadly fire that claimed just under four thousand casualties. The Battle of the Crater resulted in a bloody repulse for the troops of the IX Corps and an opportunity missed for the Union army. Pleasants's mine had exceeded expectations of producing a breach in the Confederate lines. Mismanagement of the resulting infantry attack had cost the Union a chance to split the Confederate army and possibly capture Petersburg.

Confederate engineers and troops were rarely concerned with the activities of sapping and mining. Their focus was in the construction of defensive works, not in offensive operations against such works. Even so, there were a few instances where Confederates were called upon to do some digging of their own. These were responses to Union mines, when the defenders were compelled to countermine in an effort to locate the shafts before they could be exploded. Confederate countermines were dug at both Vicksburg and Petersburg, and though in some instances they came close enough for the Federals to hear them talking, they were not successful in stopping the Union miners from completing their tasks.

CHAPTER 17

JUNIOR RESERVES

The Civil War was viewed to be the great adventure of a lifetime at its outset. Men and boys on both sides of the Mason-Dixon line felt it to be a rare opportunity for travel, excitement, and possible glory. Many boys despaired over the thought that the war would be over before they were old enough to serve. The age of enlistment on both sides was 18, but documentation of age was rarely available. Recruitment officers would often require a youth who appeared to be younger than the acceptable age to swear that they were 18. A common ruse employed on both sides was to write the number 18 on a piece of paper and place it in their shoe. Then, when asked to affirm their age, they could truthfully take an oath that they were "over 18."

Records are incomplete, especially on the Confederate side, and some historians differ as to the accuracy of those that do exist, but it is apparent that an amazing number of boys served as soldiers in both armies. Statistics reveal that more than 1,000,000 Union soldiers were 18 or under. Of these, some 800,000 were 17 or under, below the authorized age of enlistment. Of these, the 17-year-olds formed the majority, accounting for 600,000 soldiers. About 100,000 were 16, and another 100,000 were 15 or under. On the Confederate side, an examination of 11,000 soldiers' records revealed 1,000 aged 18, 366 who were 17, 100 who were only 16, and 35 who were 15 or younger.[1] Truly, boys would play an important role in the fighting of this war, and in the four years of its duration, they would have many chances for the excitement and adventure they craved. They would also learn that war is more than courage and the quest for glory. Boys on both sides would suffer the privations and hardships common to all soldiers. They would discover that doing one's duty was rarely the romantic escapade they had dreamed of. It was harsh, cruel work that demanded sacrifices beyond their tender years. In too many cases, young lives were sacrificed by boys who would not live to grow into manhood.

Incredible feats of bravery performed by individual boys in the ranks are so numerous that they could fill the pages of a book by themselves, but that is not the focus of this chapter. Instead, our interest is in units of young boys who fought together during the war. As previously stated, a great number of under-age boys were enlisted in the Union army. By 1863, the Northern government took steps to address this situation by ordering all boys under the age of 18 to be discharged from the service. The North, with its great population, could easily fill the resulting vacancies with new recruits. In the South, a far differ-ent set of circumstances existed. With a population only a fraction of the size the Union military had to draw upon, the South needed every man it could get in the ranks. While Southern leaders officially held to the rule that soldiers must be over the age of 18, they often looked the other way when it came to enforcement of that policy. By 1864, the situation in the South had become critical. Simply stated, the Confederate army was running out of men. The Confederate Congress addressed this problem by expanding the age range for men eligible to be drafted. Men and boys from the ages of 17 to 50 were open to conscription, meaning that as the North was purging the youth from its armies, the South was adding its seed corn to the pot.

While tens of thousands of youths served in the Union army during the war, there were no all-boy units organized for combat. The South, on the other hand, had already established a tradition of boy service that preceded the 1864 conscription act that opened the door to the authorized drafting of youths. In large part, this was due to the deep military heritage of the South, where private military schools were abundant. Institutions like the Virginia Military Institute, the Citadel, and the Georgia Military Institute flourished in the prewar years, filled with young boys aspiring to make a career for them-selves in the army as officers. The tradition of military service was ingrained in the youth of the Confederacy, and the military academies taught these boys of 12, 13, and older how to march, think, and live as soldiers.

A unit of boy soldiers was involved in the very first hostile action of the war. The cadet corps from the Citadel, in Charleston, South Carolina, took an active part in the opening drama of the war. The cadets had been turned out en masse to assist in servicing the cannon that ringed Union-held Fort Sumter, in Charleston Harbor. The first shot of the war, aimed at the Union resupply ship *Star of the West*, was fired by George E. Haynsworth, a Citadel cadet from nearby Sumter, South Carolina.[2] At numerous times during the conflict, the Citadel corps of cadets were turned out to man the defenses of Charleston against threatened attacks by the Union navy.

In May of 1864, another Southern military academy got the opportunity to distinguish itself when Major General Franz Sigel led an offensive down the

Shenandoah Valley. Major General John C. Breckinridge commanded the Confederate army opposed to Sigel, but his army was inferior in size to the Union invaders. Scouring the countryside for all means of support, Breckinridge issued orders to the Virginia Military Institute (VMI), in Lexington, to make the corps of cadets available for immediate service. The general had no intention of using these boys, all aged 18 or younger, as combat troops. Instead, he wished to hold them in reserve, guarding wagons and such. On May 15, the opposing armies came together at New Market, Virginia, and through some foul-up in orders the VMI cadets not only ended up on the battle line, they held the center of Breckinridge's formation. When the battle opened, the cadet corps, over two hundred strong, advanced with a cheer on the Union troops to their front. Despite galling fire from enemy muskets and cannon, the boys, led by their 24-year-old commandant, Lieutenant Colonel Scott Ship, swept forward, closing in hand-to-hand combat with the Union infantry and artillerymen. Sigel's line collapsed at this point, and the VMI cadets contributed greatly to the Confederate victory on the field of New Market. Ten cadets had been killed or died of their wounds, and another forty-seven were wounded. The VMI cadets had crowned themselves and the academy with everlasting glory. On June 9, the cadets were called to service once more, when Union forces attacked Lexington. This time, they were unsuccessful, and the Union assault of June 11 succeeded in capturing the city. In retribution for the service the cadets had rendered to the Southern cause, the Virginia Military Institute was burned to the ground.[3]

Another group of cadets went into battle as a unit in 1864, but while they performed their duty in an exemplary manner, they were denied the fame and glory extended to the boys from VMI. These were the boy soldiers of the Georgia Military Institute. During William T. Sherman's Atlanta Campaign, the cadet corps was ordered to report to General Joseph E. Johnston for service with the Army of Tennessee. Major A. P. Mason, the commandant of the academy, led the cadets into the trenches defending Atlanta, where they unsuccessfully struggled against Sherman's efforts to capture the city. Though the Georgia boys made no great charge like the one made by the cadets of VMI, they saw more than their fair share of war. Their commandant would later write of them: "In no single instance, whatever may have been the duties assigned to them or the position occupied by them, have our expectations been disappointed in either the bearing or efficiency of the command. There was fatigue and blood and death in their ranks but no white feather."[4]

In response to the government's expansion of the draft age, several Southern states began organizing battalions and regiments of reserve troops from the 17-year-old boys living within their borders. These troops were intended to be used for guard duty at bridges, railway depots, and prison camps, which would free older troops for frontline battle assignments. The boys were not expected to actually fight, except in the extreme instance of their post being attacked by the enemy. In the vast majority of cases, this plan was adhered to, but some of these boy regiments found their way to the firing line and fought in some of the closing battles of the war.

In North Carolina, Governor Zebulon Vance issued a directive that eight battalions of Junior Reserves be raised, and these were quickly filled. A great difference between these boy units and the ones from the military schools previously discussed is that the cadets had experienced extensive military training and, in most cases, had been living the life of a soldier for a few years prior to their being deployed in combat. The members of the North Carolina Junior Reserves lacked this military background and were largely boys just off the farm. In many cases, their induction into the army was to create great hardships for their families. With virtually all of the grown men already in the army, these boys had been depended upon by their families to perform the work of keeping their farms operating. Many families feared that they would not be able to subsist themselves without the assistance of their sons, and they applied for exemptions in hopes of keeping them at home. The Confederacy was starving for manpower, however, and precious few of these exemptions were ever granted.[5]

Shortly after their organization, the battalions were consolidated to form regiments, resulting in the 1st, 2nd, and 3rd North Carolina Junior Reserve Regiments, also designated as the 70th, 71st, and 72nd North Carolina Infantry. There were enough troops remaining to form an additional battalion, which was designated as the 20th Battalion North Carolina Junior Reserves. Records for the members of the Junior Reserves are incomplete, but those that survived the war attest to more than four thousand boys being registered in the three regiments and the battalion. Postwar documents account for an additional four hundred members, and there were doubtless more whose record of service was lost to history.[6]

The government tried to appoint older men to act as battalion and regimental commanders for the Junior Reserve units, but they were usually just a few short years older than the troops they were leading. An excellent example of the officers appointed to command these boy troops was Walter Clark, a mere boy himself, but at the age of 17 already the holder of two officer's commissions in the Confederate army and a veteran of a tour of duty at the front. Clark was attending Tew's Military Academy, in Hillsboro, North Carolina, when the war broke out. Though he was only 14 years old at the time, he was selected to serve as a drillmaster for the newly raised 22nd North Carolina Infantry to teach the raw recruits how to be soldiers. Clark was elected a second lieutenant by the older men of the regiment, but when they departed for the seat of war, in Virginia, he was detailed to remain behind to train the men of the 35th North Carolina Infantry. Clark felt slighted at not

Some of the boyish officers of the North Carolina Junior Reserves. (Walter Clark's *Histories of Several Regiments and Battalions from North Carolina in the Great War, 1861–1865*, vol. 4, 1901, pg. 24)

being allowed to go to the front with the 22nd North Carolina, and after a short time in camp with the 35th he resigned his commission and returned to Tew's Academy. A few months later, Clark learned that the 35th North Carolina was being reorganized in preparation for a move to Virginia, and he left the life of a schoolboy once more to seek a position with the regiment. His previous time on the drill field had so impressed the officers of the 35th that he was appointed regimental adjutant, with a rank of first lieutenant. In this capacity, Clark accompanied the regiment, as a part of Stonewall Jackson's corps, when it captured Harpers Ferry and fought at Antietam, Second Manassas, and Fredericksburg. The 35th North Carolina had suffered numerous losses in these engagements and was ordered home to perform local service while it recruited sufficient men to bring it back up to field strength. Not one for inactivity, Clark once more resigned his commission and applied for admission to the University of North Carolina. He completed the entire four-year course of studies in a single year, and on June 3, 1864, at the age of 17, received his diploma. The following day, he received word that he had been selected to be an officer in one of the newly formed boy regiments. Clark would become major of the 1st North Carolina Junior Reserve Regiment and would serve with it till the end of the war.[7]

Initially, the Junior Reserves performed the duties for which they had been raised. Thus far, North Carolina had been isolated from the war front. There had been Union coastal incursions and an occasional raid into the interior of the state, but the heavy fighting had been conducted elsewhere, in Virginia and Georgia. In the latter stages of the war, that would change, as North Carolina became a target for the Union army and navy. A joint expedition would be undertaken to silence the Confederate bastion at Fort Fisher and close the all-important port city of Wilmington. General Sherman would also march his army north from Savannah, slicing through the heart of the Carolinas in an attempt to lay waste to the Confederacy's heartland and overwhelm Robert E. Lee's Army of Northern Virginia from the rear. The boys of the North Carolina Junior Reserve did not have to be transferred to the seat of war. It was headed in their direction like a steamroller.

In December of 1864, Ulysses S. Grant gave his approval for a joint army-navy expedition against Fort Fisher, the massive earthwork bastion the Confederates had constructed at the mouth of the Cape Fear River to protect the approach to the port city of Wilmington. As the last remaining port, outside of the Trans-Mississippi Department, open to the Confederacy, Wilmington served as a lifeline to the outside world. Much-needed weapons and supplies that could not have been attained in any other fashion were smuggled into the city by blockade-runners. Grant reasoned that General Lee's Army of Northern Virginia would not be able to remain in the field without the supplies it received by way of Wilmington, and he authorized an

View of Fort Fisher, North Carolina. A large number of Junior Reserves got their first real taste of war during the Union's expedition against this place in December 1864. (Library of Congress)

infantry force from General Ben Butler's Army of the James to take part in the expedition to close the port down.

Major General Godfrey Weitzel was selected to command the army forces assigned to the expedition, the 2nd division of the XXIV Corps and the 3rd division of the XXV Corps, along with two battalions of heavy artillery and engineers. As the expedition was taking place within his department, General Butler felt he should be in command of the operation, and though General Grant objected to Butler's decision, he did not forbid him from going. The army troops were to be accompanied by the largest naval flotilla ever assembled in U.S. history to that time, nearly 60 warships, under the command of Rear Admiral David D. Porter. The combined fleet of navy warships and army transports left Hampton Roads, Virginia, on December 14, 1864, and they eventually made a rendezvous off the coast of Fort Fisher on December 19. A winter storm caused the ocean to become very rough, threatening to capsize several of the army transports, which were compelled to seek shelter at the port of Beaufort, South Carolina. When the storm finally subsided, on December 23, Admiral Porter decided to open the attack on the fort, even though the army contingent was still at Beaufort. Porter thought that his naval guns could pound the fort into submission, gaining glory for the navy that it would not have to share with the army. His plan proved to be a failure. Though some 10,000 shells were fired at Fort Fisher, very little damage was done to the works. Confederate casualties were negligible. In fact, Porter lost more men to exploding guns aboard his ships than the Confederates had lost to his bombardment. When the army transports arrived off Fort Fisher that evening, General Butler was in favor of calling off the mission. He felt that Porter's actions had warned the enemy of the coming assault, giving them ample time to make preparations to contest a landing. At length, he was convinced to put a reconnaissance force ashore to determine if an attack was still practicable. Brigadier General Adelbert Ames's division was selected, and his troops began landing on Christmas Day.

The 1st, 4th, 7th, and 8th North Carolina Junior Reserve Battalions were among the defenders of Fort Fisher during this expedition. The 1st Battalion was assigned inside the fort as part of the garrison, while the 4th, 7th, and 8th Battalions were stationed outside the fort, some of them on the beach and the remainder in a fortified camp at Sugar Loaf, a few miles north of the fort. Many members of the Junior Reserves endured the Union naval bombardment, and a few of the boys were killed or wounded. When General Ames's troops came ashore, they cut off a portion of the 4th and 8th Battalions from the rest of the Confederate defenders. Major John M. Reece of the 4th Battalion went looking for the Union commander with an offer to surrender the boys with him who had been cut off. He found Colonel Rufus Daggett of the 117th New York Infantry, but the colonel was hesitant to accept his offer. Thinking that it might be a trap, Daggett sent a subordinate officer back with Reece to confirm the story and, if true, to arrange to bring the boys in. Upon reaching his own lines, Major Reece explained to the boys that he had officially surrendered them. Lieutenant F. M. Hamlin disagreed with Reece's decision, and he and a handful of boys slipped silently away to make their way back to Confederate lines. The rest, 237 in number, stayed to accept their fate as prisoners of war. "We can't be any worse off," one was heard to comment. "We have never received a cent of pay nor scarcely anything to eat except what we picked up."[8]

The 1st and 7th Battalions of Junior Reserves, along with the remainder of the 4th and 8th Battalions, remained at their posts as Ames's troops probed the Confederate defenses. When Brigadier General Newton Martin Curtis led his brigade toward Fort Fisher, he reported that the walls of the fort had been very lightly damaged, but they also appeared to be lightly defended. Curtis was preparing to attack the fort when he received orders from Ames directing him to withdraw and return to the division. General Butler was convinced that the fort was materially undamaged and was far too strong to take by assault. Another storm was building up, and Butler feared that would further complicate the situation, so he ordered that the troops already on the beach be returned to the ships and called the whole expedition off. Then, in a very curious move, Butler left the area on his flagship, bound for Hampton Roads, before the troops ashore had been evacuated.

Following the withdrawal of the Federal army, the Junior Reserves were removed from Fort Fisher and transferred to Colerain, in eastern North Carolina, where a force of Union infantry, supported by gunboats, were threatening the area. No battle was forthcoming, however. When the boy soldiers arrived on the scene, the Union troops boarded their gunboats and evacuated the area.

The 1st and 2nd Junior Reserves were then ordered to Goldsboro, where they would spend the winter before entering upon their last campaign of the war. While at Goldsboro, all members of the regiments who had reached the age of 18 were transferred into other North Carolina regiments as replacements. Though this was not the intention, the actions of the government ensured that the Junior Reserves would remain an all-boy organization.

On February 25, 1865, General Joseph E. Johnston was restored to field command in hopes that he could do something to stop the march of Sherman's army through the Carolinas. Gathering together the remnants of the once proud Army of Tennessee, William J. Hardee's garrison troops from Savannah, Braxton Bragg's forces from Wilmington, and Wade Hampton's cavalry troopers, Johnston created a force he named the Army of the South. The Junior Reserves were added to the army, which, all told, was slightly over one-third the size of Sherman's 60,000-man army. Drastically outnumbered and overburdened with untried troops or those who were so severely demoralized by the Nashville Campaign as to make them almost unfit for service, it seemed as if there would be little Johnston could do to arrest Sherman's march northward. As if Sherman's army was not enough, Major General John Schofield was leading a sizeable column of Union troops inland from Wilmington to join with Sherman. Johnston's prospects were slim against Sherman as it was. If the two Union armies were allowed to combine, there would be little he could do but annoy and harass the Union host.

Braxton Bragg was given command of a portion of the Army of the South and directed to turn back Schofield's force. The Junior Reserves formed a part of Bragg's army, and on March 7, 1865, they fought in an engagement just east of Kinston. Bragg ordered Major General Robert Hoke to attack the Union left flank with his division. Hoke's assault drove the Federals back, capturing virtually the entire 15th Connecticut Infantry Regiment. The division of Major General Daniel H. Hill was then committed to the fight. The Junior Reserves were part of Hill's command, and this would be their first charge. As their brigade commander described the action, "The North Carolina Reserves advanced very handsomely for a time, but at length one regiment (the First, I think) broke, and the rest lay down and could not be got forward."[9] The Union flank was in danger of collapsing when Bragg disengaged Hill's troops and ordered them to another part of the field. This gave the Federals time to bring up their reserves, and the opportunity to deal a crippling blow to Schofield's army was lost. Bragg skirmished with the Federals for two days; then, on March 10, he tried another assault against the Union left flank. This was easily repulsed, causing Bragg to withdraw from the field and march toward a concentration with Johnston's main body.

The last combat the Junior Reserves were to see was in the battle of Bentonville, from March 19 to 21, 1865. Sherman was marching his army north in two wings, and they had become separated in their advance, giving General Johnston an opportunity of attacking one wing, and possibly defeating it, before the other wing could come to its assistance. On March 19, Johnston attacked the wing commanded by Major General Henry W. Slocum at Bentonville. Johnston's plan failed. He was unable to defeat Slocum's wing before Sherman and the rest of his army arrived to reinforce it, and the Confederates found themselves facing almost three-to-one odds on the battlefield. Nevertheless, the fighting lasted for three days and was some of the fiercest to take place during the war. The Junior Reserves distinguished themselves at Bentonville and fought like veterans. On the second day of the battle, Major Walter Clark commanded the skirmish line of the brigade. "We had a regular Indian fight of it behind trees," he later recalled. "They charged my line twice but were both times driven back. That night the whole skirmish line kept up an almost continuous firing as they expected our Army to leave. That together with the scamps trying to creep up on us in the dark kept us up all night."[10]

Bentonville proved to be the last battle for the Junior Reserves. They would be surrendered with the rest of Johnston's army at Bennett Place, North Carolina, on April 26, 1865. Their formation had been one of necessity, as the Confederacy struggled to find men for its depleted armies, and these boys had been forced to assume responsibilities beyond their years. In the final analysis, they acquitted themselves well in their battlefield experiences. At Fort Fisher, a portion of the command had surrendered after offering almost no resistance. But the rest of the command had stuck with the colors and saw the thing through to the end. At Kinston, they had charged heroically before being caught in a storm of bullets that caused them to waver and stop. This was their first charge, however, and most of the veteran regiments on either side had similar experiences earlier in the war, when they were still green and untried. At Bentonville, the Junior Reserves fought well and held their part of the battle line as coolly and courageously as the veterans who had passed through four years of combat.

CHAPTER 18

SENIOR RESERVES

The same diminishing manpower that had led the Confederate government to include 17-year-olds in the draft also prompted an extension of cutoff conscription age at the other end of the spectrum. The maximum age for military conscription had been 45, but this was extended to include men through the age of 50. The drafting of men 45 to 50 years of age would be a revolutionary measure by today's standards. In the 1860s, it was almost unconscionable. This was because the average life span of a man in the mid-nineteenth century was far shorter than in present times. Life expectancy in the 1860s was only 42 years, more than 30 years less than today.

The celebrated civilian hero of Gettysburg, John Burns, was a novelty for his time. At the age of 69, Burns was a veteran of the War of 1812. During the fighting on the first day at Gettysburg, Burns got his old flintlock musket, his powder horn, and his top hat and went out to fight the invaders of his town. Burns fell in with the 150th Pennsylvania Infantry, near the McPherson Farm, and was directed to go to the McPherson woods, where better shelter was to be had. A wounded soldier presented him a modern musket to replace his old flintlock, and the old soldier was ready for modern war. The 7th Wisconsin Infantry was in the woods, and Burns joined the line and blazed away at the enemy. He later moved to the eastern portion of the woods and fought with the 24th Michigan Infantry, serving in the capacity of a sharpshooter. When the Iron Brigade was pushed back toward the Lutheran Seminary, Burns received wounds in an arm and leg, as well as several minor wounds in his chest. Left behind by the troops, he was treated by Confederate surgeons, whom he convinced that he was a civilian who had been caught up in the battle while seeking aid for his invalid wife.[1] Following the battle, Burns became a national hero for his exploits, which were all the more incredible because of his highly advanced age. When President Lincoln visited Gettysburg that November to commemorate the National Cemetery, John Burns would be the only citizen of the town Lincoln expressly requested to see.

When the Senior Reserve units were raised, their ranks were filled with troops who had more in common with John Burns than they did with their other comrades in the field. These men were not middle-aged; they were fully in the sunset of their years. When people said that the Confederacy was robbing the cradle and the grave to fill its armies, the statement was only partially in jest. These elder statesmen who had anticipated a quiet finale to the story of their lives were suddenly called upon to defend their country alongside comrades in arms who were less than half their age. The graybeards, as they would come to be called, symbolized the cause they supported in 1864, as both were in the declining portion of their existence.

As with the Junior Reserves, these elder troops were not expected to serve as frontline combat troops. Instead, they were to relieve other troops for combat service by assuming responsibility for guarding important points behind the lines. Bridges, railway depots, and prisoner of war camps were to be their posts, not a line of battle on a hotly contested field. For the most part, Senior Reserve units raised throughout the South performed the function for which they had been formed, and they heard neither the rattle of enemy musketry nor the booming of their big guns. The war passed them by, and they guarded their posts undisturbed until the cessation of hostilities. For the North Carolina Senior Reserves, however, the war held an entirely different fate. These troops found themselves right in the path of General Sherman's advancing army and were called upon to actively resist the invader's march through their state. The graybeards of the North Carolina Senior Reserves would not have to wait for decades to enthrall their grandchildren with stories of what they had done in the war. They would only have to survive the ordeal and return home.

Between July of 1864 and January of 1865, five regiments, four battalions, and two independent companies of Senior Reserves were raised in North Carolina. This accounted for nearly eight thousand new recruits who could relieve younger soldiers doing guard and garrison duty for service at the front. The 4th, 5th, 6th, 7th, and 8th Senior Reserve Regiments, along with the 3rd Battalion Senior Reserves, were recruited from all parts of the state. Their official designations were the 73rd, 74th, 75th, 76th, and 77th North Carolina Infantry. The 5th Senior Reserves, or 74th Regiment, was mounted and performed cavalry service during their term of enlistment. All the rest served as infantry.

The 4th Senior Reserves were assigned to guard Union prisoners at Salisbury, North Carolina. In November of 1864, they were brigaded with

Drawing of the prisoner of war camp in Salisbury, North Carolina. Three regiments of North Carolina Senior Reserves were stationed here as prison guards. ("Bird's Eye View of the Confederate Prison Pen at Salisbury, N.C., Taken in 1864," illustration by C. A. Kraus, published by J. H. Bufford's Sons Lith., Boston, New York, and Chicago, 1886)

the 5th and 6th Senior Reserves to form the Reserve Brigade, under the command of Colonel John F. Hoke. Headquarters for the brigade was located in Salisbury. In addition to their duty as guards at Salisbury Prison, Hoke's troops were also charged with guarding the bridges and railroad in his immediate area, as well as the apprehension and arrest of all deserters from the army. The latter duty sometimes became violent, when deserters banded together into groups and resisted arrest. For these Senior Reserves, their first experience in combat would not be against the Yankees but would come against their own countrymen who had become disillusioned with the war and just wanted to go home. On November 25, 1864, several Senior Reserve members had their first encounter with the enemy, but the confrontation came from an unexpected quarter. During a changing of the guard, a squad of prisoners rushed forward to attack their captors. In the ensuing scuffle, several prisoners were able to secure muskets. As shots rang out, two Senior Reserve guards fell dead, and several more were wounded. Outer sentinels fired on the rioting prisoners, as did two pieces of artillery. When the smoke cleared, some 50 dead and wounded Union prisoners lay on the ground, and the uprising had been silenced.[2]

These Senior Reserves would have a chance to face the enemy in the final days of the war, when a Union army paid a visit to Salisbury. In late March of

1865, Major General George Stoneman embarked on a cavalry raid from East Tennessee. With six thousand troopers and four cannon, he marched out of Mossy Creek, Tennessee, bound for North Carolina. His mission was to obstruct possible lines of retreat for Lee's army, at Petersburg and Richmond, by destroying parts of the East Tennessee & Virginia Railroad, the North Carolina Railroad, and the Danville & Greensboro Railroad. Stoneman's column entered northwestern North Carolina on March 28 and made its way for the town of Boone. Reports came in that a meeting of the local home guard was taking place, so Stoneman sent a detachment ahead to capture and disperse its members. Some home guard troops, along with a few furloughed soldiers and some local citizens, attempted to resist the blue-clad troopers who swarmed through the town. The defense was short-lived, as Stoneman's cavalrymen overwhelmed the meager Confederate forces. Nine were killed and sixty-eight captured. From Boone, the Federal column confounded North Carolina officials by moving north, into Virginia. Railroads were damaged at Hillsville, Wytheville, and Christiansburg, and a portion of the command advanced as far as Lynchburg before turning south once more and heading back into North Carolina. On April 12, three days after Lee had surrendered at Appomattox, Stoneman reached Salisbury with two brigades of his command. The Federals were opposed by Brigadier General William M. Gardner and an odd collection of troops. Gardner's force included some Confederate regulars, some home guard members, government employees, civilians, and even some galvanized Yankees. It also contained members of the 4th, 5th, and 6th North Carolina Senior Reserves, as well as some Junior Reserves. Lieutenant Colonel John C. Pemberton, the same officer who had been in command of the defenses at Vicksburg as a lieutenant general, was in overall command of a battalion of veteran artillery. The size of Gardner's force was estimated between 2,500 and 5,000, but was probably closest to the lower number. The battle opened with an artillery duel in which the Confederates outgunned Stoneman's artillerists. Stoneman then ordered his troopers to attack the enemy's flanks. The Confederate right soon folded, followed by the left. The Federals then pressed their advantage against the center, which caved in as the Confederates retreated then broke to the rear in a rout. The members of the 4th, 5th, and 6th Senior Reserves had experienced their first and last combat of the war. The Federals captured 1,364 prisoners and 14 pieces of artillery.[3] A number of the captured were graybeards from the Senior Reserves.

The 7th North Carolina Senior Reserves had been sent with other North Carolina troops to try to bolster Lieutenant General William J. Hardee's forces during Sherman's March to the Sea. When Savannah was captured, the 7th Senior Reserves retreated northward through South Carolina with the rest of Hardee's command. They crossed into North Carolina and passed through Fayetteville closely pursued by the Federals. Sherman decided to stop in Fayetteville to allow his men a well-earned rest. Hardee's men also benefited from the Federal pause in Fayetteville, stopping for a rest of their own near Averasboro. It had rained almost every day during the campaign. The roads were quagmires of mud, and it was with great difficulty that the Union troops moved northward out of Fayetteville on March 14, 1865. Hardee was faced with a difficult decision. In his rear, the Black River had become a raging torrent, causing severe problems for his wagon train. Hardee must either abandon his supplies or turn to face two full corps of Sherman's army with his eight thousand men. He chose the latter, making a stand to give his wagons a chance to cross the river.[4] Nearly 30,000 veteran Union troops would be bearing down on his meager force, most of which were green troops that had never fought in an infantry battle.

In setting up his defensive position, Hardee drew upon the lessons of a famous battle that had been fought in the Carolinas in the Revolutionary War. General Daniel Morgan had dealt with a similar situation when he fought the British at the battle of Cowpens. Severely outnumbered and commanding a force of relatively untried troops, Morgan had settled on a defense in depth that made the most of his resources, and Hardee copied it at Averasboro. In a first line of battle he placed the brigade of Colonel Alfred Rhett, Confederate regulars who had spent their entire time in the service in garrison duty in Charleston. These were some of his most inexperienced troops. Two hundred yards to the rear of Rhett's position, Hardee placed a second line, manned by the brigade of Brigadier General Stephen Elliott. Six hundred yards behind Elliott's line, Hardee formed his main line, and placed four veteran brigades of Major General Lafayette McLaws's division in the works. The idea was that the green troops in the forward positions would gain courage from the fact that there were strong lines to their rear to withdraw to in case they were overpowered. If they were forced back, the Confederates would become more compressed and be able to deliver maximum firepower as the Yankees surged forward.[5]

Though they were not among the veteran troops in Hardee's command, the 7th Senior Reserves were placed in the third line among McLaws's brigades. On the evening of March 15, scattered picket fire erupted with the arrival of the Union vanguard, under the command of Brigadier General Joseph Hawley. The following morning, Hawley decided to test the enemy defenses, supported by Major General Judson Kilpatrick's cavalry. The pickets were driven back from the front of Rhett's line, exposing the fact that Hardee was there in force and ready to fight. Kilpatrick sent word back to Major General Alpheus Williams, commander of the XX Corps, that additional men would be needed, and the divisions of Brigadier Generals Nathaniel Jackson and William Ward were hurried forward. They arrived on the field at approximately 10:00 a.m., just as Confederate skirmishers were pushing back Kilpatrick's dismounted troopers. When the two divisions reached Hardee's position, they immediately deployed three batteries of artillery, which drove the Confederate skirmishers back. The Union infantry surged forward, with Ward on the right and Jackson on the left. The artillery continued to shell Hardee's first line as the Federals advanced on the position. In an hour it was all over. The Confederates had been compelled to withdraw to their second line, where they formed behind Elliott's men. Kilpatrick's troopers probed at the left flank of the Southern line but were thrown back by a brigade from McLaws's division. The Union horsemen were replaced by infantry, as pressure was brought to bear on the front and flank of Elliott's line. Facing the possibility of being cut off, the troops were withdrawn to the third and final line. Pushing forward, Ward's and Jackson's divisions slammed into the center of this final line, only to be repulsed. Several more attacks were made, all with the same result. Jackson then attempted to turn the Confederate left, but Hardee shifted forces to meet the threat and the Federals were repulsed again. As dusk gathered in the horizon, both sides settled into set lines, and only intermittent skirmishing took place until about 8:00 p.m.[6]

With his wagons safely across the Black River, Hardee withdrew his army the following day. Casualties had been just under seven hundred for the Federals and somewhere between five hundred and one thousand for the Confederates. The 7th Senior Reserves had stood to their post in this, their first battle, and had done their part in repelling the Union attacks. They would be under fire for their second and last time in just a few days.

The 8th North Carolina Senior Reserves had faced the enemy several months before their comrades in the 7th, when they formed part of the army gathered to resist Union efforts to capture Fort Fisher. During the December expedition against the fort, the 8th Senior Reserves were brigaded together with four battalions of Junior Reserves under the command of Colonel John K. Connally, and assigned to hold a position on the Sugar Loaf defensive line. Sugar Loaf was an entrenched camp six miles north of Fort Fisher, built for the Army of Wilmington and within easy supporting distance of the fort. It was connected to the fort by a series of artillery batteries and signal stations. On December 25, 1864, Union amphibious forces landed at New Inlet, five miles up the beach from Fort Fisher and one mile south of Sugar Loaf. With a beachhead established, Northern troops were pushed toward Fort Fisher to make a reconnaissance of the works, while a rear guard was faced in the opposite direction and entrenched facing Sugar Loaf to defend against a Confederate attack from the rear. There was reason for concern, as reports had come in that Major General Robert F. Hoke's division from the Army of Northern Virginia was marching toward Sugar Loaf and that his vanguard had already arrived. An inspection of the fort convinced Brigadier General Godfrey Weitzel, commanding the expeditionary force, that it could not be taken by infantry assault. He communicated this opinion to his superior, Ben Butler, who decided to cancel the attack and recall the troops from the beach.

The expedition had been a tremendous failure for the Union. The 8th Senior Reserves had taken part in their first victorious engagement without having to confront the enemy face to face. They had been under fire, however, and had been bloodied by the big guns of the Federal navy. As troops of Brigadier General William Kirkland's brigade arrived on the scene in advance of the rest of Hoke's division, they were greeted by a disconcerting sight. Several dead Confederates lay on the ground. To the battle-hardened veterans who had fought in so many campaigns with the Army of Northern Virginia, this should not have been an unusual sight, but these men were different. They were all old men with gray hair, and Kirkland's men must have reflected that they should have died at home in their beds, not on a battlefield.[7] The 8th Senior Reserves had stood to their posts, and several of them had paid for that devotion with their lives.

Less than one month later the Federals were back, however, and this time the expedition against the fort would have a very different result. Now under the command of Brigadier General Alfred Terry, the Union army force was landed on the beach on January 15, 1865. After an intense naval bombardment, the battered garrison of Fort Fisher prepared for the infantry assault that was sure to follow. Colonel William Lamb, commander of the fort, knew that his force could not possibly resist the Federals unless it received support from Confederate reserves at Sugar Loaf. The 8th Senior Reserves were once more positioned in this entrenched camp. So was General Hoke's division, along with other troops forwarded from Wilmington. General Braxton Bragg was in overall command of the department, and he was hesitant to commit his forces at Sugar Loaf in support of Lamb's garrison. Feeling that he was drastically outnumbered by the Federal army, he ignored Lamb's repeated pleas to act, and his men remained idle for the most part as the fort's garrison waged a desperate but futile fight to repel their attackers. Finally, after a portion of the works had already been captured, Bragg ordered two brigades of Hoke's division forward to assault the rear of the Union forces. The Senior Reserves would remain in their defensive positions.

The Federals had established a defensive line facing Sugar Loaf to guard against just such a move. The right of the line was held by the white brigade of Colonel Joseph Abbott. To their left was a black division under the command of Brigadier General Charles Paine. Hoke's brigades easily threw back Abbott's troops and occupied their defensive lines. Paine's black troops were another matter. They offered stiff resistance and refused to be brushed away.

At this time, the situation on the beach became known to the Federal navy, and the Confederates began to be shelled by the big guns of the fleet. The troops in Hoke's brigades knew that the Federals must stop shelling them as soon as they advanced against Paine's troops, for fear of hitting their own men, and they readied themselves to make the assault. But the orders to advance were not forthcoming. Instead, they were directed to withdraw back to their original position at Sugar Loaf. General Bragg had become unnerved by the fleet's bombardment and had called off the attack. Fort Fisher would be allowed to fall without being actively supported by the reinforcements at Sugar Loaf.[8]

With the loss of Fort Fisher, General Bragg concentrated his available forces around Wilmington. As important as the city was to the life of the Confederacy, it was expected that he would make a fight of it before allowing the last major port to the outside world to be closed. But Bragg had become convinced that saving Wilmington was impossible and that he did not have nearly enough men to confront the Federals. Instead, he withdrew his army inland, in the direction of Goldsboro. General Joseph E. Johnston was gathering together forces in an effort to stop Sherman's march through North Carolina, and Bragg's troops, including the 8th Senior Reserves, would become a part of this newly formed Army of the South. General Hardee's troops, after their engagement at Averasboro, were also falling back for a rendezvous with Johnston. The 7th and 8th Senior Reserves would soon be united to fight in one of the last great battles of the war, at Bentonville.

Johnston was creating his Army of the South using all the resources still available in the southeastern states. The skeletal remnant of the once proud Army of Tennessee, Hardee's garrison forces from Savannah, Bragg's troops from Wilmington, and units of Junior and Senior Reserves were all brought together for a decisive stand against Sherman before his army could reach Virginia and assault Lee's Richmond and Petersburg defenses from the rear. Johnston's entire concentration numbered slightly less than 30,000 men. They would be opposed by Sherman's army, some 60,000 strong. In addition, Major General John Schofield was advancing from Wilmington with another Federal force of 20,000. There was little Johnston could do, given the overwhelming odds against him. His only chance was if he could attack and defeat a part of Sherman's army and even the odds a little. That opportunity presented itself as a result of General Hardee's stand at Averasboro. A gap was created between the left and right wings of the Federal army that the Confederates estimated to be at least a day's march. Johnston decided that there was a chance for him to fall on the left wing and defeat it before the rest of Sherman's forces could come to its support. Accordingly, he concentrated his army at Bentonville and waited to spring his trap.

On the morning of March 19, 1865, Brigadier General William P. Carlin's division of the XIV Corps made contact with the Confederates one mile south

The battle of Bentonville, where members of the Senior Reserves participated in the last great battle of the war. (Library of Congress)

of Bentonville. The left wing commander, Major General Henry W. Slocum, felt that it was nothing more than a cavalry screen, and ordered Carlin to brush them aside. The resulting Union attack ran headlong into Southern infantry in a prepared position and was repulsed. Brigadier General Absalom Baird's division joined the fray in support of Carlin, but both divisions were driven back. By this time, Slocum was aware that he was facing an entire Confederate army. Brigadier General James D. Morgan's division had reached the field, but Slocum did not order another assault. Instead, the three divisions assumed a defensive posture, with Carlin's division on the left, Baird's in the center, and Morgan's on the right. While awaiting the arrival of the XX Corps, Morgan's troops constructed strong fieldworks that would play a key role in the battle. At 3:00 p.m., the Confederates launched an attack with what would be the last great infantry charge of the war. Carlin's and Baird's divisions were driven back, leaving Morgan's men alone on the field to face the Southern onslaught. In a series of attacks, Morgan's men were assaulted from all sides but, owing to the uncoordinated nature of the attacks, were able to hold firm behind their entrenchments. As elements of the XX Corps arrived on the field, they were fed into the fight, which lasted throughout the afternoon and evening.

Unable to dislodge the Federals from their last position, General Johnston approved a rare night attack against Morgan's position, to be made under the command of General Hardee. Colonel Washington Hardy led a brigade in this attack that included the 7th North Carolina Senior Reserves. The brigade also included the 50th North Carolina Infantry and the 10th North Carolina Battalion. Battlefield casualties, illness, and desertion had greatly reduced the numbers of men in the ranks, and Hardy's brigade had been reduced to 329 men at the time of the attack.[9] Hardy advanced without skirmishers, and as his brigade marched forward it drifted to the left and lost contact with the rest of the Confederate battle line. An officer from Hardy's command went forward to ascertain if troops to their front were friend or foe and was captured by members of the 113th Ohio, a regiment in Colonel John G. Mitchell's brigade. The officer, not yet realizing that he was in the presence of the enemy, inadvertently advised Mitchell that Hardy was in his front and stated that officer "asks that you will apprise your line that he is forming in your front to charge the Yankee lines on your left." Mitchell, who had been preparing to go to bed, sprang to his feet and asked the officer to repeat the message. He then inquired if the young man had eaten his supper yet, and when told he had not, he sent the unsuspecting prisoner to the rear to be fed, later recalling that the "information was well worth a better supper than could be improvised." Mitchell ordered his pickets to be drawn in and directed that a volley be fired by the entire brigade when a signal was given, which was to be the sound of a drum. Mitchell had barely given the order before Hardy's men appeared before his line. The Confederates were so close that the Union troops could hear their footsteps and the conversation in the ranks. One loud tap was given on a bass drum, and Mitchell's line erupted in a sheet of flame. Hardy's troops, including the 7th Senior Reserves, were swept away by the murderous fire. Mitchell would later write, "I never expect to hear again such a volume of mingled cries, groans, screams and curses. The next morning there was displayed in front of our works, among the dead, a line of new Enfield rifles and knapsacks, almost as straight as if laid out for a Sunday morning inspection."[10] One Confederate reported that 51 of Hardy's men had been shot down by the volley; the remainder fell to the ground to protect themselves before retreating to the rear. The 7th Senior Reserves had been bloodied in this attack, the only one they would make during the war, and they had been summarily repulsed in the effort. They would return to their place in the line to await the future developments of the battle.

The following day, on March 20, Major General Oliver O. Howard's right wing of Sherman's army, along with the commanding general himself, was on the field. Johnston's opportunity to deal the Federals a crippling blow had been lost, and he was now confronted by a force more than twice his size. Johnston remained on the field, hoping to induce Sherman into making a frontal assault on his lines, as he had at Kennesaw Mountain the previous summer. But Sherman would not take the bait, and the day was marked by only desultory skirmishing and probing. On March 21, Johnston was still on the field, but his hopes of baiting Sherman into dashing his army against the Confederate fieldworks were all but gone. Major General Joseph Mower had been granted permission to make a reconnaissance of the extreme left of the Confederate line with his division. Mower exceeded his orders and turned the reconnaissance into a full-scale attack with two of his brigades. The Confederates were driven back, and Mower's men came close to capturing a bridge over Mill Creek that served as Johnston's only line of retreat, before General Sherman peremptorily ordered him to cease his advance and pull back. That night, Johnston pulled his army out of its lines and retreated across the Mill Creek Bridge. The Confederates retired to Smithfield, 16 miles northwest of Bentonville, where he reorganized and refitted his army. Here, the 8th Senior Reserves were reunited with their comrades. They had been part of Colonel George Jackson's brigade that had been left at the town and had missed the fighting at Bentonville.[11]

For the next month, the 7th and 8th Senior Reserves would accompany Johnston's army as it maneuvered to try to avoid being trapped by the Federal forces converging upon it. On April 26, nearly three weeks after Robert E. Lee's Army of Northern Virginia had surrendered at Appomattox Court House, General Johnston decided that all hopes of Confederate victory were gone, and he surrendered what was left of his own army to General Sherman at Bennett Place, North Carolina. The Senior Reserves had written no glorious chapters in the annals of the war. They had been on the winning side at the first expedition against Fort Fisher and at Averasboro, but they had been recruited at a time when the demise of the Confederacy was all but certain, and they fought in engagements that were more forlorn hopes than practical solutions to the military situation at the time. While it is true that large numbers of Senior Reserves deserted the ranks, those that remained seem to have done their duty. Their mere existence highlighted the dire situation the Confederate army found itself in after three years of bloody war that had all but drained the lifeblood out of the South. These graybeards indeed formed a unique fighting unit in the Civil War, and their service is worthy of remembrance.

CHAPTER 19

THE SUBMARINERS

Man had long envisioned the construction of a device that would allow exploration of what lay beneath the surface of the world's oceans, a submersible vehicle that would allow access to the mysteries of the deep. Though many designs had previously been forwarded for such a vessel, it would appear that the first successful attempt at constructing a submarine was in 1620, when Cornelius Drebbel built one for England. Drebbel, a Dutch citizen, was in the service of King James I. The king was a scholar in his own right, a patron of the arts and sciences, and is best known for his sponsorship of the translation of the Bible into the English language, which became known as the King James version.[1] Military leaders quickly appreciated the advantages a submarine would provide in warfare, as efforts were focused on devising a workable prototype model capable of attacking enemy shipping. The United States was the first country to develop a working submarine, during the Revolutionary War. David Bushnell, a Connecticut inventor, constructed an acorn-shaped submersible he named the *Turtle*, because of the way it looked in the water. Bushnell's design allowed for a one-man crew and incorporated a screw propulsion system. The *Turtle* was built in 1775 but saw its first action against the British on September 7, 1776, when Sergeant Ezra Lee made an attack against the English warship HMS *Eagle* in New York Harbor. Lee failed to sink the enemy vessel, but the enterprise served to increase interest in submersible design.

Americans continued to play a leading role in submarine development, as Robert Fulton's design was adopted by the French when they built the *Nautilus* in 1804. In 1814, Silas Halsey was killed while making an unsuccessful attack on a British warship in the harbor of New London, Connecticut, during the War of 1812. Over the next 50 years, submersible technology was much improved, and by the time hostilities erupted in the

Civil War there were several inventors having plans for viable prototypes of military submarines. Both sides displayed early interest in the construction of submarines when the war commenced, for very different reasons. In the North, the Navy looked at the craft as a possible means for clearing obstacles away from Southern harbors. In the South, submarines were looked upon as a stealthy way to combat the vastly superior Union navy and break the blockade of important ports.

Brutus de Villeroi was a French engineer who had become one of the foremost experts on submarines in the world. In 1832 he had built a submersible that was slightly over 10 feet long, but only 27 inches high and 25 inches wide. The craft required a crew of three men, and was propelled by three sets of duck-foot paddles. Villeroi conducted a test of his submarine near Nantes on August 12, 1832. The sub was able to remain submerged for two hours, and was proclaimed to be a complete success.[2] Villeroi tried unsuccessfully to sell his submarine design to the French government, and in 1856 he immigrated to the United States, eventually settling in Philadelphia, Pennsylvania. On May 16, 1861, a submarine built by Villeroi was seized by the Philadelphia police after it had been spotted sailing in the Delaware River. As it turned out, this submersible had been built by Villeroi for its possible use in salvage operations of sunken ships, but the inventor was quick to offer his expertise to the Federal government to design a larger version of his submarine capable of performing military tasks.

At the insistence of Abraham Lincoln, Villeroi's submarine was tested by the navy, and a contract was subsequently issued for a larger model to be built. By November of 1861, the Navy Department placed an order for construction of the craft. This first submarine of the U.S. Navy (the *Turtle* was created before there was a U.S. Navy) was to be named the USS *Alligator*, the fourth vessel of the navy to bear that name. The submarine was built by the firm of Neafie & Levy. It was 30 feet long and had a diameter of 6 to 8 feet. The iron tube had several small, circular glass plates on top to allow light into the craft. Two tubes connected the ship to floats on the surface of the water, through which air pumps brought oxygen into the *Alligator*. The submarine was powered by means of 16 hand-powered paddles protruding from the sides. The navy was interested in using the *Alligator* to counter the new ironclad ram the Confederates were reported to be building at the Norfolk Navy Yard. The contract called for the submarine to be completed in forty days, but the work progressed very slowly, and it took more than six months before the *Alligator* was ready to be launched. Part of the reason for the delay was fighting that erupted between Villeroi and the contractor over the propulsion system and the fresh air system. Before the craft had been completed, Villeroi quit the project in disgust and offered no further service to the war effort.[3]

The USS *Alligator*, one of the North's first submarines. (U.S. Navy)

Following its May 1, 1862, launching, Gideon Welles, secretary of the navy, instructed Flag Officer Louis Goldsborough to send "one of your small and swift steamers" to tow the *Alligator* from the Philadelphia Navy Yard to the James River, where the craft would undergo a shakedown cruise before possibly being sent against the Confederate ironclad *Virginia*.[4] When the *Alligator* reached Hampton Roads, it did little more than poke around on the bottom.[5] Commander John Rodgers quickly determined that the vessel was too large to be able to maneuver in either the James or Appomattox Rivers. What Rodgers feared was that the *Alligator* might fall into enemy hands and be used against the ships of his fleet. The submarine was taken to the Washington Navy Yard, where its oars were replaced with a hand-cranked screw propeller. It was at this time that Rear Admiral Samuel F. DuPont decided that the *Alligator* might be useful in his offensive plans against Charleston, South Carolina. On March 31, 1863, the *Alligator* got underway for Charleston, under tow by the USS *Sumpter*. The following day, the two ships ran into a storm at sea. By April 2, the sea had become so rough that the commander of the *Sumpter* was forced to cut loose the *Alligator* off Cape Hatteras, North Carolina, in order to save his own ship. The *Alligator* sank in waters in close proximity to where the ironclad *Monitor* had found a watery grave.[6] The first submarine of the U.S. Navy had been an innovation of design and technology but had failed to make any contribution to the Northern war effort.

The North was not deterred by the less than favorable results achieved by the *Alligator*. In 1863, work was begun on the *Sub Marine Explorer*, a submarine designed by Julius H. Kroehl and Ariel Patterson. The *Explorer* was an improvement on Van Buren Ryerson's 1858 patent for a diving bell. It was 36 feet long, 12 feet high, and 13 feet broad, having a flat bottom and two hatches. The craft was said to resemble "the upper segment of a short, thick cigar, with a turret in the middle of the top part for the entrance of the men who descend in it."[7] The *Sub Marine Explorer* featured a pressurized compartment for its crew and utilized a water ballast system for the descent and ascent of the craft. Construction on the sub was not completed until after the close of the Civil War, and the *Explorer* was employed in gathering pearls from the oyster beds off the coast of Panama. Problems with the pressurized compartment led to continual episodes of decompression sickness with the vessel's crews and the death of numerous crew members. In 1869, the *Sub Marine Explorer* was abandoned in Panama's Pearl Islands.

A third Northern submarine begun during the war was the *Intelligent Whale*, designed by Scovel S. Merriam. In November 1863, Merriam contracted Augustus Price and Cornelius Bushnell to construct the submarine for the sum of $15,000. Merriam's design called for a vessel made of half-inch-thick boiler iron, to be 28 feet 8 inches long, 9 feet high, and 7 feet wide. The *Intelligent Whale* was driven by a hand-cranked propeller, operated by four of the six to thirteen men it could accommodate as a crew, and could attain a speed of four knots. The submarine carried two tanks of compressed air, capable of allowing the crew to be submerged for as many as ten hours, and had a device that sprayed water through the air, as well as a release valve to cleanse the ship of foul air. The crew embarked and disembarked via a hatch located topside, in the middle of the craft. The *Intelligent Whale* carried no torpedoes. Her method of attack was by means of deploying divers through two wooden doors in the floor of the craft. The diver would then make his way to the enemy ship and place a charge under the scow. Returning to the *Intelligent Whale*, the diver could then explode the charge by using a lanyard and a friction primer.[8]

In April of 1864, the American Submarine Company replaced Price and Bushnell as the builders. Cost overruns plagued the construction of the submarine, which cost about $60,000 by the time of its completion in April of 1866, a year after the end of the Civil War. The *Intelligent Whale* was sold to the U.S. Navy in 1869, pending the results of test trials. These were not completed until 1872, at which time the navy determined the craft to be unfit for its needs and abandoned the project.[9] The *Intelligent Whale* survived scrapping and for a number of years has been on display at the National Guard Militia Museum, in Sea Girt, New Jersey. Plans are to move the sub to the navy's small boat repair facility in Annapolis, Maryland, where she is to be refitted and made seaworthy for a PBS documentary being produced by NOVA. Though the *Intelligent Whale* never saw service during the Civil

The *Intelligent Whale*. Begun during the Civil War, its completion in 1866 was too late for it to be employed in service. (U.S. Navy)

War, she is the most complete example of the 1860s technology that went into designing and building these pioneer scourges of the deep.

The Confederacy also began building submarines in the early days of the war, but the names and designs of several of them have been lost to history. It is estimated by historians that there were as many as 20 different submarines built during the war, by both sides, but records are only available for some half dozen or so. Southern submarine production was not carried out under the auspices of the Confederate Navy, but was instead assigned to the Confederate Secret Service, and the evidence of some of the earliest models is shrouded in mystery. Part of the reason for this lies in the fact that Confederate officials believed that the employment of submarines was outside the boundaries of the normal and accepted rules of war. As such, they felt that individuals connected with Southern submarines would be treated harshly if captured by the Federals. At the close of the war, many official records pertaining to the development of Confederate submarines were destroyed, in an effort to protect those who had worked on the projects. The history of submarine service in the Civil War was greatly thwarted by the destruction of these records. As early as the fall of 1861, Confederate submarines were spotted in the James River and at New Orleans, but no information about these early craft survived the war.

William G. Cheeney, an underwater explosives engineer, may have designed as many as two submarines of similar design for Confederate service that were built at the Tredegar Iron Works in Richmond. One or both of these submarines probably account for the sightings in the James River in

1861. Though no schematics or drawings of either craft survive, it is known that the vessels required only a crew of two men and were powered by a hand-cranked propeller. Mrs. E. L. Baker, a Union spy in Richmond, left an account of a test voyage of one of Cheeney's submarines, in which an old barge was used as a target and successfully sunk by the Confederate craft. Mrs. Baker's report caused an official stir in Washington, as naval officers scrambled to develop effective means to deal with this new enemy threat. A system of antisubmarine nets was finally adopted, whereby heavy netting or chains were attached to spars encircling the ship. It was hoped that an enemy submarine would become tangled if it approached a ship, leaving it helpless for possible destruction or capture. In October of 1861, one of Cheeney's submarines made an attack against the USS *Minnesota*, near Sewell's Point, Virginia. Union countermeasures were effective, as the sub got caught in the protective netting and was barely able to extricate itself. Three weeks later, one of Cheeney's subs attempted another attack but was thwarted when an alert sailor spotted its camouflaged float, which supplied fresh air to the crew. The sailor lifted up the float and cut the attached hose, which quickly sank into the water. It is not known if the vessel or crew survived this incident, but there were no further sightings of Cheeney's submarines from that point forward.[10]

The earliest design about which there is reliable information is the *Pioneer*. This Confederate submarine was the collective venture of James McClintock, Baxter Watson, Horace Hunley, J. K. Scott, and Henry Leovy. McClintock and Watson were partners in a machine shop business in New Orleans that manufactured steam gauges. At the outbreak of the war, the partners secured a government contract to produce minié balls on a high-speed machine invented by McClintock. During the summer of 1861, the city of New Orleans was threatened by two U.S. steamers operating on Lake Pontchartrain, and McClintock set his mind to work on a way to eliminate the Federal menace. He designed a submarine for use in the lake, and his plans quickly attracted the attention of Horace Hunley. Hunley was a wealthy New Orleans lawyer and plantation owner, who had served a term in the Louisiana legislature. Always on the lookout for a good business opportunity, he had taken command of a blockade-runner in the early months of the war, motivated as much by the promise of financial rewards as by patriotic fervor or the thrill of adventure.[11] The blockade-running trade proved to be unsuccessful, and Hunley was quick to join in on the venture to construct a submarine.

The craft was made from quarter-inch iron plates that had been cut from old boilers. The plates were then riveted together to form the outer casing of the vessel. McClintock stated in a postwar interview that it was 30 feet long and 4 feet in diameter, being in the shape of a cigar. (Actual measurements, taken by W. M. Robinson in 1926 after the *Pioneer* had been salvaged, showed the craft to be 20 feet long, 3 feet 2 inches wide, and 6 feet deep.)

The *Pioneer* had a conning tower with manholes in the top, and small, circular glass windows in her sides. She was propelled by means of a hand-cranked screw that was operated by a single crew member. She incorporated diving planes with an iron ballast keel of sufficient weight that it barely enabled the craft to float on the surface. The *Pioneer* was armed with a mine towed by a 200-foot cable that was intended to be pulled into an enemy vessel for detonation. The *Pioneer* was completed early in 1862, and on March 12 she was granted a letter of marque to operate as a privateer against enemy shipping. Tests were conducted in Lake Pontchartrain in which the *Pioneer* successfully sank a small schooner and several rafts. Before she could be used to attack any Union ships, Admiral David Farragut captured New Orleans on April 25, 1862. With the Crescent City now in Federal hands, the owners of the *Pioneer* worried that she would be captured by the enemy and had her scuttled to prevent that from happening.[12]

McClintock, Watson, and Hunley had succeeded in building a working submarine, and their enterprise was foiled only by the inopportune capture of New Orleans. With the Confederate government paying as much as $50,000 for the sinking of a Federal warship, the trio decided to move their operation to another location and try again. Accordingly, they packed up their plans and tools and relocated to Mobile, Alabama, where work was soon begun on the *Pioneer II*, also known as the *American Diver*. Work was begun as soon as the trio could find suitable space to work, in the machine shop of Park and Lyons, and by the end of 1862 the submarine was nearing completion. The partners were greatly assisted in the project by the efforts of William A. Alexander, a Confederate army engineer from the 21st Alabama Infantry, along with Lieutenant G. E. Dixon of the same regiment. The *Pioneer II* was delayed in her final completion because of failed attempts to improve her means of propulsion. Initially, the vessel was fitted with an electromagnetic engine. When this failed to provide the desired effect, the possibilities of using a steam engine were explored. Upon exhausting this possibility, a hand-cranked propeller was installed. The finished craft measured 36 feet long, 3 feet wide, and 4 feet deep. It was tapered inward from the tip for a distance of 12 feet, on each end, to facilitate underwater movement. The *Pioneer II* carried a crew of five, with four of those crew members being needed to operate the hand-cranked propeller. Initial trials left the creators less than satisfied, as the submarine was unable to attain the sufficient speed necessary to make an attack on a Federal ship. Nonetheless, in February 1863, the *Pioneer II* prepared to assault a Union warship in Mobile Bay. According to a Confederate deserter who had witnessed scene,

> On or about the 14th, an infernal machine, consisting of a submarine boat, capable of holding 5 persons, and having a torpedo which was to be attached

to the bottom of a vessel and exploded by means of clockwork, left Fort Morgan at 8 p.m. . . . The instruction was to come up at Sand Island, get the bearing and distance of the nearest vessel, dive under again and operate upon her; but on emerging they found themselves so far outside the island and in so strong a current that they were forced to cut the torpedo adrift and make the best of their way back.

What the deserter failed to include in his report was that the mission took place in foul weather that had churned up the water, making the expedition hazardous from the beginning.[13] Though all members of the crew were able to escape when the *Pioneer II* went to the bottom of Mobile Bay, the submarine was not able to be recovered, and the second attempt of McClintock, Watson, and Hunley to build a submarine for privateer service had ended in failure.

The loss of the *Pioneer II* did not dampen the enthusiasm of Hunley, McClintock, and Watson, but it left them seriously short of funds. The first two submarines had cost $15,000, exhausting most of the capital the partnership had to work with. Additional investors would have to be found if another submarine was to be built. Edgar Singer, of the Texas family that had made a fortune manufacturing sewing machines, agreed to help fund the venture. So did A. Whitney, a businessman who had made considerable money manufacturing torpedoes for the Confederate navy. With the necessary resources acquired, the partners began work on their third submarine. Apprehensive that Union spies might discover their purpose, they moved their boat-building operations from the Park and Lyons facility to the abandoned Seaman's Bethel Church, also in Mobile. Work was immediately begun on a craft referred to as the "fish boat" or the "fish torpedo boat." It was a long-held belief that the vessel was constructed from a steam boiler. This was due to a drawing of the craft, made by William A. Alexander in 1863, depicting the submarine as being short and stubby. The fact is that Alexander's drawing was somewhat incorrect, and the *Hunley* was a sleek, modern-looking submarine constructed out of new materials, not cast-off boilers.

The *Hunley* was 39.5 feet long. She had two short conning towers, one fore and one aft, containing the hatches through which the crew entered and exited the craft. These hatches were extremely small, being only 14 by 15.75 inches in size. The hull of the *Hunley* was 4 feet 3 inches in height, and the overall weight of the submarine was 7.5 tons. The *Hunley* was equipped with a diving plane and was submerged by means of ballast tanks on either end of the vessel that could be filled with water through the use of valves and pumped out with hand pumps. Additional ballast was provided through the use of iron weights, bolted to the bottom of the hull, which could be unscrewed from within the *Hunley* in case there was a need to acquire additional buoyancy in an

Sketch of the CSS *Hunley* drawn by William Alexander, one of Hunley's partners in constructing the submarine. (Naval History and Heritage Command)

emergency. An iron shaft ran through the length of the submarine, bent to form handles, that connected to propeller that gave the craft motion. Seven crew members were needed to work the crank and achieve a maximum surface speed of four knots. The *Hunley* was armed with a torpedo towed on a 200-foot rope, meaning that its method of attack would be the same as its predecessors. The *Hunley* would make for an enemy vessel, dive under it, and continue onward until the torpedo it had in tow made contact with the hull of the Union ship. Work on the submarine was completed in July of 1863, and tests were begun in Mobile Bay. On her first test run, the *Hunley* successfully sank a flatboat target. The waters of Mobile Bay proved to be too rough for the craft, however, and though it is not certain, the *Hunley*'s first crew may have been lost there.[14]

By late summer in 1863, the *Hunley* was transferred to Charleston, South Carolina, at the request of General Pierre G. T. Beauregard. Suffering tremendously from the tight Union blockade around Charleston Harbor, Beauregard saw the *Hunley* as a way to loosen the grip the Federals had on the city. A new crew was assembled, with Lieutenant John Payne, an Alabama infantry officer, serving as the ship's captain. Initial tests served as a foreboding omen of things to come, however, when the *Hunley* was sunk by the wake of a passing steamer that forced water into her open hatch as she made ready to make a dive. The hold quickly filled with water, sending her to the bottom with all hands aboard. Lieutenant Payne, who was about to close the hatch when the steamer sailed by, was able to squeeze through the hole and make his way to the surface. All other hands were lost.[15]

General Beauregard lost much of his enthusiasm for the project following the sinking of the *Hunley*, but this was rekindled when the torpedo boat, CSS *David*, succeeded in damaging the USS *New Ironsides* in Charleston Harbor. Lieutenant Payne acquired a new crew of volunteers, and the raised *Hunley* was put through another series of tests. But the hard-luck submarine continued to be a source of peril. She sunk again, and though Payne and two other crew members were able to escape through the hatches, four more crew members were killed in the accident. Beauregard was ready to pull the plug on the experiment when Horace Hunley arrived in Charleston. Hunley convinced the general to give his submarine one more chance. He assured Beauregard that he would take personal charge of the craft and assumed command of the vessel from Payne. The *Hunley* conducted a successful test run with the creator for which she was named in command, but on October 15, 1863, she sunk again, taking Horace Hunley and her seven other crew members to their death.[16]

Following Hunley's death, William Alexander and George Dixon traveled from Mobile to Charleston to press their case for the submarine. Having been so instrumental in her construction, Alexander and Dixon were convinced that the vessel could perform her mission and prevailed upon Beauregard to allow the *Hunley* one final chance. Beauregard agreed, in part because certain modifications were made concerning the armament and usage of the *Hunley*. One of his staff officers suggested that the *Hunley* be armed with a spar torpedo, similar to the one the torpedo boat *David* had earlier so successfully employed. The second suggestion was that the *Hunley* be operated more like a torpedo boat and not fully submerge during its attack. With these revisions in place, Beauregard agreed to salvage the sunken *Hunley* and give her another opportunity. Volunteers for a new crew came from the CSS *Indian Chief*, but Beauregard insisted that the gruesome history of the submarine be explained in detail to each man offering his services, in order that they might have the chance to reconsider before volunteering.[17]

The crew trained extensively for weeks, but high winds and heavy surf prevented any attacks being made upon Federal ships. For nearly three months, the *Hunley* made several voyages a week in search of a Union ship the sub could successfully attack. The craft made its nighttime forays from Battery Marshall, located at Beach Inlet on Sullivan's Island. Lieutenant Dixon used compass bearings, taken from the beach, to plot his course toward enemy ships. The problem was that Federal ships rarely anchored for the night any closer than 6–7 miles from Sullivan's Island. This distance was too great for the *Hunley* and her crew. Such a long cruise was exhausting on the men, who propelled the craft laboriously by working the crankshaft. At the distance the Federals ships usually anchored outside the harbor, a round-trip voyage would tax the endurance of the crew to the limit, risking the chance of losing the sub. Such a long trip would also place the craft in danger of being swept out to sea by the heavy tides outside the harbor, with a crew too weak to power the sub back to calmer waters.[18]

On the night of February 17, 1864, the *Hunley* was finally presented with a suitable opportunity to prove what she could do, when a Federal ship anchored within the range of the sub and her crew. The USS *Housatonic*, a steam-powered sloop-of-war, had stopped for the night in the north channel entrance to Charleston Harbor, some two miles from Battery Marshall, in 27 feet of water. Though the waters of the harbor were calm, the night sky was brightly illuminated by the moon, which would make it more difficult for the sub to approach her prey undetected. Nevertheless, Dixon prepared his crew to make an attack on the Union ship, not willing to allow this first target in months to go unchallenged. The *Hunley* made her silent approach toward the *Housatonic*, coming to within 100 yards of the objective before being spotted by lookouts on the Federal ship. The alarm was sounded, and the crew of the *Housatonic* sprang into action. The guns of the ship were manned, but the *Hunley* was already too close, and the cannon could not be depressed sufficiently to be brought to bear. Shipboard sailors opened fire on the *Hunley* with muskets as the ship's captain ordered the cable be slipped, in an effort to back away from the attacker. The attempt to flee was too late. The torpedo of the *Hunley* struck the *Housatonic* under the water, just abaft of the mizzenmast. The resulting explosion sent timbers from the ship as high as the top of the mizzenmast, as a plume of heavy smoke rose into the sky. The *Housatonic* settled to the bottom of the harbor floor, but owing to the shallow water she had been anchored in, most of the rigging remained unsubmerged, providing safe refuge for the crew. Five sailors aboard the *Housatonic* had been killed by the explosion or by drowning, but the vast majority of the crew were rescued by other Federal ships that quickly came to their assistance.[19]

The *Hunley* had been successful in accomplishing her mission, becoming the first submarine to ever sink an enemy ship. But the ship and crew did not return from the foray against the *Housatonic*. Lieutenant Dixon and his brave volunteers lost their lives while performing their historic feat, and the cause of their demise became a source of speculation and discussion for more than a century. It was thought that the *Hunley* might have been swamped by waves from the sinking *Housatonic*, or that she may have been swept out to sea by the tides. It was also speculated that the force of the torpedo explosion might have damaged the submarine. The resting place of the *Hunley* was discovered in 1970 by underwater archaeologist E. Lee Spence, about one hundred yards away from the site where the *Housatonic* had sunk. The craft was covered with silt but remained in a well-preserved condition. In 2000, the *Hunley* was recovered through the combined efforts of several state and federal agencies. The sub was taken to the Warren Lasch Conservation Center, at the former Charleston Navy Yard, where it can be seen today.

An examination of the crew compartment of the *Hunley* revealed little to end the conjecture or speculation. All eight crew members were found to be at their stations, but there was nothing that conclusively pointed to either a quick death or a slow one. The crew may have been rendered unconscious by the explosion of the torpedo, sunk to the bottom, and later drowned. They also may have sailed beyond the sinking *Housatonic*—in an effort to elude the approaching USS *Canandaigua*, sailing to assist the survivors of the attack—and rested on the floor of the harbor before attempting to make their way back with the help of incoming tides. While in this state, it would have been possible that the crew used up all the oxygen in the craft and suc-cumbed to a lack of the life-giving air. It may also be possible that once the ballast tanks were filled, the crew found it impossible to pump the water back out of them and rise to the surface.[20] Additional research and analysis may someday provide clues to the final fate of the crew of the *Hunley*, but for now, the submarine's final moments are still the topic of conjecture and edu-cated guessing. That her crew was successful in mounting the first triumphant attack on an enemy vessel is without question, however, and this fact alone makes the *Hunley* one of the most innovative weapons of war to emerge from the U.S. Civil War and assures her place in the annals of military history.

As previously stated, it is estimated that as many as 20 submarines were built by the Union and Confederacy during the Civil War. Though most of these failed to accomplish the mission for which they were constructed, the world watched with great interest as the United States assumed the leading technological role in submarine development. The lessons learned through these early experiments paved the way for the successful craft to follow, and the turn of the century would witness the full potential of submarine warfare, when the wolf packs of the German navy thrust the world into a new era of fighting on and under the seas. U.S. maritime innovations had led the way and, in the process, had pioneered the path to forever changing the world's navies. In many ways, U.S. innovations in regard to submarine warfare were far ahead of their time. The next successful attack of a submarine on an enemy ship would not take place for fully 50 years following the loss of the *Hunley*, when the German submarine *U-21* fired a torpedo into the magazine of the British cruiser *Pathfinder*, off Scotland's Firth of Forth, on September 5, 1914.[21] The age of the submarine, which had begun with the *Hunley* and her predecessors, had finally come to fruition, and the navies of the world would never be the same.

CHAPTER 20

THE IRONCLADS

The U.S. Civil War witnessed the first engagement between armored warships to take place in naval history. When the USS *Monitor* and the CSS *Virginia* (*Merrimack*) fought their epic battle at Hampton Roads, Virginia, on March 9, 1862, the era of wooden warships was brought to a close, as the navies of the world scrambled to update their own naval forces and bring them into the industrial age. But the story of ironclad naval vessels did not begin with the *Monitor* or the *Virginia*. These two vessels were the first of their kind to engage in combat against one another, but they were not the first to be used in warfare. That distinction belongs to the floating batteries built by the French and British in 1855 and 1856 for use in the Crimean War. These floating batteries were light-draught vessels, capable of moving about under their own steam power, but they could hardly be considered warships in the modern sense of the word. Bulky and unmaneuverable, they had a top speed of only four knots and usually had to be towed to the place where they were to be used. Furthermore, they were not seaworthy, which confined their usage to coastal operations. Nevertheless, these iron-plated platforms proved their worth in combat, enabling batteries of guns to be brought to bear against enemy fortifications in a way that offered more protection to the gunners than could be had on a wooden ship.[1]

By the end of the 1850s, the French and British had already adopted designs for seaworthy naval ships having iron plating and steam engines. In 1859, the French navy commissioned the *La Gloire*, a 36-gun vessel having 4.5-inch iron plates and capable of doing 13 knots. The British responded in 1860 by constructing the HMS *Warrior*, a 40-gun frigate, also boasting 4.5-inch iron plating, and capable of top speeds of 14.3 knots. A new arms race was on, and by 1862, each nation would have 16 ironclad ships in their navy, as the rest of Europe scrambled to keep pace with the new technology.[2]

The Confederacy had no existing navy when it declared its independence from the United States in 1861. As such, Southern leaders were faced with the problem of creating a naval department capable of dealing with the extensive pressure the Union navy could bring to bear against Confederate shipping and coastal areas. Southern leaders decided that their best course of action was to acquire a fleet of the most modern vessels, and ironclads seemed their best option. Since all of the ships of the U.S. Navy were wooden vessels, the Confederates felt that they could best offset the Union's advantage in numbers by employing superior armored technology. In May of 1861, the Confederate Congress appropriated $2 million to purchase ironclad vessels overseas. Inquiries were made concerning the willingness of the French to sell *La Gloire*, but these proved to be fruitless. France was not inclined to part with the ship it considered to be the jewel of its fleet, and the French were not interested, at this early stage of the war, in violating international laws of neutrality. Unable to procure the desired vessels abroad, the Confederacy was forced to undertake construction efforts to convert several existing wooden ships into ironclads in July of 1861.[3]

The first ironclad vessel to be converted and commissioned by the Confederate navy was the CSS *Manassas*. The ship had been built as the steamer *Enoch Train*, but had been captured by a Confederate privateer in the opening months of the war. It was purchased by John A. Stevenson, a New Orleans commission merchant, with the intention of converting the craft into a privateer ship. Stevenson had the ship taken to Algiers, Louisiana, where she was stripped down to her deck, and the work of converting her to an ironclad was begun. Stevenson lengthened the ship from 128 feet to 143 feet and increased her beam from 26 feet to 33 feet. The draft of the ship was made deeper, increasing her 12 feet 6 inches to 17 feet. In addition, 17-inch-thick, 20-foot-long beams were added to her bow to strengthen her for ramming, and a pointed iron ram was installed as her principal weapon. The ship was then covered with a layer of iron plating, 1.25 inches thick, fashioned in a curved manner that resembled a turtle's shell or an elongated floating cigar. She carried but one gun, a forward-firing cannon mounted in a gun port behind an armored shutter. Depending on the weight she was carrying, the ironclad hull of the vessel projected only 2–4 feet above the water line, presenting a scant target for an enemy ship to fire at. The curvature of the plating would also cause enemy shells to glance off, preventing any direct hits to be scored. Stevenson commissioned his ship the CSS *Manassas* on September 12, 1861, but before she could embark on the life of a privateer, the *Manassas* was seized by Flag Officer G. N. Hollins, CSN, for use by the Confederate navy.[4]

On October 12, 1861, the *Manassas*, under the command of Lieutenant A. F. Warley, took part in a naval engagement at Head of Passes, at the mouth of the Mississippi River. The *Manassas* led a small flotilla of ships, commanded by Flag Officer Hollins, in a surprise attack against Union blockading ships at the mouth of the river. Though the armored ram proved to be impervious to the shells fired at it from the Union warships, its performance in the engagement was less than glorious. In attempting to ram the USS *Richmond*, the ship's iron prow was broken off by a coal barge tied alongside the intended victim. The impact caused the *Manassas* to lose one of its smokestacks, and one of its two engines came loose from its mountings. Partially disabled and missing its main offensive weapon, the *Manassas* was forced to retire from the fight. In April of 1862, the *Manassas* once more engaged the Union navy during the battle of Forts Jackson and Saint Philip. In this engagement, the *Manassas* attempted to ram the USS *Pensacola*, but the Union ship turned before a full blow could be delivered. The *Manassas* then turned its attention to the USS *Mississippi* but failed to deliver more than a glancing blow. Finally, she rammed the USS *Brooklyn*, causing severe damage but failing to sink the enemy ship. Once the Union flotilla had successfully sailed past Forts Jackson and Saint Philip, Commodore David Farragut set his course for the city of New Orleans. The *Manassas* followed the Union ships until she ran aground following an attack by the USS *Mississippi*. The crew evacuated the ship, which eventually freed itself and began drifting down the Mississippi River. Union Commander David D. Porter attempted to save the ship so the Northern navy could examine it, but the *Manassas* exploded and sank to the bottom of the river.[5]

The North was not to be outdone in the construction of armored warships, and efforts to provide the Union navy with ironclad vessels were undertaken shortly after the firing on Fort Sumter. James B. Eads, a retired operator of salvage boats on the Mississippi River, went to Washington with a proposal to convert one of his salvage ships into an ironclad for Union service. Eads described his plan to Secretary of the Navy Gideon Welles, who was intrigued by the idea. But the inland waters were not under the jurisdiction of the navy, so Eads was referred to Secretary of War Simon Cameron. Eads's proposal met with little enthusiasm at the War Department. The army was not interested in a converted salvage boat. What was needed was a fleet of light-draft gunboats, capable of providing offensive punch for Union armies operating along the inland waters of the Mississippi, Ohio, Cumberland, and Tennessee Rivers. Commander John Rodgers had been detached from the navy to provide technical assistance to the army in creating such a fleet and, together with Eads, began drawing up designs for a suitable ship. Rodgers asked the navy to provide an officer to lend technical expertise to the project, and the services of Samuel M. Pook were obtained. Pook was a civilian contractor, with a wealth of experience in designing river vessels, who was, at that time, working in Cairo, Illinois. Pook came up with a design for a ship that was 175 feet long and 52 feet wide, having casemated oaken sides, two feet thick, which protected the engines, guns, and rear-mounted paddle wheel that propelled the ship. The ship was designed to take only six feet of water and was to be armed with three large guns in the front, four lesser guns on each side, and two light guns in the rear. The casemate was covered with iron plating 2.5 inches thick in the front and part way back the sides. This was due to the fact that Pook intended the ships to do the greater part of their fighting head-on, reducing the need to cover the entire vessel in iron plate, and thereby making it less weighty and ponderous.[6]

Pook's design bore a striking resemblance to the CSS *Virginia*, which the Confederates would later build, but his ships would be less powerful and more lightly armored than the Southern titan. The War Department approved Pook's design, and Eads was awarded a contract to build seven of the vessels at a cost of $89,600 each. The ships were to be named for cities along the Mississippi River or its tributaries, which led to their being named the City-class ironclads. They were the USS *Cairo, Carondelet, Cincinnati, Louisville, Mound City, Pittsburgh*, and *St. Louis* (later renamed the *Baron de Kalb*). The first four ironclads were built at St. Louis, and the remaining three were constructed at Mound City. Eads's contract called for delivery of the ships by October 10, 1861, but changes in design during construction delayed their completion for several months. They also more than doubled the cost of each ship. By late January 1862, however, all of the City-class ironclads had been completed and were ready to be turned over to the army to serve as the core of the Western Gunboat Flotilla.[7]

The fighting vessels were a novelty to all who saw them. Nothing of their kind had ever been seen in the United States before, and their strange appearance soon led to the nickname of Pook's Turtles, which stuck with them to the end of the war. The completion of the ships proved to be a stroke of luck for Brigadier General Ulysses S. Grant and the Union war effort in the West. Grant proposed to mount a campaign against Forts Henry and Donelson, in western Tennessee. These works had been built by the Confederates to prevent the North from using the Tennessee and Cumberland Rivers and served as an anchor for a Confederate defensive line that stretched through much of Tennessee and a portion of Kentucky. If the western flank of the Confederate's position could be turned, their entire line would become untenable, opening large portions of Tennessee to Union invasion. Grant contacted Flag Officer Andrew H. Foote, the naval officer assigned to command the Western Gunboat Flotilla, seeking his assistance in a combined operation against the forts. In Foote, Grant found a willing and resourceful ally. Foote agreed to participate in the expedition with four ironclads, the *Carondelet, Cincinnati, St. Louis*, and *Essex*. The latter ship was a converted ironclad, built on the hull of the steam ferry *New Era* by Eads and purchased by the army for the Western Gunboat Flotilla. Foote could not employ all of the City-class ironclads Eads had built because he did not have enough sailors to supply crews for all the ships. Foote and Grant began the expedition from Cairo, Illinois, sailing down the Ohio River to the mouth of the Tennessee, and then sailing the 50 miles up that river to Fort Henry. Grant's troops were put ashore, where they were quickly mired down in the swampy land that surrounded the Confederate fortification. Foote and his gunboats proceeded on, engaging the Southern batteries of Fort Henry alone. The fort was an earthwork structure, built low to the ground and susceptible to the naval fire. In addition, it was partially submerged in floodwaters from the Tennessee River. The position was virtually untenable, prompting the fort's commander, Brigadier General Lloyd Tilghman, to transfer all but 54 of his 4,000-man garrison to nearby Fort Donelson. The remaining Confederates manned the fort's guns in a delaying action, but they were greatly outmatched by the firepower of Foote's fleet. The Union flotilla opened fire when it was a mile away from the fort and continued to steam up the river until the ships came within five hundred yards of the works, where they held fast to deliver a heavy bombardment. Fort Henry's guns responded, hitting each of the vessels numerous times, with the *Cincinnati* being struck by 32 shells. Though some of the iron plates were cracked, none of the shells were able to penetrate the armor. At this juncture, the *Essex* drifted with the current, turning the ship sideways to the fort. A shell pierced the unarmored portion of the casemate, hitting the boiler and filling the ship with steam and boiling water. Several crew members were killed by the blast, and the survivors jumped overboard to escape the deadly situation. The *Essex* was out of the fight and was helplessly carried downriver by the current. Foote's remaining ironclads continued shelling the fort, knocking out two of the Confederate's big guns and covering the fort with a pall of heavy smoke that obscured the ships from the enemy's view. Steaming the ships forward to the very edge of the fort, Foote compelled General Tilghman to surrender his force, and the works were taken without the aid of Grant's infantry.[8]

The success of the ironclads against Fort Henry convinced Flag Officer Foote that his ships could stand up against anything the enemy threw against them. He went back to Cairo to replace the battered *Essex* and *Cincinnati* with the *Pittsburgh* and *St. Louis*, and then he pushed his fleet up the Cumberland River toward Fort Donelson. Donelson would prove a much tougher nut to crack than Henry, however. Situated on a bluff, high above the river, the guns of Donelson would be a much harder target to hit for the ironclad gunners, while the plunging fire from the fort would lessen the advantage of the ship's armored sides. Encouraged by the success at Fort Henry, Foote ordered his ironclads to sail in close to Donelson to open their bombardment, exposing the ships to an effective and deadly fire. The *St. Louis* and the *Louisville* both had their wheel ropes shot away, and they drifted helplessly down the river, out of the fight. The *Pittsburgh* developed a serious leak as a result of the enemy shellfire and was also forced to withdraw. This left the *Carondelet* to stand alone against the combined weight of Donelson's batteries. Her captain and crew tried valiantly to keep the ship in the fight, but she could not long withstand the concentrated firepower coming from the fort. In a very short time, the *Carondelet* lost her stack, pilothouse, anchor, and boat cranes. Then one of her own bow guns exploded, setting the ship on fire. When two enemy shells blew through the bow ports, the captain ordered a withdrawal, backing the ship downriver in order to keep her more heavily armored head toward the fort. Donelson would not be taken by the flotilla. That honor would fall to General Grant and his infantry, who had arrived to encircle and cut off the fort from the land side. The experience at Fort Donelson had shown that while Pook's Turtles were a vast improvement over any wooden naval craft fighting on the inland waters, their somewhat thin iron plates were still vulnerable to the heavy ordnance mounted in most of the Confederate river fortifications.[9] Even so, the City-class ironclads would provide invaluable service to the Union's western operations for the remainder of the war, seeing action at places like Island Number 10, Memphis, Vicksburg, and the Red River Campaign. Though the vessels had weaknesses and flaws, they were a vast improvement over any fighting vessels that had plied the nation's inland waters prior to that time, and they paved the way for later, more sophisticated ships that followed.

The two most famous armored ships to come out of the Civil War were the *Monitor* and the *Virginia* (*Merrimack*). On April 20, 1861, Confederate forces seized control of the important Union Gosport Naval Yard at Portsmouth, Virginia. Though the Union sailors had orders to destroy anything in the yard that might be of value to the Confederates, the work was only partially completed. The Confederates were able to capture a treasure trove of naval supplies, including an intact dry dock, a large quantity of heavy-bore cannon, and a large cache of powder and shot. They were also able to salvage several ships that had been badly damaged but were not destroyed. One of these was the USS *Merrimack*, a steam frigate that had sunk in shallow waters before being completely burned. When the Confederate government took possession of the yard, Flag Officer French Forrest was commissioned to salvage the wreck of the *Merrimack*. By May 30, the ship had been raised from the bottom of the Elizabeth River and was towed to a dock in Gosport, where work was begun to remove the burned portions.[10]

Confederate Secretary of the Navy Stephen Mallory had been an advocate of ironclad ships since first reading about the successful efforts of the French and British. Having failed in his attempts to purchase an armored ship for Confederate service overseas, Mallory determined to construct an ironclad vessel on the hull of the *Merrimack*. The Confederacy did not have the facilities to build a new ship, but it did have the capacity to rebuild an old one. In searching for a naval builder to design his new ship, Mallory found John Porter, a civilian contractor at the Gosport Navy Yard. Porter had previous experience designing ironclad vessels, having submitted plans for an armored ship to the U.S. government before the war, which were turned down by the naval department. He quickly adapted his previous design to be built on the hull of the *Merrimack* and submitted the plans to Mallory. The navy secretary was enthusiastic about what he saw, and on June 30, he granted Porter permission to begin construction, without waiting for approval of the project from the Confederate Congress. Eighty skilled workers were assigned to the construction, laboring from daylight till eight in the evening each day. Work progressed throughout the summer and into the fall, and by Thanksgiving week the *Virginia* was ready to have her guns mounted and her armor plates installed. It would take nine months for the ship to be completed, and on February 24, 1862, the *Virginia* was launched and officially commissioned into the Confederate navy.[11]

The completed vessel was an imposing weapon indeed, and it had cost the Confederate government $110,000. It measured 262.9 feet in length and had a beam of 51.2 feet. The *Virginia* weighed 3,500 tons and had a draft of 22 feet. A casemated super-structure had been built on the hull of the ship, which was covered with two layers of two-inch iron plates. The armament of the *Virginia* consisted of ten guns: two 7-inch Brooke rifles, two 6-inch Brooke rifles, and six 9-inch Dahlgren guns. The ship was powered by four boilers that turned the massive 17.5-foot propeller, giving the *Virginia* a top speed of six knots. With a crew of 350, commanded by Flag Officer Franklin Buchanan, the Confederate ship was indeed a monster, capable of defeating any ship in the world, but she did have a few weaknesses. The *Virginia* was bulky and hard to maneuver, taking 30–40 minutes to make a full circle turn, and her 22-foot draft made her a candidate for grounding in the shallow waters of the Virginia coast.[12] Union authorities were unaware of these weaknesses, and it would probably have made little difference in their thinking if they had been advised. Northern spies had been reporting on the progress of the *Virginia* all through the summer and fall of 1861, and the information they provided caused a near panic among the government officials in Washington. It was speculated that the *Virginia* would be capable of lifting the Union blockade all by itself, and that it might be capable of attacking the port cities of Philadelphia, New York, or even steaming up the Potomac River to lay waste to Washington. When news reached Washington that the *Virginia* had been launched, there were those in the government who advised taking steps to remove the government from the city in the event the *Virginia* headed their way.

Officials in Washington were anxiously looking toward Brooklyn, New York, as they anticipated the reign of terror the *Virginia* might soon embark upon. There, at the Green Point Ship Yard, work was progressing at a feverish pace to complete an ironclad vessel to challenge the *Virginia*. The ship was being built under the supervision of John Ericsson, a noted inventor and engineer responsible for building the first steam-powered fire engine and the first warship driven by a screw propeller instead of a paddle wheel. In September of 1861, Cornelius S. Bushnell visited Ericsson in New York City to get his opinion on Bushnell's design for an ironclad ship. Ericsson looked over the plans and told Bushnell that his design looked feasible. He then asked if Bushnell would like to see a superior ironclad ship that could be built in only 90 days. Ericsson handed Bushnell a cardboard model of an odd-looking vessel that resembled a tin can on a raft. He explained that the tin can part was actually a turret, capable of revolving 360 degrees and bringing the two large guns to bear at any point needed. It was intended to be a light-draft vessel, with very little of the deck area rising above the surface of the water. Bushnell recognized Ericsson's ship to be superior to his own design and took the model back to Washington with him to show to Secretary Welles. The secretary called a meeting of top navy officials for September 10 to present Ericsson's model, and President Lincoln was invited to attend. Though Lincoln voiced his approval, the board did not reach a unanimous decision to adopt Ericsson's design until the inventor came to Washington to personally answer their questions. It took Ericsson only an hour to convince the naval board members that his ship offered the best chance for the Union to combat the ironclad the Confederates were building. He was awarded the contract and left the capital immediately to begin construction on what was to become the USS *Monitor*.[13]

Back in Brooklyn, Ericsson set to work on the *Monitor* at a feverish pace. Parts were manufactured for the ship at several different factories, from Baltimore to New York, and then assembled in Brooklyn. This was done to expedite the construction process, in order to meet the three-month timetable promised for completion of the ship. Ericsson was in a state of constant motion during construction, traveling between the various cities where the components of his ship were being made to supervise every detail of the process. Numerous problems and difficulties arose requiring Ericsson's personal attention and expertise. By the time the ship was completed, Ericsson had filed for more than 40 patents for the innovative designs he had incorporated into the *Monitor*.[14]

The need for numerous revisions to the plans for the ship caused Ericsson to miss his proposed completion date for the *Monitor*, but only by a slight margin. The ship was ready on January 30, 1862, and that morning she was launched into the East River for a test cruise. Curious onlookers watched the launching of the odd-looking ship and speculated on whether the unseemly craft would even float. The *Monitor* was unlike anything ever seen

Crew on the deck of the USS *Monitor*. (Library of Congress)

before. Looking like a cheese can sitting on a raft, she was 172 feet long and 41 feet wide and weighed 776 tons. Her turret was positioned in the center of the ship and mounted two 11-inch Dahlgren guns. The armor plating on the *Monitor* was 8 inches thick—double that of the *Virginia*. Her draft was only 11 feet 4 inches, half that of the *Virginia*, and her speed was eight knots. The time needed to turn the ship in a full circle was only five minutes, or about half an hour quicker than the *Virginia*. All in all, the *Monitor* was a very impressive warship, but she still seemed overmatched by the 10-gun monster the Confederates were constructing.[15]

The test cruise of the *Monitor* uncovered the need for several revisions, which were completed by February 27. In the meantime, work on the *Virginia* had been completed, and the Confederate ironclad was launched on February 24. The two iron monsters were destined to meet, and the only question would be if the *Monitor* could make it to Virginia coastal waters before the Confederate ironclad played havoc with the Union blockading fleet. The *Monitor* sailed out into the open sea on March 6, headed south, towed by the tugboat *Seth Low*. She was under the command of Lieutenant John L. Worden and carried a crew of 59 men, all volunteers. On March 7, the ship ran into rough waters, as a storm whipped the ocean into heavy waves. The

Monitor took on water, which extinguished the engines and filled the hold with suffocating fumes. For two days, the crew struggled to keep the helpless ship afloat, till finally the seas calmed and the crisis was over. On the afternoon of March 8, the *Monitor* steamed into the Chesapeake Bay, where her exhausted crew could hear the blasts from cannon and see the smoke rising upward from exploding shells. A naval battle was in progress, and the crew of the *Monitor* wondered if they had arrived too late.[16]

The sounds that greeted the *Monitor* were indeed from a naval battle. The *Virginia* had steamed out of the Gosport Naval Yard a little before noon that morning to engage the wooden ships of the Union blockading fleet. Flag Officer Buchanan sailed his ship down the Elizabeth River in search of prey. His attention was focused on the USS *Cumberland* and the USS *Congress*, laying close to shore batteries at Newport News. The *Virginia* engaged both ships, inflicting severe damage on the enemy craft while suffering only slightly from the Union guns. Buchanan sailed away from the Union ships, then turned about and gave the order to prepare to ram. The *Virginia* bore down on the helpless *Cumberland*, driving her iron ram deep into the wooden hull of the Union ship. The *Cumberland* was doomed. Her crew fired three broadsides into the *Virginia* at point-blank range before she went down, but the shells merely cracked some of the iron plates. While all this was going on, the *Congress* was towed to shallow waters to escape being rammed herself. But the *Virginia* opened with her deck guns, tearing the ship to pieces and littering her decks with killed and wounded. At length, a white flag was seen to be flying from the *Congress*, and Buchanan directed two small gunboats that had accompanied him to sail in and accept the surrender of the ship. When the Confederate boats were fired on by Union troops on shore, Buchanan became enraged and ordered hot shot to be fired into the side of the *Congress*. The vessel was soon aflame, as her crew scrambled to abandon ship. Buchanan was no longer in command of the *Virginia*, however. In a fit of temper, when his boats had been fired upon under a white flag, the officer had climbed atop the casemate of the *Virginia* to fire at the enemy with a musket. He was hit in the thigh by a Union infantryman, and command of the *Virginia* passed to Lieutenant Catesby Jones, who immediately turned his attention to the USS *Minnesota*, which had run aground while trying to reach the battle. Jones had to postpone his attack on the stranded ship, however. Night was rapidly coming on, as was the low tide. Deciding not to chance becoming grounded himself, Jones called off the attack on the *Minnesota*. He would return to base and finish off the Union warship the following morning.[17]

The *Monitor* reached Hampton Roads late in the evening of March 8. Her crew could see the flames still burning on the *Congress*. Lieutenant Worden reported for duty and was given his assignment for the next day. The *Monitor* was to protect the still-grounded *Minnesota* if the *Virginia* returned to finish her off. Worden did not have long to wait. At 6:00 a.m. on the morning of March 9, the *Virginia* appeared on the horizon, sailing toward the *Minnesota*. The *Monitor* sailed out from behind the *Minnesota*, placing itself in a blocking position between that ship and the *Virginia*. Jones was the first to open fire, but his initial shots passed harmlessly over the *Monitor*. Worden sailed his ship out to meet the enemy, and the two ironclads locked together in mortal combat for three hours. The two iron monsters circled one another, looking like David and Goliath, firing point-blank volleys. Hit after hit was recorded on both ships, but only minor damage was sustained. Finally, Jones decided to ram the *Monitor*. Lieutenant Worden held his place, inviting Jones to use his iron prow. The *Virginia* crashed into the *Monitor* with a mighty thud, but the impact was absorbed by the iron plating. In fact, it was the *Virginia* that sustained major damage as a result of the ramming, when her iron prow was broken off in striking the *Monitor*'s iron plating. Lieutenant Worden seized the initiative and wheeled his ship around to press home an attack on the Confederate vessel. A shot from the *Virginia* struck the pilothouse of the *Monitor*, blinding Worden, and command of the ship passed to Lieutenant S. Dana Greene. As Worden was being carried to his cabin, the *Monitor* drifted away from the *Virginia*, and Catesby Jones thought she was giving up the fight. Feeling he had forced the Union ship to retire, Jones sailed his own ship back to Norfolk, where necessary repairs could be made.[18] The first meeting of naval ironclads was over. Neither ship had been able to inflict serious damage to her opponent, and both sides had to consider the engagement a draw. The overall advantage went to the North, however, as the timely arrival of the *Monitor* had prevented the *Virginia* from completing its mission of destroying the Union blockading fleet.

The *Monitor* and the *Virginia* signaled the end of wooden warships for the navies of the world, as all nations scrambled to modernize their fleets in a new iron age. In the North, construction was immediately undertaken to build a fleet of monitors. First of these was the Passaic class, a single-turret vessel closely resembling the *Monitor*, of which 10 ships were built. Nine monitors of the Canonicus class were constructed, boasting 15-inch Dahlgren guns. Fifteen monitors of the Casco class were built, while another five were finished as torpedo boats. The USS *Onondaga* was built having two turrets, as was the USS *Monadnock*. The latter ship served as the production model for four ships that would constitute the Monadnock class. Though the Union focused mainly on the construction of monitor-type vessels, other ironclad designs also found their way into the U.S. Navy. The USS *Galena* was an armored sloop, while the USS *New Ironsides*, thought to be the most powerful of the Union ironclads, was an armored frigate. The USS *Keokuk* was a twin-casemated ironclad that resembled the *Virginia* with its middle portion

The USS *Onondaga* on duty in the James River. This was a twin turret style of monitor. (Library of Congress)

missing. In all, the Union would build some 60 coastal ironclads to be used against the Southern shoreline by the time the war ended.

The South did its best to keep pace with the Northern buildup of ironclad vessels. Approximately 59 ironclads were commissioned by the Confederate navy, but only 24 were completed by the end of the war. Southern ironclads generally conformed to the casemated design used on the *Virginia* because of the lack of Confederate resources to build a ship from the keel up. Ships like the CSS *Albemarle*, *Arkansas*, and *Richmond* performed admirably against their Union counterparts, providing offensive punch for the undersized Southern navy. The South also built a fleet of more than 20 David-class armored torpedo boats that were used to attack blockading ships. Though a few of the Southern ironclads were captured or sunk by Union ships, the majority were scuttled to prevent them from falling into enemy hands.

Armored ships had already begun to appear in European navies before the Civil War, but the practical experience gained by the Union and Confederate navies along the U.S. coast and inland waters proved beyond question that the age of wooden ships had ended. Naval warfare would be forever changed, as smoke-belching ironclad monsters took the place of the sleek, mast-bearing vessels that had plied the waters of the world for centuries. Over the next several decades, the ships would get larger and larger and would carry an ever-increasing number of guns, but the massive battleships and aircraft carriers that formed the core of the twentieth century navies could all trace their ancestry back to those first ironclads that had sailed under Union and Confederate banners in the Civil War.

CHAPTER 21

THE WOMEN

The Civil War was responsible for many innovations in the technology of warfare. The Industrial Revolution made possible the implementation of many advanced and revolutionary ideas that would have been unthinkable only a generation before. These changing norms could also be seen in the evolving fabric of U.S. society. Women of the Victorian age were viewed to be the fairer sex, or the weaker sex if you will, and they were prevented from taking part in most phases of daily life in the United States. During the American Revolution, women had stepped out of their traditional roles to serve the cause of freedom in a variety of ways. A number of them had gone so far as to break through the all-male barrier that was the army to serve as soldiers on the battlefield. Indeed, the names of such patriotic heroines as Molly Pitcher, Deborah Sampson, Margaret Cochran, and Nancy Hart were well known to every child of school age in the country. Women patriots had given such great aid to the cause that in some places they were even granted the vote in the years immediately following the conclusion of the war. All of the advancements they had made were quickly lost, however, because of the manner in which American women were viewed by the world community. American women were thought to be brutish and manly, not at all the picture of femininity expected by cultured society. In the end, U.S. society conformed to the status quo then in fashion in Western Europe, and women in the United States were once more relegated to a role as second-class citizens and specta-tors to most of the historic events of their time. The Civil War would give American women the opportunity to once more challenge these archaic social norms. This time, however, the advances made by women would not so easily be surrendered following the end of the war. The seeds of social change had been sewn, and they would continue to grow in the ensuing decades until women had achieved suffrage and a more equal place in U.S. society.

American women stepped forward to do their part and aid their cause in numerous ways during the war. The efforts of women like Clara Barton and Dorothea Dix threw open the doors of the nursing profession to thousands of women, causing what was an all-male system to become overwhelmingly female. Many women joined with Mary Livermore in supporting relief organizations like the Sanitary Commission, to ease the hardships of the soldiers in the field. Countless other women across the country assumed traditionally male roles by working in factories or by taking over the management of family farms or plantations when husbands, fathers, and sons joined the military. The lure of adventure and excitement caused women like Belle Boyd, Rose Greenhow, and Elizabeth Van Lew to undertake life in the cloak-and-dagger world of espionage. Along with numerous other women, these ladies gathered information on the enemy to aid the cause of their convictions. For many women, however, the prospect of becoming nurses, spies, or social workers did not fulfill their need to contribute personal service to the cause. This group needed to give more active support to the great struggle taking place in the land, by placing themselves at the post of danger on the battlefield.

In the early 1700s, the French army instituted a practice of allowing female vivandières to accompany the troops into the field. These vivandières served the purpose of later sutlers in providing commissary items for the soldiers beyond the limited scope of their normal rations. As time went on, the role of the vivandières expanded in the French army to include such duties as cooking and nursing; some even fought in the ranks. At the outbreak of the Civil War, many regiments, both North and South, adopted the French system of vivandières, also referred to as daughters of the regiment. It is unknown exactly how many women served as vivandières during the war, as they were not officially soldiers and therefore were not listed on the rolls of the regiments in which they served. It can be assumed that their numbers were great, however, as a significant number of regiments marching off to war in 1861 contained a complement of vivandières.

The 2nd Michigan Infantry provides a good example of how numerous vivandières could be in an individual regiment. In April 1861, 20 women from Detroit stepped forward to offer their services to the regiment when it was formed. The most distinguished member of the group would be Anna Etheridge. Anna had accompanied her husband into the service, but when he deserted from the regiment, she remained behind to faithfully perform her duties. Etheridge would serve in the capacity of a vivandièere with the 2nd, 3rd, and 5th Michigan Infantry Regiments during the war, and she remained at her post for the full four years of the conflict. She saw her first combat at Blackburn's Ford, Virginia, on June 18, 1861, where she fearlessly braved enemy fire to tend the wounded. She was on the field of battle at First Manassas, during the Peninsula Campaign, Second Manassas, Antietam, Fredericksburg, Chancellorsville, Gettysburg, and Spotsylvania, rallying the troops and providing care and comfort to the wounded. Anna never carried a musket in battle, but she was known to have two pistols stuck into her belt for personal defense. It is not recorded if she ever had cause to use them during a battle. Anna's bravery under fire earned her great admiration, not only from the men in her regiment but from everyone she came in contact with. In 1863, she was awarded the Kearny Cross, an award issued to members of General Phil Kearny's old division who had displayed exceptional courage and gallantry on the battlefield. Etheridge was the only woman so honored during the war. In 1864, when General Ulysses S. Grant proclaimed that all women must leave the camps of the Army of the Potomac, a petition was circulated throughout the army to make an exception in the case of Etheridge. Grant denied the petition, so Anna volunteered for nursing duty at the army hospital at City Point, Virginia. A soldier who served with her described Anna during the battle of Deep Bottom, Virginia, in 1864:

> Anna has remained with the colors, but this time we are up too close to the front line, and unless we get back we may be captured. So we have to do some tall walking to get out of this swamp we have gotten into. Anna falls back with us in good order, but her dress is a little torn by the brush. One of our boys is borne back wounded, our heroine does up his wound. The balls fall thick and fast around her, but she fears them not, and performs her task as coolly as if she was in camp and out of danger.

Anna's exploits made her one of the best-known vivandières in the war, and her devotion to duty brought her great acclaim and admiration. After the war, Etheridge would be granted a pension of $25 per month for her services, a high tribute to her courageous service. Upon her death, in 1913, she was afforded the singular honor of being buried in Arlington National Cemetery, with full military honors.[1]

Kady Brownell was another famous vivandière from the war who went far above what was expected in the performance of her duties. Kady joined the 1st Rhode Island Infantry in 1861, when her husband, Robert, enrolled as a private in the regiment's company of sharpshooters. Despite her sex, Kady was given the honor of being a color bearer for the regiment, presumably only for the period they were in training camp, as the post of color bearer was usually reserved for the bravest men in the regiment. Not content with this honorary position, Kady began drilling as a sharpshooter. In a short period of time, she had attained a level of proficiency making her as quick and accurate as any man in the regiment. She also began training with a sword, and soon attained the same level of competence she had achieved with a musket. At the battle of First Manassas, the 1st Rhode Island was positioned on the left of the Union line of battle, and Kady proudly bore the colors of the regiment throughout the fray. When the right of the Union line began to crumble, panic quickly seized all of the Northern troops, including the members of the 1st Rhode Island, on the left. Kady defiantly waved her flag, calling on the soldiers in her regiment to stand firm, but her efforts were in vain. By ones and twos, then by large groups, the 1st Rhode Island boys started breaking for the rear. Kady remained, calling for the men to rally. Her efforts were in vain, but she refused to leave her post, gallantly displaying the regimental banner in the face of the onrushing enemy. A soldier from a Pennsylvania regiment spotted Kady, in imminent danger of being killed or captured, and forcibly removed her from the field. The 1st Rhode Island was a 90-day unit and was mustered out shortly after Manassas. Kady and her husband then joined the 5th Rhode Island Infantry. This regiment was one of the units assigned to Major General Ambrose Burnside's expeditionary force that was going to attack coastal North Carolina. During the Union assault on the Southern works at New Bern, Kady begged to be allowed to carry the colors of the regiment into battle. Her wish was granted, but as the 5th Rhode Island marched forward, it arrived on the field from a direction that confused the other regiments making up the assault wave. Kady quickly surmised that the other Union troops mistakenly believed the 5th Rhode Island to be an enemy regiment and were preparing to open fire. She rushed forward, frantically waving the colors she bore, exposing herself to almost certain death until she had convinced the other troops that they were about to fire on friends. Following this incident and the crisis that almost ensued, Kady was ordered to turn the flag over to the regular bearer and go to the rear. Her husband was wounded in the engagement that followed, leading to his discharge from the service. Kady left the regiment as well, following her husband back into civilian life the way she had followed him into the army. In 1884, she petitioned the government for a military pension. Affidavits from soldiers she had served with convinced the government to grant her a pension of $8 a month for the rest of her life.[2]

Marie Tebe was yet another famous woman who joined the ranks as a vivandière. As with the previous two ladies, Marie offered her services when her husband joined the 27th Pennsylvania Infantry in April 1861. Marie received full pay as a soldier as well as receiving an extra 25 cents per day for hospital and headquarters services. She was under fire with the 27th Pennsylvania on 13 different occasions, from First Manassas through the Peninsula Campaign. During the fighting on the Peninsula, her work came under the eye of Colonel Charles H. T. Collis, commander of the 114th Pennsylvania Infantry, know as Collis's Zouaves. The colonel persuaded

Marie Tebe, a vivandière with the 114th Pennsylvania Infantry. (National Archives)

Marie to join his regiment once the Peninsula Campaign was over, and she served the Zouaves with distinction for the remainder of the war, being in the thick of battle at Gettysburg, the Wilderness, Spotsylvania Court House, and Cold Harbor, and she was wounded in the left ankle while performing her duty. Marie's bravery on the battlefield earned her the Kearny Cross, the same award bestowed on Anna Etheridge. She and Etheridge were the only women to be so honored during the war.[3]

The vivandière spirit was not confined to women of the North. Southern women entered the Confederate army in large numbers to do exactly the same service. Lucy Ann Cox was one such woman who followed her husband into the army when he enlisted in the 13th Virginia Infantry. Lucy endured all the privations of a soldier with the regiment, and as one veteran recalled, "No march was too long or weather too inclement to deter this patriotic woman from doing what she considered her duty." Lucy served with the 13th Virginia continuously through all the campaigns of the Army of Northern Virginia, until they were eventually surrendered at Appomattox Court House in 1865. Rose Quinn Rooney served with the 15th Louisiana Infantry from June of 1861 through to the end of the war. She saw her first combat at First Manassas where she "signalized her courage and devotion by bravely pulling down a fence in the midst of bursting shells to let the Battery of Washington Artillery pass through." Rooney's actions were conspicuous at Gettysburg when her regiment assaulted Culp's Hill on the second day of the battle. One observer stated that she "served with undaunted bravery which led her to risk the dangers of every battle-field where the regiment was engaged, unheeding the zip of miniés, the shock of shells, or the horrible havoc made by solid shot, so that she might give timely succor to the wounded or comfort the dying." At Appomattox, following the formal surrender of General Lee's army, several members of the 15th Louisiana were put under arrest by Union troops for acts of open defiance. Rooney demanded the Federals arrest her too, and she subsequently spent two weeks serving as a nurse in a hospital in Burkesville, Virginia, where both Union and Confederate troops were being treated.[4]

It is estimated that as many as four hundred women disguised themselves as men to serve in the army as full-fledged soldiers. The numerous documented examples in existence suggest that the actual number could be much higher than that, however. The majority of the women who attempted to become soldiers were quickly discovered and sent home, but there are numerous cases where the deception went undetected, and these female warriors went to war, shoulder to shoulder with their male counterparts. Some were not detected until they had become wounded or succumbed to illness. Others were able to conceal their true identity for the duration of their term of service.

Sarah Edmonds was one of the women whose true identity was never discovered while she was in the army. Born in Canada in 1841, Sarah was a resident of Michigan when the Civil War broke out. Disguising herself as a man, she joined the 2nd Michigan Infantry early in 1861 under the alias of Franklin Flint Thompson. She had been unsuccessful in three previous attempts to get into the service. The 2nd Michigan, it may be remembered, also had another famous woman in its ranks in the person of Anna Etheridge. Being somewhat small and frail, Sarah was assigned to serve as a nurse for the regiment. This was at a time when all nurses were male. She also served as a courier and performed acts of scouting and spying for the regiment. In a book detailing her wartime experiences, Edmonds claimed a number of experiences that have never been verified and are highly unlikely. For instance, she alleged that she had served as an aide for several Union generals, including Phil Kearny, Winfield Scott Hancock, Oliver O. Howard, and George B. McClellan. If such had been the case, Edmonds, or her alias of Thompson, should have been listed in orders, dispatches, or correspondence, but such is not the case. It is documented that after the regiment was transferred to the Western Theater following the battle of Fredericksburg, Edmonds deserted and evaded capture by resuming life as a woman. She gave the reason for her desertion as contracting malaria.

An unidentified Union vivandière. (U.S. Army Military History Institute)

Fearing that her true sex would be discovered if she were hospitalized, she decided to desert instead. Even so, in 1884, she applied for and was granted a soldier's pension of $12 per month for her services as Frank Thompson. In 1897 she became the only female member of the Grand Army of the Republic, and upon her death in 1901, she was buried in the Grand Army of the Republic plot in Houston's Washington Cemetery.[5]

Frances Hook enlisted in the 65th Illinois Home Guard with her brother during the opening days of the war. They had both been orphaned at an early age and were nearly inseparable. Disguising herself as a man, she used the name of Frank Miller. The 65th Illinois was a three-month unit, and Frances served her entire term of enlistment without her true sex being discovered. After being mustered out, she enlisted in the 90th Illinois Infantry. Frances took part in the Vicksburg Campaign before the 90th Illinois was transferred east to participate in the battles for Chattanooga. It was here that she was taken prisoner. While attempting to escape, she was shot through the calf, and medical examination revealed her true gender. Nonetheless, she was sent to a prison camp in Atlanta, where she was at least provided with a separate room. When Jefferson Davis heard about Frances he was much impressed. The Confederate president wrote to her offering a commission as a lieutenant if she would enlist in the Southern army. Frances declined, stating that she would rather die as a private in the Union army than hold a commission with the Confederacy. In time, she was duly exchanged. Before leaving the prison camp, her captors tried to persuade her to return to her home and not go back to the army. Frances was enraged. "Go home," she said, "my only brother was killed at Pittsburgh Landing, and I have no home—no friends."[6]

Lizzie Compton served in a number of regiments during the course of the war. Each time her gender was discovered, she would move on to another unit and enlist again. Lizzie served in regiments in the Army of the Potomac and the Army of the Cumberland, seeing combat on several fields of battle. She was wounded at Fredericksburg and again at Green River Bridge. Toward the end of the war, she presented herself to the commanding officer of her regiment, which was then the 11th Kentucky Cavalry. Lizzie revealed her true gender and was given a discharge. At the time, she was still only sixteen years of age. During her time in the army, she had served in seven or eight different regiments and had competently performed the duties of a soldier in each one until her ruse was discovered.[7]

One woman who did not have to conceal her identity to serve in the army was Maria Lewis. Maria was a runaway slave who enlisted in the 8th New York Cavalry at Alexandria, Virginia. She never tried to disguise the fact that she was a woman, and it is unclear as to why she was allowed to enlist. A possible explanation is that she was very familiar with the area and could act as a scout and guide. Whatever the reason for accepting her, Maria served with distinction in the regiment, undergoing all the rigors of a soldier. She was even detailed with a detachment from the regiment to present 22 Confederate banners captured by the regiment to the War Department.[8]

Thus far, we have discussed only women who served as individuals in the army, surrounded by men. There were also several instances of women who sought to serve in all-female organizations. One of the earliest of these was the brainchild of Sallie Reneau, a 23-year-old resident of Panola County, Mississippi. Reneau was a strong advocate for women's rights, and in 1856 she had petitioned the state legislature to fund a female academy of higher learning. In April of 1861, Reneau wrote to Governor John J. Pettus that she had organized a number of women from Panola County she referred to as the Mississippi Nightingales. Reneau proposed her women be used to nurse sick and wounded soldiers, but she went a step further in requesting the governor provide them with small arms and uniforms in order that they might also defend their charges against all enemies. Governor Pettus did not respond to her letter, and Reneau lost the opportunity of organizing the first armed female detachment on either side during the war.[9]

In Bascom, Georgia, the women of the town formed a home guard unit to protect themselves after all of the men of military age had departed to join the army. The unit, called the Bascom Home Guard, was formed in 1861 and regularly drilled in the school of the soldier. As one member described in a letter:

> We have formed a female Company in Bascom for the purpose of learning to shoot, so that if all the men go to war we can protect our homes and selves ... The name of our Company is the Bascom Home Guards. You know how nervous timid Mollie was. Well, now she can load and fire and hit a spot at a good distance ... We are delighted with the idea of learning to shoot. Father thinks our uniform is prettier than the boys although ours is made of calico.[10]

Another company of female home guard was raised in Lagrange, Georgia. This town was located between Atlanta, Georgia, and Montgomery, Alabama, along an important railroad line. In 1861, some 1,300 men from Lagrange enlisted in the Confederate army, leaving the town with young boys, old men, and women. Two wives of the departed soldiers, Nancy Hill Morgan and Mary Alford Heard, decided a woman's home guard unit should be formed to protect the town from possible Union incursions. A meeting was called at the local schoolhouse in May, and all interested women were instructed to bring whatever muskets or pistols they had with them. Approximately 40 women responded to the call, and the result of the meeting was the formation of a militia company. Nancy Morgan was elected captain, Mary Heard, Andelia Bull, and Aley Smith were elected lieutenants, and Augusta Hill and M. E. Colquitt were named sergeants. The company was named the Nancy Harts, in honor of a Georgia heroine of Revolutionary War fame. The ladies then approached Dr. Augustus Ware with a request for him to serve as drillmaster for the company. Dr. Ware was physically disabled to the point that he could not perform military service, but he was proficient in the use of firearms and familiar with military drill procedures. Ware readily agreed to train the women, and he determined to use William J. Hardee's *Rifle and Light Infantry Tactics* as his manual of instruction. The company met twice a week to drill, and Ware focused his primary attention to developing their marksmanship skills. The officers regularly awarded prizes to the top shooters, and in a short time the Nancy Harts had attained a reputation of being crack shots.[11]

The Nancy Harts continued to train and drill, but their anticipated attack by Federal forces did not materialize. Instead, Lagrange became filled with Confederate soldiers. Its position along the rail line made it a perfect place for a hospital town, and its buildings were soon filled to capacity with wounded and sick soldiers from the battlefields of Virginia, Tennessee, Mississippi, and Georgia. The Nancy Harts responded to the situation with the same patriotic fervor that had led them to organize their company of militia. Nursing duties were quickly added to their daily tasks of caring for their families and homes and training for military service.

In the spring of 1865, the Confederacy was breathing its dead rattle, and the end of the war seemed near. Atlanta and Savannah had both fallen to General William T. Sherman's army, and Northern troops traveled through Georgia almost at will. On April 16, the people of Lagrange received a telegram from Brigadier General Robert Tyler, in nearby West Point. Tyler reported a Federal force to be approaching West Point and requested every able-bodied man of Lagrange to come to his assistance. A number of elderly men from Lagrange, along with the walking wounded from the hospital, answered Tyler's call and boarded a train for West Point. Even with these reinforcements, Tyler had only three hundred men with which to resist the Federals, numbering ten times his own strength. The general fought a desperate battle but was soon defeated, and he was killed in the process. The following day, word reached Lagrange that the Federals were approaching the town. The Nancy Harts responded to the warning, meeting at the home of Lieutenant Mary Heard before marching to the Lagrange Female College on the outskirts of town to meet the oncoming foe. A small band of Confederate cavalry soon came galloping down the road, fleeing from a full regiment of Union troopers. The Confederate horsemen beseeched the women to return to their homes and bar their doors, before sinking spurs to their mounts and continuing their retreat. But the Nancy Harts stood firm, forming a line of battle bisecting the road leading into their town. When the main body of the Union force came into view, Captain Nancy Morgan marched out to greet the invaders. Ironically, Colonel Oscar Lagrange happened to be the officer in command of the Union troops, and he met with Morgan, who informed him of the intent of her and her company to resist any depredations against the town. Colonel Lagrange examined the female line of battle formed behind Lieutenant Heard and complimented Morgan on the military bearing and unbounded courage of her militia troops. He then promised that all private property would be respected by the men in his command. With this assurance, Morgan decided a defense of the town would not be necessary, and Colonel Lagrange was tendered the surrender of the town of Lagrange. The Federals kept their word, and none of the homes in Lagrange were molested. The Nancy Harts had been prepared to fight, but in the end, they achieved their objective in a bloodless victory.[12]

Yet another women's military unit was formed in Rhea County, Tennessee, in 1862. (Recent scholarship may suggest that it was formed in 1861, but that is still open to some debate.) Mary McDonald and her sister-in-law Caroline McDonald were instrumental in forming the company and were subsequently elected captain and first lieutenant of the unit. Anne Paine and Rhoda Tomison were selected as second and third lieutenants, and the sergeants were Jane Keith, Rachel Howard, Sallie Mitchell, and Minerva Tucker. The ladies determined that their company would be cavalry, and they took the name of the Rhea County Spartans. While the Spartans did not participate in any military engagements, it is possible that they did a small amount of scouting and spying for Confederate units operating in East Tennessee. In April of 1865, John P. Walker, a captain in the 6th Tennessee Mounted Infantry and a resident of Rhea County, decided to round up the girls as Confederate irregulars. With the permission of his commander, Lieutenant Colonel George Gowin, Walker led his company into the county to arrest the young ladies on April 5, 1865. Eventually, 16 of the girls were rounded up and marched to the Tennessee River, at Bell's Landing, where they were loaded on a crude steamer for passage to Chattanooga. Upon arriving in the city, they were marched, under guard, to the provost marshal's office, presumably to be turned over for incarceration. Captain Seth Moe, the assistant adjutant general, notified Major General James B. Steedman of the situation. Steedman's quick response was not what Walker anticipated. The general sternly rebuked Captain Walker for wasting everyone's time with such foolishness. He then directed Captain Moe to escort the ladies to the Central House Hotel, where they were allowed to refresh themselves before being treated to the best meal the hotel could offer. Once they were fed, Steedman directed Walker to escort the women back to their homes in Rhea County. Walker accompanied them only across the river, however, abandoning them to their own resources once the opposite shore was reached. When the girls were once again safely back in Rhea County, the Spartans were disbanded, and they faded into the fog of Americana trivia.[13]

Women of the Civil War era stepped forward to shoulder what had previously been considered a man's portion of responsibility and sacrifice. As a group, they excelled in every endeavor undertaken, turning the social norms of the time upside down. But the end of the war forced most women back into the traditional roles of polite society. They were not content to remain there. Their experiences in the war convinced many women that they were entitled to equal status and rights in a United States that was expanding its role as the land of the free. The fight for equality would begin with the woman's suffrage movement and would be waged with the same undaunted courage many of their compatriots had displayed on the battlefield.

CHAPTER 22

THE U.S. COLORED TROOPS

Nearly 200,000 African-Americans served in the Union army during the Civil War, providing a much-needed boost for the North in the last two years of the war. A strong argument can be made that without the enlistment of these black troops the Union may not have been able to emerge victorious in the struggle. War weariness had caused a tremendous drop-off of enlistments, forcing the government to institute conscription to keep the ranks filled at the front. City, county, and state bounties came into fashion, as local governments endeavored to avoid the unpopular drafts by inducing men to enlist with cash inducements. A large number of bounty men were unreliable, however, skulking on the battlefield and deserting when an opportunity presented itself. The large enlistments of black troops not only provided the Union war effort with badly needed numbers of men, it also provided a core of passionate soldiers who were fighting for more than money. Fighting for the cause of freedom took on a new perspective for these troops, many of them being ex-slaves or runaway slaves. These men were fighting not only for their own future lives and freedoms; they were fighting for the future of their families and for an entire race.

Early in the war, black volunteers on both sides stepped forward to offer their services to cause and country. Four days before the firing on Fort Sumter, Levin Tilmon of New York wrote to President Lincoln that all he need do was signify his acceptance to have black troops from that state. Lincoln never responded. On April 16, 1861, Burr Porter wrote to Secretary of War Simon Cameron requesting that regiments of black troops be raised from the border states. A week later, Jacob Dodson, a free black employed as an attendant in the Senate Chamber, offered Secretary Cameron "300 reliable free colored citizens of this city (Washington) who desire to enter this

Members of the 4th U.S. Colored Troops, some of the nearly 200,000 black troops that served in the Union army during the war. (Library of Congress)

service for the defense of the city." In July of 1861, three full regiments of black troops were offered for Federal service to the governor of New York. The black residents of the state promised not only to arm, clothe, and equip these troops but also to pay them for their entire term of enlistment. Once again, the offer was declined. At this time, the Lincoln administration was adverse to accepting black volunteers because of the supposed effect it might have in the border states, where there were a large number of slave holders. It was felt that these states might be lost to the Union if the question of slavery was brought to the forefront at this time, and Lincoln was not willing to risk them falling to the Confederacy.[1]

Black recruits found an easier path to service in the South, as least in the early days of the war. While the Confederate government established an official policy forbidding black enlistment in the army, most regiments were formed by the individual states and came under their state laws regarding the raising of militia units. In March of 1861, a Shreveport, Louisiana, newspaper ran a story about "a very large meeting of the free colored men of New Orleans," who were taking measures to form a military organization that would be offered to the governor of the state. A Baton Rouge paper added, "Our honored and respected friend and fellow citizen Capt. H. B. Favrot is at work mustering into the service the free colored men of the city and has already about thirty of them enrolled." This unit called itself the Louisiana Native Guards and would figure prominently in the war at a later date. In Mobile, G. Huggins Cleveland offered to raise a regiment of free black men for Alabama service. In Lynchburg, Virginia, some 70 local blacks offered to fight for the Confederacy, while 60 black men of Richmond, bearing a Confederate flag, asked to be enlisted. In June of 1861, Tennessee became the first Confederate state to sanction the enrollment of black troops when the state legislature authorized the use in "military service of the state all free male persons of color between the ages of fifteen and fifty." The city of Nashville formed a company of black troops, and Fort Smith, Arkansas, surpassed that by forming two companies from among the free black residents of the city.[2]

Indeed, black troops were serving in the military in 1861, but it may be surprising to find that most of these were in the South. No less a personage than Frederick Douglass reported that there were armed blacks serving as soldiers with the Confederate forces at the battle of First Manassas. During the Peninsula Campaign in 1862, there were several reports of blacks serving in the ranks of the Confederate army. Black snipers fired on Union troops at Yorktown, while at least one Southern cannon was reported as being served entirely by a black artillery crew.[3] There were even several armed black troops among the prisoners taken at the battle of Gettysburg in 1863.[4]

A black man bears the distinction of shedding the first blood spilled in the Civil War. Nicholas Biddle was a 65-year-old runaway slave who had been living in Pottsville, Pennsylvania, for many years. When the Washington Artillery was raised in Schuylkill County, Biddle offered his services and attached himself to the company of cannoneers. (This company would become part of the 25th Pennsylvania Infantry.) When Biddle and his comrades marched through Baltimore, Maryland, on April 18, 1861, en route for Washington, a crowd of angry pro-Southern residents gathered to taunt and jeer them. Biddle's race was quickly noticed by the crowd, and objects were soon being thrown in his direction. A brick struck Biddle in the face, cutting him so badly as to expose the bone. He would have fallen, were he not supported by First Lieutenant James Russell of his company. The 6th Massachusetts Infantry would pass through Baltimore the following day, sparking the Baltimore Riot about which so much has been written. The casualties resulting from that confrontation are generally regarded as being the first bloodshed spilled in the war, but Nicholas Biddle holds that honor by a full day, as the first man to be wounded in a struggle that would witness more than 600,000 casualties.[5]

The Union did not begin to enlist black troops into the service until 1862. In March of that year, Major General David Hunter set in motion events that would lead to the creation of the first black regiment in the Northern army. Hunter was in command of the recently captured coastal town of Port Royal, South Carolina, where he had begun enrolling fugitive slaves within his lines for military service. On April 3, 1862, he wired Secretary of War Edwin Stanton requesting 50,000 muskets and authority to arm such loyal men as he found in the country. Hunter organized a regiment from among the slaves in his department, which he called the 1st South Carolina Infantry (Union). A large number of these men had not volunteered but were pressed into service, as Hunter sought not only to augment his own military force but also to deprive the Confederates of this source of manpower and labor. But the 1st South Carolina was neither recognized nor provisioned by the Federal government. The men in the regiment served with no pay, and after a few months, desertions reached a point where men could be kept in camp only through the use of armed white guards. In August of 1862, General Hunter had to admit that his experiment had been a failure, and he announced the disbandment of the regiment. The story of the 1st South Carolina Infantry was an inglorious end for the first black unit to serve with the Union army.[6]

At approximately the same time, another attempt to enlist blacks into the army was taking place in Kansas. Brigadier General James Lane, who was at the time also a senator from Kansas, sought to raise a regiment of black soldiers with which to combat the guerillas and border ruffians operating out of Missouri. On August 5, 1862, he wired Secretary Stanton of his intentions to recruit blacks for the 1st Kansas Colored Regiment. Stanton sent two messages ordering Lane to stop this activity, but the general continued nonetheless, raising seven full companies by the end of September. By October the 1st Kansas Colored Regiment was at full strength, and Lane began sending them out on raiding missions in the countryside. Later that month, a portion of the regiment took part in an engagement with Confederate forces at Island Mound, in Bates County, Missouri. The Kansas troops acquitted themselves admirably in the engagement, which proved to be a Union victory, becoming the first black soldiers to fight in a battle in the Civil War.[7]

In Louisiana, Major General Benjamin Butler was busy raising black regiments of his own. Initially, Butler had scorned the idea of black enlistments, which had been proposed by one of his subordinates, Brigadier General John W. Phelps. In early August of 1862, fighting in the vicinity of Baton Rouge had convinced Butler that his force was too small to perform its occupation duties in the Federal-held portion of Louisiana as well as deal with the military threat from Confederate forces. He contacted Secretary Stanton to request reinforcements but was informed that there were no additional troops to spare. On August 14, Butler sent Stanton a message stating, "I shall call on Africa to intervene, and I do not think I shall call in vain." Butler's first move was to contact several of the officers of the Louisiana Native Guards. Though they had originally formed to serve the Confederacy, they had never been officially mustered into Confederate service and had been left behind when Southern forces retreated from New Orleans. Butler convinced these men to fight for the Union and assured them that black officers would be retained as line officers in any units that were raised. On August 22, he issued a general order authorizing the enlistment of black troops, stipulating that only free blacks could be enrolled. This prerequisite was largely ignored by recruiting officers, however, and though the previous members of the Louisiana Native Guard made up the nucleus of the regiment, it was mostly filled by runaway slaves. By September 27, the rolls were complete, and General Butler mustered the 1st Louisiana Native Guards into Federal service. The 1st South Carolina had been the first black regiment raised for Northern service, but the 1st Louisiana Native Guards bore the distinction of being the first to be officially mustered in. Enlistments continued to come in at a steady pace, and Butler decided to organize as many regiments as he could. On October 12, the 2nd Louisiana Native Guards were mustered in, followed by the 3rd Louisiana Native Guards on November 24. In the space of less than two months, General Butler had eliminated his worries over the deficiency of his command by enlisting a full brigade of black troops. All of this had been done on Butler's own initiative and without approval from the War Department.[8]

President Lincoln's Emancipation Proclamation, issued in September of 1862, officially changed the government's stance on the status of blacks in society and opened the door for their inclusion into the army as soldiers. Frederick Douglass had long been advocating the enlistment of blacks and felt that by fighting for their freedom, they could also earn the right to full citizenship. "Once let the black man get upon his person the brass letters 'U.S.,' let him get an eagle on his button, and a musket on his shoulder and bullets in his pocket, and there is no power on earth which can deny that he has earned the right to citizenship in the United States."[9]

When the Emancipation Proclamation took effect, on January 1, 1863, the Federal government instituted a program to actively recruit black regiments for service in the Union army. A shifting of public opinion made this move possible and even necessary. Enlistments of white troops had fallen off dramatically in the last year, forcing the government to enact the Conscription Act to draft men into the ranks. Each state was given a quota of recruits it was to raise for military service. If there were not enough volunteers to meet this quota, then a draft would be instituted to make up the difference. The draft was highly unpopular with Northern citizens, who felt it to be unfairly biased in favor of the wealthy. A provision of the law allowed anyone who was drafted to hire a substitute to take his place or pay a fee of $300 to be excused from service. In 1863, that sum was a huge amount of money, far beyond the means of the average working man to raise. Most citizens felt the law to be unfair, and they complained that it was a rich man's war but a poor man's fight. Civil unrest led to violent confrontations in New York City, the coalfields of eastern Pennsylvania, and many other places. In order to increase enlistments and eliminate the need for a draft, many cities, counties, and states offered enlistment bounties to volunteers. The amounts varied, but most volunteers could attain a sizeable sum of money upon enlistment, and many Northern men took advantage of this inducement. But the number of volunteers coming into the army was still below that which was needed to sustain the armies in the field. The enlistment of black troops could offset that, and when it was decided that black volunteers would be counted against the quota assigned to a state, it became very attractive to several northeastern state governments to actively recruit black regiments.

Massachusetts was one of the first states granted permission to raise black regiments for state service. In this instance, the rush to recruit black troops was not a result of a desire to fill quotas or reduce the possibility of a draft. The governor of Massachusetts, John Andrew, was an ardent abolitionist who sought to not only further the cause of freedom but to prove to white society that blacks could perform on an equal footing with whites and were deserving of an equal measure of rights as full citizens of the nation. Andrew did not want to raise an ordinary regiment; he wanted a regiment that would serve as a model, one that would show to the world what blacks could do if given the opportunity.

Governor Andrew appointed Robert Gould Shaw to be the colonel of his model regiment. Shaw was currently serving as a captain in a Massachusetts regiment and had seen combat, but the primary reason for his selection is that he came from one of the leading abolitionist families in Boston.[10] By the direction of Secretary Stanton, all officers of the regiment were to be white, and Shaw and his second in command, Lieutenant Colonel Norwood P. Hallowell, carefully screened the potential candidates to ensure they were acceptable, both militarily and morally.[11] Recruiting of volunteers was met with a brisk response, but it soon became evident that Massachusetts did not have enough black recruits to fill out a regiment. Recruiting officers were sent to other states to make up the shortfall, under the supervision of George Stearns. Among the first to enlist from outside Massachusetts were Charles and Lewis Douglass, the sons of Frederick Douglass. By March of 1864, four companies had been filled, and it was decided to continue recruitment beyond what was needed to complete the regiment so that a second regiment might be formed. The volunteers were trained at Camp Meigs, outside Readville, Massachusetts, and the troops were quickly transformed into efficient and well-drilled soldiers. Everything was going exceedingly well until an edict from the War Department threatened to disrupt the entire project.

Washington had decided that black troops were to be paid a lesser sum than that being given to whites. Black soldiers would receive $10 per month, as opposed to the $13 a month white troops were paid. The men of the 54th had been promised equal status with white troops, and this pay differential flew in the face of that equality. The Massachusetts legislature offered to make up the difference, but the men of the 54th declined, feeling the national government was responsible for correcting the inequity. Officers and men of the regiment chose another route. They would accept no pay from the government for their services until such time as Washington relented and paid them the same as white troops.[12]

On May 28, 1863, the regiment left Boston, bound for Beaufort, South Carolina, where it was brigaded together with the 2nd South Carolina Volunteers, a regiment of South Carolina freedmen. The brigade was under the command of Colonel James Montgomery, a Jayhawker from Kansas. On June 11, 1863, Montgomery led the regiments on a raid against Darien, Georgia, where he ordered the looting and burning of the empty town. Colonel Shaw objected strongly to this action, and after it was over he went over Montgomery's head to complain that this was not the sort of action suitable for his model black regiment.[13]

The regiment was removed from Montgomery's control, and on July 16 it saw its first combat in a skirmish on James Island, South Carolina, where it fought admirably in repulsing an attack of Confederate troops. Two days later the 54th gained national fame when it spearheaded an assault against the Confederate stronghold of Battery Wagner, near Charleston. The attack failed, costing the regiment 272 casualties out of the 600 men it took into the fight—including Colonel Shaw, who was killed at the head of his attacking forces—but the gallantry and courage of the troops gained the attention and respect of all who witnessed them. The model regiment had indeed proven that black soldiers could be the equal of white troops and that they could be depended upon to shoulder a significant role in the war.

The 54th would go on to fight with distinction at the battles of Olustee, Florida, and at Honey Hill, South Carolina, in 1864. They would take part in the engagement at Boykin's Mill, South Carolina, on April 18, 1865, more than a week following the surrender of Robert E. Lee's Army of Northern Virginia, in what was one of the last battles of the war. The much-heralded fame of the 54th Massachusetts paved the way for the Federal government to grant approval for black regiments to serve in combat by erasing many of the prejudices then commonly held by top commanders. Andrew and Shaw had been successful in proving that blacks would not only fight but also that they could be depended upon to conduct themselves in the highest traditions of the military.

Though the 54th Massachusetts was the most famous of the black regiments serving in the war, it was not the first black regiment to actually see

The charge of the 54th Massachusetts at Battery Wagner in 1863 proved that black troops would fight with distinction if given the chance. (Library of Congress)

combat. In fact, the 54th missed that distinction by more than a year. On May 27, 1862, the 1st and 3rd Louisiana Native Guard Regiments took part in the Union assault on Port Hudson, Louisiana. In a forlorn charge, the regiments advanced against the Confederate works, with the Mississippi River on their left, an enemy infantry regiment and battery of light artillery on their right, and heavily fortified infantry and large-caliber coastal artillery guns in their front. Nevertheless, the regiments surged forward despite the fearful crossfire, led by Captain Andre Cailloux, a free black man from New Orleans, shouting orders in both English and French. Losses in the regiments were horrendous, including the heroic Captain Cailloux, and the troops retreated only after it had been proven that to remain longer was a useless sacrifice of human lives. Though their valor did not obtain the same newspaper coverage the 54th Massachusetts would later receive, the actions of the Native Guards were indispensable in proving to the commanders of the western armies that black troops would fight.[14]

The successful battlefield performances of the 54th Massachusetts and the Louisiana Native Guards spurred the government to recruit black regiments on a large scale. Inspector General Lorenzo Thomas was given the task of overseeing the recruitment of black troops in the Mississippi Valley as well as finding suitable white officers to command them. Thomas diligently performed his mission, and by the end of 1863 he could report that he had successfully raised 20 full regiments of black troops. By the end of 1864, he had added another 30 regiments to that total. In all, General Thomas was personally responsible for recruiting some 78,000 black soldiers for the Union army, more than 40 percent of the total that would serve in the war.[15]

In June of 1863, the 1st Regiment, U.S. Colored Troops was mustered into Federal service, in accordance with a directive from the War Department the previous month formally establishing the Bureau of Colored Troops. From that point onward, all recruitment and organization of black regiments would be conducted under the auspices of the federal government. By the time the war was concluded, the Bureau of Colored Troops consisted of 135 regiments of infantry, 6 regiments of cavalry, 12 regiments of heavy artillery, and 10 batteries of light artillery. These included regiments raised by 14 states that would be redesignated as U.S. Colored Troops units. Most of the regiments that had been raised prior to the establishment of the Bureau of Colored Troops were also renamed. The 1st, 2nd, and 3rd Regiments Louisiana Native Guards became the 33rd, 73rd, and 74th U.S. Colored Troops, and the 1st Regiment Kansas Colored Infantry became the 79th U.S.C.T. One notable exception was the Massachusetts troops, the 54th and 55th Infantry Regiments, who were allowed to retain their state designation. By the end of the war, 178,975 black recruits had enlisted in the Union army, and 9,695 more volunteered to serve in the Union navy. They would fight in 39 major battles of the war and more than 400 lesser engagements, and 29 of their number were awarded the Congressional Medal of Honor for the conspicuous gallantry they displayed in combat.[16]

U.S. Colored Troops took part in every theater of the war, but they were especially well represented in Virginia and Tennessee. On December 3, 1864, the 24th Army Corps was created when black regiments from the 9th, 10th, and 18th Corps were brought together to form the first all-black corps in U.S. military history. The corps, under the command of Major General Godfrey Weitzel, contained nearly 14,000 troops and was divided into three divisions.[17] The corps performed exceptional service during the siege of Petersburg and in the final phases of the Appomattox Campaign. But its greatest laurels were perhaps won when a portion of the corps took part in the two expeditions against the Confederate bastion of Fort Fisher, guarding the vital Southern port at Wilmington, North Carolina. A failed effort on December 15, 1864, was followed by another try on January 15, 1865, when Union ground forces stormed the land face of the fort, overpowering the Southern garrison and capturing the works. Two brigades of the 3rd Division, 25th Corps were employed in the expedition. During the fighting on January 15, the Union offensive had bogged down, and as the sun began to set in the sky the members of the 27th U.S.C.T. were ordered forward to add their weight to the attack. These fresh troops, along with a detachment of fresh white troops, proved to be too much for the Confederate defenders to hold, and the Confederate lines began to crumble. The 27th fought with conspicuous gallantry and was instrumental in the capture of Battery Buchanan as well as a number of Confederates who were trying to escape from the fort.[18]

The troops of the 25th Corps had the signal honor of accepting the official surrender of the city of Richmond. On April 3, 1865, General Weitzel was tendered the surrender of the city by Confederate officials, and the troops of his corps were among the first Union soldiers to take possession. Furthermore, the black soldiers of the 25th Corps were assigned to garrison duty in Richmond, charged with maintaining law and order in the abandoned Confederate capital.

To the west, General George Henry Thomas relied on black troops to secure the most decisive victory of the war, and one of the most decisive victories in the annals of military history. When William T. Sherman moved east from Atlanta on his celebrated March to the Sea, General Thomas was left behind to deal with General John Bell Hood and his Confederate Army of Tennessee. Hood had invaded Tennessee in hopes of drawing Sherman and his forces away from Atlanta, but the Union commander paid him no mind and directed Thomas to deal with the threat to the state and to the important Union supply hub in Nashville. The problem was that Thomas had very little with which to confront Hood, and the forces under his command were spread terribly thin guarding various important points in the state. Thomas's first order of business was to gather together an army capable of dealing with the Confederate threat, and the general leaned heavily on black troops when putting his force together. In the formation of a Provisional Division, Thomas incorporated eight full regiments of black infantry and a black artillery battery that he had helped to train and organize following the battle of Missionary Ridge. These regiments, the 12th, 13th, 14th, 16th, 17th, 18th, 44th, and 100th U.S.C.T. Infantry and the 2nd U.S.C.T. Light Artillery, accounted for about half the men in the Provisional Division.[19]

Thomas had been worried whether the black troops would fight or not, as they were all green and untested in combat, but he nevertheless assigned them a key position in his line when he prepared to fight Hood's army at Nashville on December 15, 1864. The Provisional Division, under the command of Major General James B. Steedman, was placed on the left of the Union lines with orders to open the fighting by demonstrating against the right of the enemy line. It was hoped that they would draw Confederate reserves away from the Confederate center, where Thomas planned to launch his main attack. The black troops were up to the challenge and became so caught up in their feint that it developed into a full-fledged attack. They were eventually repulsed, but their actions had indeed caused Hood to shift reinforcements to his right, softening his center for Thomas's main thrust. The Union attack that followed drove the Confederates back, and by nightfall they were tenuously holding on to their defensive positions. The next day, Thomas resumed the offensive, launching such a crushing attack on the Southern lines that the Army of Tennessee all but ceased to exist as a military organization. It was the most complete victory of the war, and military historians rate it second only to Napoléon's victory at Austerlitz as being the most decisive victory in military history. The soldiers of the U.S.C.T. regiments that had taken part in the battle had proven themselves, despite the fact that they had never been in battle before. They had shouldered a substantial portion of the fighting and had added another glorious chapter to the history of black troops in the war.

Toward the end of the war, the Confederacy was running out of everything needed to maintain its armies in the field. Its most critical shortage was in manpower. The cradle and the grave had already been robbed, as boyish youths and gray-bearded old men were inducted into the service, but there were simply not enough men in the South to replace the battlefield losses and keep the armies at fighting strength. Major General Patrick Cleburne had been a strong advocate of arming blacks and enlisting them in the Confederate army in 1864, but his advice was generally derided and ridiculed in both military and civilian circles. Cleburne would be killed at the battle of Franklin in November of 1864, two months before his advice became a prophecy. By January of 1865, President Jefferson Davis realized that revolutionary steps must be taken if the Confederacy hoped to stave off the impending defeat of its armies. Blacks in the South must be induced to fight for the Confederacy, in a last-gasp hope for final victory. Davis knew that this move would bring about an end to slavery, as the government would need to promise freedom as a reward for enlistment, and he realized that there would be many in the South that would cry out against his plan. Nonetheless, he regarded it to be the only viable option to fill his depleted ranks and continue the struggle. Accordingly, on February 8, 1865, a bill was introduced in the Confederate Senate to have 200,000 slaves freed so that they might be enlisted in the military. The bill met with strong resistance, and it was not until March 9 that it finally gained the necessary votes to pass, even though Robert E. Lee had endorsed the measure.[20] By the time Davis had come to the conclusion the measure was needed, its prospect of success was little more than a fleeting hope. The delay caused in the passage of the bill by the Confederate Congress made it an exercise in futility. Grant's army was daily threatening to break Lee's lines and capture Richmond and Petersburg. The measure might have worked if it had been enacted several months earlier, but it was now too little, too late.

Amazingly, even at this late date, a couple hundred black volunteers were organized into the nucleus of the 1st Regiment Confederate States Colored

Black soldiers in the field. (Library of Congress)

Troops. The men quickly took to drill and training and were already starting to display a level of martial competence by the time General Lee was compelled to abandon his lines around Richmond and Petersburg on April 3. The following day, the Confederate black troops were detailed to guard a wagon train near Amelia Court House. They were attacked by Union cavalry, and they repulsed the enemy with a display of military skill that belied their short time in the service. The Union troopers were not to be denied, however, and they reformed for another charge. This time, their charge overwhelmed the black Confederate troops. It was a dubious debut for the Confederate States Colored Troops. In their first engagement they had experienced their first victory, had experienced their first defeat, and had ceased to exist as a military unit.[21]

Black soldiers contributed greatly to the final outcome of the war. Without their numbers and passion, it is doubtful if the North could have won the war in 1865, if at all. One can only speculate what course the struggle could have taken if the Confederate government had embraced the policy of emancipation and enlisted black troops earlier in the conflict. The courage, discipline, and manliness displayed by black troops on fields of battle across the country was undeniable, and it effected a shift in public opinion that not only led to their freedom but to their full citizenship. Issues of race and equality would continue to surface for decades, as the American people struggled to become truly integrated as a society. The valor of the tens of thousands of freemen and ex-slaves who fought in the Civil War ensured that this process, however rocky, would continue to move forward and would never be permitted to regress.

CHAPTER 23

THE NATIVE AMERICANS

Native Americans took an active part in the Civil War despite the fact that they were not regarded as citizens of either the United States or the Confederacy. With little to gain and everything to lose, it is astounding that nearly 29,000 Native Americans served in the Union and Confederate armies during the four-year struggle. In the East, native tribes tended to align themselves according to the section of the country in which they resided. For the most part, Northern tribes sided with the Union and Southern tribes allied themselves with the Confederacy. There were, however, exceptions to that rule. In Virginia and North Carolina, the Pamunkey and Lumbee tribes chose to honor their allegiance to the Union. The Pamunkey served as civilian and naval pilots for Union ships sailing in the region, while the Lumbee fought an isolated guerilla war deep within Confederate territory. While they were forced to provide menial labor for the Confederacy, many Lumbee performed acts of sabotage against their oppressors that benefited the Union.[1]

Two of the primary native peoples that took part in the war in the East were the Iroquois and the Cherokee. The Iroquois people consisted of the tribes of the Cayuga, Mohawk, Oneida, Onondaga, Seneca, and Tuscarora. Located in New York State, the Iroquois lived primarily on several small reservations. A small number of the tribe had been relocated to the Indian Territory, and there was also a small Oneida reservation located in Wisconsin, near Green Bay. The Iroquois people wanted to support the Union. In fact, they felt it was their responsibility to do so, as they had signed treaties with the Federal government pledging themselves to be allies. The only problem was that the state of New York did not want the Iroquois to enlist in the army. Confrontations over Native American land had been boiling over for decades, and there were many whites in the state who wished for all the Iroquois to be

removed to the Indian Territory and their lands in New York opened for settle-
ment. The state government flatly refused to allow the recruitment of soldiers
from the Iroquois Nation. Twelve young Iroquois men would not be denied,
however, and traveled to Harrisburg, Pennsylvania, to enlist in the 57th
Pennsylvania Infantry.

Three prominent tribal members, Ely and Newt Parker and Cornelius
Cusick, championed the cause for Iroquois enlistment. The Parker brothers
were from the Seneca tribe, while Cusick was a member of the Tuscarora
tribe, and all came from families having a rich tradition of military service
to the United States. Ely Parker was a sachem of his tribe, a lawyer, and a
trained engineer who had served as a captain in the New York militia in
1853. Having numerous official contacts in the New York government, he
began to press the case for Iroquois enlistment through proper channels.
Two other members of the Seneca tribe, Peter Wilson and Chauncey
Jemison, took an entirely different route. Wilson and Jemison contacted
Orlando Allen, a land speculator who had swindled the Iroquois out of large
tracts of land. Though Allen had never proven himself to be a friend of the
Indians, he was well connected, and Wilson and Jemison correctly surmised
that his influence could be substantial. They pleaded their case for Iroquois
enlistment to Allen, who was moved by the patriotic fervor the two men
exuded. He pledged his support, and he was as good as his word in pressing
the case with all his political acquaintances. By March of 1862, all the efforts
began to pay off. Recruiting offices in Buffalo were instructed to accept the
enlistment of Iroquois volunteers.[2]

The prevailing custom of Native American enlistment in the East was for
individual volunteers joining predominantly white units. One group of 25
Iroquois joined Company D of the 132nd New York Infantry. John Cusick
was appointed a lieutenant in the company, and Newt Parker became a company sergeant. The unit soon became known as the Tuscarora Company,
largely because Cusick came from that tribe; the majority of the men in the
company were of German descent, and the larger portion of the Indian volunteers were Seneca. The 132nd New York was sent to North Carolina, where it
performed garrison duty around New Bern. While the regiment saw limited
fighting during the war, the men of the Tuscarora Company did have the
opportunity to distinguish themselves in February 1863. General George E.
Pickett had been assigned to command the Confederate forces in the New
Bern area and undertook an offensive to drive the Federal troops out of the
region. On February 1, 1863, the Tuscarora Company was heavily engaged
at Batchelder's Creek, when Pickett's troops attempted to force their way
across the Neuse Road Bridge. The Confederate attack force was a few thousand strong, while the Union defenders numbered only about two hundred
men. Despite the disparity of numbers, the Union troops kept Pickett's men

from capturing the bridge, even after the Confederates ordered an artillery barrage to drive them away. The Tuscarora Company men fought bravely, fending off every assault until the Confederates built another bridge, below their defensive position, and crossed there in strength. Assailed by front, flank, and rear, the Tuscarora men were finally compelled to retreat, but not before suffering some 91 casualties. The action at Batchelder's Creek established the heroism of the Iroquois men throughout the army. It also established Lieutenant Cusick as being a born leader of men. Cusick found military life to his liking and would continue to serve in the army until his retirement in 1892, as a captain in the 22nd U.S. Infantry.[3]

Ely Parker took a different route to enter the service of the Union army. He petitioned the War Department for a commission. It took more than a year, but Parker was finally granted a commission as captain of volunteers in May of 1863 and was assigned to General Ulysses S. Grant's army, in Mississippi. Parker would serve as Grant's assistant adjutant general and as a division engineer before being assigned as a personal secretary to Grant himself. In this capacity, he was responsible for writing out Grant's terms of surrender to Robert E. Lee at Appomattox Court House on April 9, 1865. When Lee was introduced to Parker, he is reported to have remarked, "I'm glad to see a real American here," referring to the fact that Parker was a Native American. Parker took the Confederate leader's hand and responded, "We are all Americans here."

The 14th Wisconsin Infantry enlisted 49 Oneida men from the Green Bay area into its ranks in the fall and winter of 1863–64, 39 of them serving together in Company F. These troops proved to be exceptional skirmishers and were heavily engaged in the battles of the Atlanta Campaign and the Red River Campaign. They were especially noted within the regiment for being excellent marksmen and squirrel hunters, and their abilities to procure wild game benefited many of their white comrades. The reputation earned as sharpshooters by the Oneida of the 14th Wisconsin was eclipsed by other Indian troops, however. The men of Company K, 1st Michigan Sharpshooters became famous for their shooting abilities and were, perhaps, the best-known Indian unit fighting in the Eastern Theater of the war. All members of the company were Native Americans, most of them coming from Michigan. The vast majority came from the Ottawa tribe, but there was also representation from the Delaware, Huron, Oneida, Potawatomi, and Ojibwa tribes. The regiment was raised during the summer of 1863, and Garrett A. Graveraet was commissioned a second lieutenant in Company K. Graveraet was half Ottawa himself and had long been an advocate for Indian rights. The 1st Michigan Sharpshooters took part in all of the battles of General Grant's Overland Campaign of 1864, including the engagements at the Wilderness, Spotsylvania Court House, and Cold Harbor. The regiment took part in the attacks on the Confederate defenses at Petersburg, Virginia, in June of 1864, where Lieutenant Graveraet was mortally wounded. They took an active role in the Mine Explosion battle that took place on July 30 and in all of the siege operations from June of 1864 to April of 1865. When Petersburg and Richmond fell, the regiment participated in the pursuit of General Lee's army that resulted in the surrender of the Army of Northern Virginia at Appomattox Court House on April 9, 1865. After taking part in the Grand Review of the Army of the Potomac on May 23 in Washington, D.C., the regiment was mustered out of the service on July 28, 1865. The Ottawa and other tribal members of Company K had earned a well-deserved reputation for their marksmanship and bravery. An admiring Union soldier from another regiment praised the members of Company K during the siege of Petersburg, noting that there were "only some 20 of them left out of over 100 that commenced the campaign," some three months before.[4] The Indian company of the 1st Michigan Sharpshooters had paid a heavy price for their reputation on the bloodstained fields of Virginia, and, in the end, there were too few left to keep the reputation going.

The most famous Native American unit to serve in the Confederate army east of the Mississippi River was the Thomas Legion from North Carolina. Some four hundred Cherokee from the Oconaluftee tribe of North Carolina would serve in the unit by the end of the war. The unit was raised by William Holland Thomas, a native of Waynesville, North Carolina. As a boy, Thomas became fascinated with the Cherokee who lived near his home, and he was a regular visitor in their villages. Thomas was twelve when his father died, and he was immediately adopted by Yonaguska, chief of the Oconaluftee tribe. The boy learned the Cherokee language and was instructed in all things Yonaguska thought he needed to know to become a man. The bond that was created between Thomas and the tribe would pay dividends during the Cherokee removal and relocation that took place in the 1830s. The vast majority of the Cherokee tribes were forced to relinquish their lands in the East and move to reservations in the Indian Territory in what became known as the Trail of Tears. By this time, Thomas had become a successful businessman and lawyer, and the Oconaluftee retained him to represent their interests with the government. Thomas was able to convince the authorities that the Oconaluftee were separate from the rest of the Cherokee Nation and should be dealt with individually. He portrayed the members of the tribe as being peaceful, law-abiding people who only wanted to be citizens of the state of North Carolina. In the end, the Oconaluftee were successful in maintaining their lands and avoiding the removal that befell the other tribes of the Cherokee. At the outbreak of the Civil War, Thomas determined to raise a command for Confederate service, and the first place he turned for recruits was the Oconaluftee tribe.[5]

Thomas was able to raise two full companies of volunteers from the tribe, and they were mustered into Confederate service on April 9, 1862. The companies were ordered to East Tennessee, but Thomas had other service in mind. He shortly began petitioning Governor Zebulon Vance for permission to raise a larger force to be used for local defense in the Carolinas, Virginia, and East Tennessee. Being granted authorization, Thomas spent the summer of 1862 recruiting volunteers. By September, he had succeeded in raising 8 companies of white troops and had a regiment boasting 1,100 men. By October, he had enlisted enough additional volunteers to form a 700-man battalion of infantry and cavalry. The unit was named the Thomas Legion and was assigned the unpleasant duty of rounding up deserters and enforcing conscription in the mountains within their sphere of influence. The Cherokee members of the legion proved to be especially proficient in tracking down deserters due to their intimate knowledge of the area, but Thomas protested the duty as being humiliating and unmanly. He desired combat duty, not service doing police work.[6]

On September 14, 1862, a portion of the legion saw action at Rogersville, Tennessee, when one of the Cherokee companies was ambushed by Union troops. The second Cherokee company was sent to counterattack the Federals and succeeded in driving them from the field. The commander of the second company, Captain Astooga Stoga, was killed in this engagement. By April of 1863, the Thomas Legion had swelled to about 2,800 soldiers, including a company of artillery. The unit was divided, with Thomas assigned to take a portion of the legion to Madison County, North Carolina, to eliminate the activities of Union partisans in the area. The bulk of the legion was detailed to guard the East Tennessee and Virginia Railroad. When the unit was reunited, it was placed under the command of Brigadier General Alfred E. Jackson. Jackson and Thomas had a bitter relationship that led to Jackson preferring court martial charges against his subordinate three different times. In all cases, the charges were dismissed. When Thomas was ordered to report to Major General Simon B. Buckner in East Tennessee with his two Indian companies, it must have been a bittersweet parting. Thomas was no longer under the command of Jackson, but his legion was still divided, and he was commanding only a small portion of it.[7]

While attached to General Buckner, several of the Cherokee were captured by the Federals and jailed near Sevierville, Tennessee. Thomas sent a large portion of his Indian companies to free them, and the mission was a huge success. Not only were all of the Cherokee captives recovered, but six Union soldiers and sixty East Tennessee Unionists were captured as well.

The Thomas Legion participated, as a unit or by detachments, in numerous engagements in East Tennessee and in all of the battles of the Valley Campaign of 1864. As a testament to their bravery, it can be noted that of the six hundred men of the legion that began the Valley Campaign, only about one hundred were left by its conclusion. Losses to the Thomas Legion had been extreme, and by the end of 1864 the unit was a mere shadow of its former self. Thomas received permission from the War Department to recruit volunteers to fill his ranks, and by April of 1865 he had secured several hundred new recruits, four hundred of them being Cherokee. But by April of 1865 the war was coming to a close in the East. Before the month was over, both of the principal Confederate armies east of the Mississippi River had surrendered. May found the Thomas Legion as the only organized Confederate military unit still in the field in the East. On May 9, the legion engaged Union forces at Waynesville, North Carolina. Thomas's men surrounded the Union troops and demanded their surrender. During the course of negotiations, however, it was impressed upon the Confederates that they were the last remaining Southern forces in the field in the state and that their further resistance was futile. Good sense prevailed, and the men of the legion surrendered rather than engaging in what would have been a useless effusion of blood. The Oconaluftee Cherokee of the Thomas Legion had proven themselves brave and conscientious soldiers on numerous fields of battle throughout the war, and they also bore the distinction of being among the last Confederate soldiers to surrender east of the Mississippi.[8]

It was in the West, however, where the greatest impact of Indian troops was made during the Civil War. With a larger Native American population to draw from, Indian units in the West were both larger and more numerous. At the outbreak of the war, both sides courted the support of the Five Civilized Tribes living in the Indian Territory of Oklahoma. These were the Cherokee, Choctaw, Chickasaw, Creek, and Seminole. All of these tribes had treaties with the United States, but many of their members had adopted the Southern plantation culture and were allied to the Confederacy by lifestyle and values. The Confederacy assigned Albert Pike as a special envoy to the Indian Territory for the purpose of negotiating treaties with the various tribes. Pike found his assignment difficult, as John Ross, chief of the Cherokee, stated he wanted the Cherokee to remain neutral and take no part in this white man's war. Pike had greater success with Stand Watie, leader of a segment of mixed-blood Cherokee, who readily adopted the Southern cause and raised volunteers to serve in the Confederate army. The Choctaw and Chickasaw tribes proved to be easy converts to the Confederacy, and recruitment for Confederate soldiers among the tribal members was begun as soon as the treaties were signed. Pike found the Creek and Seminole tribes to be especially hard to deal with. Both tribes were split in their allegiance, the full-blooded members preferring to remain loyal to the United States and the mixed-blood members favoring the Confederacy. The Creek chief Opothleyahola actually favored neutrality at the start of the war but was convinced to support

the Union due to the pro-Confederate efforts of the McIntosh brothers, Chilly
and Daniel, who were leaders of the mixed-blood faction. The Seminole split
along similar lines, with Chief Alligator advocating neutrality before being
pushed into the Union camp by the activities of mixed-blood leader John
Jumper. Hostilities between the rival factions erupted in November 1861, creating a civil war within the Civil War.[9]

Opothleyahola gathered together his followers at his plantation, near
present-day Eufaula, Oklahoma. He was joined there by Alligator and his
loyal Seminole, as well as by loyal members of the Shawnee, Delaware,
Wichita, and Comanche tribes. In all, some 5,000 Indians answered
Opothleyahola's call, including 1,300 warriors. The chief intended to lead
his people on an exodus out of Oklahoma, to seek Union protection in
Kansas. On November 5, 1861, Opothleyahola started his people northward.
Confederate authorities were informed of the movement, and a military
detachment was sent to prevent the Creek from leaving the territory. The
Confederate force included some five hundred Texas cavalry, but it was pre-
dominantly made up of Indian units, including the 1st Choctaw and
Chickasaw Mounted Rifles, 1st Creek Cavalry, and 1st Seminole Cavalry
Battalion, all under the command of Colonel Douglas Cooper. On
November 19, the Confederates caught up to Opothleyahola's force at
Round Mountain, in present-day Payne County. The Texas cavalrymen
promptly charged the camp of the loyal Creek, but they discovered that
Opothleyahola had prepared a careful ambush for them. Fighting continued
until darkness fell, at which time Opothleyahola withdrew his
people to the north, toward Bird Creek.[10]

Cooper would later pursue the Creek and would be joined by Colonel John
Drew and his five hundred troopers of the 1st Cherokee Mounted Rifles.
When the Confederates caught up to Opothleyahola at Bird Creek on
December 8, all knew that another engagement was imminent the following
day. Some four hundred Cherokee of Colonel Drew's 1st Mounted Rifles
deserted that night and went over to join with Opothlcyahola. On
December 9, when Colonel Cooper ordered his men forward to the attack,
he found that Opothleyahola and his followers had prepared a formidable
defense against them. The fighting lasted for four hours, and by nightfall
Opothleyahola's warriors were forced to give ground and retreat. Cooper
was unable to pursue, however, due to a shortage of ammunition, and he
was forced to withdraw from the field himself to replenish his supplies.[11]

Cooper's column would be joined by Texas and Arkansas troops under the
command of Colonel James M. McIntosh in a new expedition to prevent
Opothleyahola and his followers from gaining the safety of Kansas. Stand
Watie's 2nd Cherokee Mounted Rifles would also take part in the pursuit.
On December 25, the Confederates overtook Opothleyahola's followers at

Chustenahlah, in Osage County, Oklahoma. Colonel James McIntosh decided to attack, even though Colonel Cooper's column had not yet arrived. Opothleyahola's followers had, by this time, swelled to some 9,000 people, of which about 1,700 were warriors. McIntosh had slightly less than 1,400 men with him, but the Confederates were better armed and equipped than the loyal Indians. On December 26, McIntosh attacked, and Opothleyahola's followers were forced to give ground. By the time the Confederates reached the camp of the loyal Indians, the retreat turned into a rout. The fleeing Indians split into several smaller groups as they tried to make good their escape to Kansas. Stand Watie and his 2nd Cherokee Mounted Rifles pursued the group containing Opothleyahola and engaged them on December 27, about 25 miles north of Chustenahlah. Watie's men killed 11 of Opothleyahola's warriors and captured 75 women and children, but they were unable to capture the chief and the bulk of his followers. Colonel McIntosh, satisfied that his mission had been accomplished, prepared to return to Arkansas. Colonel Cooper, irate that the attack had been made before the arrival of his column and anxious to bag all of Opothleyahola's followers, pushed his men forward. Cooper's command made contact with Opothleyahola's remaining force near the Kansas border on December 31, 1861. After a brief and indecisive engagement, on January 1, 1862, Cooper decided to call off the pursuit and return to Fort Gibson, largely because of inclement weather and fearfully cold temperatures. Opothleyahola's followers were suffering horribly from exposure to the same harsh elements. Approximately 2,000 of his people would freeze to death before they reached the safety of Kansas. Of the 9,000 followers who had begun the exodus, only 3,168 made it safely across the border. By April of 1862 their numbers would swell to 7,600, however, as more Indians fled the Indian Territory in search of sanctuary.[12]

With the Indian Territory firmly in Southern hands, the Confederacy began to consolidate its holdings. Albert Pike had been commissioned a brigadier general and given command of the Indian Territory on November 22, 1861. Pike's first priority was to bring the Indian regiments that had been recruited up to full strength, so they could take a significant part in the war. Though he never fully completed his mission to fill out the Indian regiments under his command, by March of 1862 Pike could boast approximately 2,500 troops in his various commands. These included the 1st and 2nd Cherokee Mounted Rifles, the 1st Choctaw and Chickasaw Cavalry, the 1st Creek Cavalry, the 1st Seminole Cavalry Battalion, and a few other smaller independent units. According to the treaties Pike had signed with the various tribes, Indian soldiers were to be used solely for the protection of the Indian Territory and could not be compelled to serve outside Indian lands without their consent. On January 19, 1862, Major General Earl Van Dorn was assigned to

Albert Pike led a brigade of Native American troops at the battle of Pea Ridge in 1862. (Library of Congress)

command the Trans-Mississippi District, which included the Indian Territory. Van Dorn cared little about the stipulations of the treaties signed with the various tribes and considered the troops under Pike's command to be just another part of his available forces. He ordered Pike to take part in a planned offensive to invade Missouri and capture Saint Louis that was due to be initiated in March. Pike's Indian brigade was assigned to the division of Brigadier General Ben McCulloch, which was to constitute the right wing of Van Dorn's army. General Sterling Price's Missouri militia troops would make up the left wing.[13]

By March of 1862, Van Dorn was ready to move. Brigadier General Samuel R. Curtis, commander of the Union Army of the Southwest, had entered northeast Arkansas with a force of 10,500 men. Van Dorn's combined wings numbered about 16,500 men, but a large portion of these were relatively untrained and undisciplined. The Confederates marched into the Boston Mountains, where Van Dorn made contact with Curtis at Elkhorn Tavern, on March 6. Van Dorn had divided his command, ordering his two wing commanders to envelop the Union position and strike it from the rear. McCulloch's wing was delayed in its march, but by 11:30 a.m. on the

morning of March 7, it had made contact with Union forces at Leetown. The
Federals were greatly outnumbered, but their commander, Colonel Peter
Osterhaus, decided to attack. After his initial surprise, McCulloch counterat-
tacked, driving the Union forces before him. Two companies of the 3rd
Iowa Infantry ran into the Cherokee under Pike's command and were routed.
The Iowa troops lost 24 killed and 17 wounded in the engagement with the
Cherokee. It was later discovered that eight of the Iowa troops had been scalped,
and allegations were made that several of the dead had been wounded troops
that were murdered by the Indians. Pike's troops were unnerved by Federal artillery, and many of them took cover in a line of trees, firing at anyone dressed in a
blue uniform, despite the fact that many Confederates were wearing blue. In the
course of the battle, General McCulloch and Colonel James McIntosh were both
killed, and Brigadier General Louis Hebert was captured, leaving Pike as the
senior officer on the field. Pike ordered a retreat of the units in his immediate
sphere of influence, creating a confused situation in which several regiments
were left behind on the field of battle. Pike's performance at the battle of
Elkhorn Tavern, along with charges of mishandling of money and material
intended for his command, would later lead to Major General Thomas
Hindman ordering his arrest. Pike eluded arrest and tendered his resignation to
the Confederate War Department. His resignation was accepted, and the charges
were dropped.[14]

The units Pike had commanded at Elkhorn Tavern would continue to serve
the Confederacy for the remainder of the war. By the conclusion of hostilities,
the 1st Cherokee Mounted Rifles had fought in 27 major engagements as well
as numerous smaller affairs. Most of the other tribal units from the Indian
Territory boasted similar records. Stand Watie was promoted to brigadier general in 1864 and given command of the Indian Division, consisting of Native
American troops from the Indian Territory. Watie would prove himself to be a
dogged supporter of the Confederate cause, keeping his soldiers in the field
long after most other Southern commands had surrendered. He would become
the last Confederate general to lay down his arms when he surrendered himself and his forces in June of 1865.

Many of the Indians who followed Opothleyahola into Kansas ended up
joining the Union army. The Federal government desired to retake control
of the Indian Territory and to facilitate the relocation of the displaced
Indians in Kansas back to their abandoned homes. To this end, it was proposed that two regiments of Indian troops be raised to accompany Union
forces in an expedition into Indian Territory. Brigadier General James G.
Blunt, commander of the Department of Kansas, heartily endorsed the program, and recruitment among the displaced Indians began in early
May 1862. By May 22, enough volunteers had come forward to form the 1st
Kansas Indian Home Guard, under the command of Colonel Robert

W. Furnas. The regiment was a tri-racial unit, having white officers and Native American and black members of the Creek and Seminole tribes. The 2nd Kansas Indian Home Guard was formed in June and early July of 1862, under the command of Colonel John Ritchie, and was composed of volunteers from the Delaware, Kickapoo, Osage, Shawnee, and Seneca tribes, with a smattering of recruits from the Five Civilized Tribes. The 3rd Kansas Indian Home Guard was raised in July 1862 and was commanded by Colonel William A. Phillips. The majority of the volunteers in this regiment were Cherokee, many of them being deserters from the Confederate First Cherokee Mounted Rifles who had come over to Opothleyahola during his exodus to Kansas.[15]

The 1st Kansas Indian Home Guard took part in an expedition into Indian Territory under the command of Colonel William Weer that took place in June and July of 1862. On July 3, a portion of Weer's command, including members of the 1st Kansas Indian Home Guard, surrounded and surprised a Confederate force under the command of Colonel James Clarkson at Locust Grove, in present-day Mayes County, Oklahoma. Clarkson's force, approximately 250 strong, was virtually annihilated by the Union attack, with some 100 being killed and 110 being captured, including Colonel Clarkson. The Union force captured Tahlequah, capital of the Cherokee Nation, on July 16 and Fort Gibson, on the Arkansas River, on July 18. On that day, Colonel Weer was placed under arrest by his second-in-command, Colonel Frederick Salomon, on charges of habitual drunkenness and neglect of duty. Salomon decided that his troops were exhausted from the heat and running low on supplies. He therefore gave the order to withdraw his force from Indian Territory, leaving behind the Indian regiment to guard points along the Arkansas, Grand, and Verdigris Rivers.[16]

The three Indian home guard regiments would serve till the end of the war, seeing battle at Prairie Grove, Honey Springs, Cabin Creek, and numerous other locations in the Indian Territory, Arkansas, and Kansas. The Confederates of Stand Watie's Indian Brigade were a constant nemesis, as were the raiders of Colonel William Quantrill, who frequently rode into Indian Territory in search of plunder. Though the situation in the Indian Territory was often chaotic and unorganized, the members of the three Kansas Indian home guard regiments performed faithful service to the United States and contributed significantly to defeating Confederate ambitions in the region. They performed an even greater service to their own people. The fact that so many of these Indians had aided the Union cause ensured that they would retain ownership of the tribal lands ceded to them in Oklahoma after the conclusion of the war. Had all the members of the tribes living within the Indian Territory sided with the Confederacy, it is probable that much or all of their land would have been seized by the Federal government as punishment for supporting the Southern cause.

Stand Watie was a Cherokee chief who became a brigadier general in the Confederate army. His Native American troops were the last significant body of Confederate soldiers to surrender after the war. (National Archives)

The Native American units mentioned here are some of the more famous to serve in the Civil War, but they are only a sampling of the Indian involvement in that conflict. More than 28,000 Native Americans participated in this white man's war, serving in many of the most fiercely fought battles ever to be waged in the Western Hemisphere. Though there were some isolated instances of scalping and other atrocities, the vast majority of Native Americans, both North and South, conducted themselves as soldiers, earning for themselves the gratitude and admiration of the cause they supported.

CHAPTER 24

SUMMATION OF COMBAT EFFICIENCY

To summarize the various units described in this text, the archaic units that were still in existence during the war, like the lancers and pikemen, performed as one would expect them to when faced with weapons and tactics from a more modern period. Pikemen were thankfully never called on to pit their spears against rifled muskets or artillery, and the pikes served as a weapon while awaiting the arrival of a unit's muskets or for guard duty far removed from the front. Rush's Lancers was the only lancer unit to go into combat with their lances, and though they fought bravely and did comparatively well, Rush's superiors realized the impracticality of these weapons and issued carbines to the troopers instead.

The Zouaves' colorful uniforms easily distinguished them in camp and on the battlefield, but what other contributions did they make to the war? The light infantry tactics that Zouave units were supposed to employ were ideal for skirmishing, and they could have been used to great advantage by the Union and Confederate armies if the commanders of those armies had not been so thoroughly mired in the concepts of Napoleonic tactics. Instead of being used to their full potential, the Zouave regiments were most often merely assigned a position in the massed columns of shoulder-to shoulder infantry in the concentrated formations of the day. By the second year of the war, many of these units had done away with their colorful garb and were dressed in standard-issue uniforms. It did not take a year for the army commanders to also strip them of their specialized fighting ability. Because of the manner in which they were used, the Zouaves earned their place as elite units based on the extreme courage and élan they displayed on numerous battlefields, and not because of special or unique qualities brought to the army.

Horse artillery demonstrated a great ability to decide the course of battles during the war. The capacity to mass heavy guns at a critical point on the line, in a rapid manner, gave offensive and defensive power to the infantry and cavalry that was a key in securing victory on many hard-fought fields. In the age of mechanized fighting, tanks and self-propelled guns would replace horses as the means of getting the ordnance where it needed to be in a timely fashion, but the concept that had proven itself so successful in the Civil War remained unchanged.

Machine gunners could have made an enormous difference in the war, had they been utilized to their full potential. Ordnance officers and field commanders placed little faith in these newfangled contraptions, however, and their development was shelved until after the war. The machine gun became a staple of the world's armies in World War I, and the carnage they exacted was horrific. One can only imagine the effects machine guns might have made on the war if their development and employment had been more actively pursued. When thinking of the great charges on the fields of Fredericksburg, Gettysburg, Spotsylvania, and the like, one can speculate that machine guns would have given the defenders an insurmountable advantage.

The operations of the Chemical Corps were in their infancy at the time of the war. Continued scientific and technological advances would bring this service to the forefront in later wars, when chemical weapons became the most hated and feared component of an enemy's arsenal. The gas attacks of World War I were so terrible that following that conflict, the civilized nations of the world agreed to ban their further use. The Union and Confederate soldiers of the Civil War had enough horror to contend with and were luckily spared this gruesome aspect of warfare.

Through their invaluable services to the armies to which they were attached, the sharpshooters more than earned a spot as an elite unit of the war. Their deadly fire and long-range shooting ability made them terrors of the battlefield, winning the respect of friend and foe alike. In later years, the U.S. Army would give greater training in marksmanship to the common soldier in the ranks, improving their overall shooting ability and decreasing the need for sharpshooters as large bodies of men. Instead, these talented marksmen would be employed primarily as snipers, working alone or in pairs to keep their foe ever vigilant when operating in enemy territory.

Ironclad ships forever changed the navies of the world and ushered in a new chapter in maritime warfare. These vessels upset the balance of power that land-based fortifications had held for centuries and made it possible for relatively small numbers of ships to successfully engage fixed works. On the water, the ironclads led to an arms race of sorts, as the nations of the world sought to gain an advantage by building ever-larger ships with ever-larger armaments. The result would find expression in the majestic battleships of

World War I and II, when the feared dreadnaughts ruled the waves as ocean-going fortresses.

Submarine development was largely a failure during the Civil War, especially when it came to application. True, the *Hunley* did make history when it successfully sank the *Housatonic*, but in doing so it shared the fate of so many submarines before it by sinking and taking its crew to their deaths. Submarines were more a novelty of the war than an effective fighting arm, and they played almost no role in the outcome of the conflict. The day of the submarine would come several decades later, when German wolf packs roamed the Atlantic spreading fear and consternation. Union and Confederate submarines were the forerunners of these terrors of the deep and provided significant advancements in the technological and developmental science needed to create the submarine as we know it today.

The light division was an idea that was a little ahead of its time. Civil War field commanders were so imbued with the strategy and tactics of the Napoleonic era that they failed to fully grasp the benefits to be derived from the use of fast-moving, light infantry on the battlefield. Most commanders had still not learned this lesson in World War I, which accounts for the great slaughter found in most battles of that time, when massed formations of men were thrown against artillery, machine guns, and tanks. It would take until World War II for the U.S. Army to fully embrace the concepts of light infantry tactics. The German army had perfected their usage in the adoption of their blitzkrieg strategy, showing the world what could be accomplished by celerity of movement with adequate fire support.

The rocket battalion had little impact on the war. This was owing to both the inferior rockets being used at the time and the fact that horse artillery was so proficient in providing fire support for the army. Future wars would be charged with the task of fully developing the technology for battlefield application. Once more, the Germans would step forward to become leaders in this field of endeavor. The V-1 and V-2 rockets that Germany employed in World War II paved the way for the intercontinental ballistic missiles, capable of laying waste to entire cities, that emerged in the atomic age.

Black troops were a deciding factor in the North's ability to prosecute the war to its final conclusion, and their heroism, service, and sacrifice were decisive in making it possible for the Union to be victorious. In the years that followed, soldiers of African-American descent continued to be segregated in the army. They served with distinction in taming the West and during the Spanish-American War and both World Wars. It was not until the Korean Conflict that black troops were fully integrated and the all-black units disappeared. In the meantime, these men had forged a tradition of military accomplishment crowned with glory and respect.

Women would seek to do their part in all of this nation's conflicts, and though no women were successful in joining the ranks as many had done during the Civil War, they still found ways to serve. The WAAFs, WACs, and WAVEs of later generations became a modern-day equivalent for women desiring to do more than work in a factory or volunteer time in a canteen. Many of the duties they performed freed up men to serve in combat, as these brave ladies did their part in uniform.

The marines are the unit that experienced the greatest shift in responsibility in the decades following the war. In their limited appearances in the Civil War, they performed with great courage and devotion, but neither the Confederates nor the Union employed enough marines to make a real impact on the outcome. In World War II, their role was expanded from shipboard and garrison duty to become a premier strike force of the U.S. military. As elite and special forces, they have generally become the country's first responders in times of military necessity. Though still the smallest of the nation's four primary branches of service, the fighting men of the Marine Corps are among the most respected in the world.

Native American units, for the most part, fought gallantly when called upon to do so in the war. Following that conflict, they were incorporated into the mainstream of the military and, unlike blacks, were no longer segregated in individual units. One notable exception to this is the Navajo code talkers of World War II, when the nation adopted the complex native language of the Navajo upon which to base a secret code. Fighting in the Pacific Theater, the code talkers played a critical part in keeping U.S. messages and intelligence from falling into enemy hands.

The Signal Corps performed spectacularly during the war, providing officers in the field with rapid and accurate communications. They helped to achieve a cohesiveness to the chain of command that was essential in the management of such large bodies of men and gave field commanders the ability to react to the ever-changing conditions on the battlefield in real time. The work of the Signal Corps continued to grow in the postwar years, as new technology pushed the frontiers of communication. Signal flags were replaced with telephone packs and walkie-talkies as science improved methods for the transferal of information. Through it all, the Signal Corps had steadfastly attained its mission, the transmission and receiving of critical intelligence and orders in combat zones throughout the world.

The Junior and Senior Reserves were units seen only in the Civil War. In no other period of U.S. military history have such units existed. They were formed out of a dire necessity to increase manpower in a Confederate army that had been bled beyond its available resources during the four years of war. Long on determination but short on troops, the South was forced to adopt radical measures or accept the defeat of its cause. Possessed of the same gritty spirit that had sustained an army at Valley Forge, in another civil war, the Confederacy opted to fight on to the bitter end, using every able-bodied man and boy at its disposal. The reserves allowed the Confederate army to gain strength through the addition of troops that would have been otherwise occupied if they had not been formed. In this respect, they were a great success, and their organization can be understood. Their limited exposure to trials of battle were not exemplary, but they were little different from any other raw troops, regardless of their age. The war ended before these soldiers had an opportunity to become veterans and show their full capabilities.

Sappers and miners had limited use, and that was principally on the side of the Union. Vicksburg and Petersburg served as the main arenas for this sort of activity, and even then much of what was done was accomplished by common soldiers in the ranks instead of by trained engineers. The threat of engineering operations had convinced Joe Johnston to evacuate his position at Yorktown without making a stand and was a key to the campaign. Likewise, at Vicksburg, the sapping and mining activities of the Union army played a part in the Union victory. General Pemberton, surrounded and cut off, had endured a month-long siege in his works. His troops were running low on everything, especially food. The knowledge that his army was soon to lose the protection of their earthen fortifications as well must have had a great influence on his decision to surrender his army and give Grant possession of the strategic city of Vicksburg.

As with many other units to see their debut in the Civil War, the Balloon Corps was not fully utilized and never achieved the success that it might have. Aerial observation of the enemy was in its formative stages, and though the Balloon Corps accredited itself well in the somewhat limited nature in which it was used, army commanders, for the most part, failed to grasp the advantage this form of intelligence could have provided if properly harnessed and employed. The U.S. Balloon Corps would be resurrected 50 years after its predecessor had ceased to exist, when it was called on again to provide needed observation and intelligence in the French countryside during World War I.

The Ambulance Corps made one of the greatest contributions to the war effort of any of the specialized units. Though they played no role in the outcome of battles, the medical professionals who made up the corps saved tens of thousands of lives through the advancement of the evacuation and treatment of the wounded. The Ambulance Corps operated as a well-oiled machine in the performance of its duties and served as a model for the armies of the world. The concepts upon which Letterman based its developments are still in use today, where they continue to save lives.

Partisan rangers have existed in many wars, where bands of dedicated men harassed and confounded their enemies by preying on their lines of communication and supply. In the Civil War, some were more successful at accomplishing this mission than others. John Singleton Mosby achieved legendary status operating behind enemy-controlled lines and was a source of major irritation and embarrassment to Federal authorities, causing an inordinate number of troops to be siphoned away from the front to guard against his incursions. Some units of rangers, like Quantrill's Raiders, took advantage of the situation to acquire profit or to settle old blood feuds that had nothing to do with the war. In all cases, the existence of partisan ranger units in a theater of operations kept the enemy ever vigilant and in a state of alarm, never knowing when or where the next strike might take place.

The spies and scouts of both North and South risked their lives to gain and convey information that could turn the tide of battle for their respective side. In this cloak-and-dagger world, they operated in shadows and secrecy, rarely gaining the attention or approval their deeds deserved. In many cases, they were aided by the carelessness and indifference of their enemies, who failed to realize the importance of securing their motives and plans. The United States was still very much in a state of innocence during the war, and to many the deadly game of espionage seemed like a thrilling adventure. In later wars, espionage and counterespionage would assume a greater and more serious tone, as the business of gathering information became even more dangerous and deadly.

CONCLUSION

There is an old saying that military leaders usually employ tactics and strategies that are one war behind the military technology currently available to them. This was certainly the case in the Civil War. Commanders on both sides had been instructed in the science of war according to the philosophies of Napoléon. While these tactics and strategies had been revolutionary in Europe at the turn of the nineteenth century, they were outdated and obsolete half a century later when they were used on the North American continent. The principle of massed infantry worked well with smoothbore muskets having an accurate range of only 50 yards, but it was the next thing to murder when sending lines of closely formed troops against rifled muskets having a range six times that distance. The primary reason why the Civil War became the bloodiest in U.S. history is due to the fact that field commanders continued to fight with old ideas while facing new and improved weapons.

The Civil War is considered to be the first modern war. In many respects, this is true. This war, fought during the rise of the Industrial Revolution, incorporated many scientific and technological advances. Among these were the machine gun, the telegraph, ironclad ships, the first successful submarine, and the first use of railroads in war, to name a few. Indeed, the Civil War ushered in a new era of warfare for the world, and future wars would be deadlier and more horrible than any in the history of mankind. It is also true that the Civil War was the last romantic war, the last to be fought with visions of glory and fame in the minds of the combatants. The citizen soldiers that filled the ranks of both armies were as affected by the old ideals of war as were the commanders who led them. It is for this reason that lances and pikes could be issued to recruits as weapons of war at a time when repeating rifles were making their appearance on the battlefield. Courage and audacity were held in high esteem, and it was felt that these qualities could turn the tide of battle on any field. In reality, firepower and mobility had replaced courage and audacity as the most important factors for winning battles.

Much of the lure of the Civil War comes from the blending of old and new that was such a part of this conflict. To be sure, the martial pageantry displayed on so many fields of battle was the stuff of legend. It is difficult to think of Pickett's sweeping charge across the fields of Gettysburg without being caught up in the grandeur of the spectacle. It is also true that Pickett's Charge ended so disastrously because of the rifled muskets and artillery into which they charged. The capacity to kill had exceeded the capacity of bravery to over-come obstacles, the power of sheer will to drive an enemy from his post. The greatest tribute that can be paid to the soldiers and sailors of the Civil War is that they continued to do their duty in spite of this new capacity for killing. They adapted, as best they could, to the new developments of warfare and stood fast to the cause they espoused with a dedication born of innocence. In doing so, they established a record of service that is a source of pride to all Americans.

I hope you have enjoyed these stories about the unique and unusual units to fight in the Civil War. May they give you a fuller understanding of this climac-tic period in our nation's history and a deeper appreciation for the men and women who did their part to mold the country in which we all now live.

NOTES

CHAPTER 1

1. Brown, Jacob, *Brown's Miscellaneous Writings Upon a Great Variety of Subjects*, J. J. Miller, Cumberland, MD, 1896, pgs. 37–38.

2. Randall, Ruth Painter, *Colonel Elmer Ellsworth*, Little, Brown and Company, Boston, MA, 1960, pg. 229.

3. Ingraham, Charles A., *Elmer E. Ellsworth and the Zouaves of '61*, University of Chicago Press, Chicago, IL, 1925, pg. 128.

4. Randall, pgs. 257–258.

5. Murray, R. L., *"They Fought Like Tigers": The 11th New York Fire Zouaves, 14th Brooklyn and the Irish 69th at First Bull Run*, Benedum Books, Wolcott, NY, 2005, pg. 110.

6. Poland, Charles P., Jr., *The Glories of War: Small Battles and Early Heroes of 1861*, Author House, Bloomington, IN, 2006, pg. 213.

7. Dyer, Frederick H., *A Compendium of the War of the Rebellion*, Thomas Yoseloff, New York, NY, 1959, pgs. 1406–1407.

8. Bates, Samuel P., *History of Pennsylvania Volunteers 1861–5,* vol. 3, B. Singerly, Harrisburg, PA, 1869–71, pgs. 1183–1187.

9. Bates, vol. 2, pg. 945; and Campbell, Joseph, *Marching Orders: The Civil War Diary of Alexander Crawford Gwin*, Daisy Publishing, Altoona, PA, 1999, pg. 23.

10. Bates, vol. 2, pgs. 956–949.

11. Brooks, Ross, "Desperate Stand: Wheat's First Special Battalion, Louisiana Volunteer Infantry on Matthew's Hill, 21 July 1861," *Military Collector and Historian*, Fall 2007, pg. 157.

12. Bergeron, Arthur W., Jr., *Guide to Louisiana Confederate Military Units 1861–1865*, Louisiana State University Press, Baton Rouge, LA, 1989, pgs. 149–150.

CHAPTER 2

1. Cabot, Stephen, *Report of the Draft Riot in Boston July 14, 1863*, Veterans Association of the 1st Massachusetts Heavy Artillery, Boston, MA, 1863, pg. 5.

2. Garrison, Webb, *Civil War Curiosities: Strange Stories, Oddities, Events and Coincidences*, Rutledge Hill Press, Nashville, TN, 1994, pgs. 129–130.

3. Taylor, Frank H., *Philadelphia in the Civil War*, published by the author, Philadelphia, PA, 1879, pgs. 48–184.

4. Bates, vol. 2, pg. 741; and Meade, George, *The Life and Letters of George Gordon Meade*, vol. 1, Charles Scribner's Sons, New York, NY, 1913, pgs. XV–1.

5. Garrison, pg. 129; and Blaschek, Joseph, "The Story of Rush's Lancers," *The National Tribune*, June 24, 1897.

6. Bates, vol. 2, pg. 741.

7. Ibid., pg. 742.

8. Ibid.

9. Brooksher, William R., and Snider, David K., *Glory at a Gallop: Tales of the Confederate Cavalry*, Brassey's, Washington, DC, 1993, pgs. 10–15.

10. Bates, vol. 2, pgs. 744–745.

CHAPTER 3

1. Albaugh, William A., III, *Confederate Edged Weapons*, Harper & Brothers, New York, NY, 1960, pgs. 146–148.

2. Ibid., pgs. 148–149; and Lord, Francis A., *Civil War Collector's Encyclopedia: Arms, Uniforms, and Equipment of the Union and Confederacy*, Stackpole Company, Harrisburg, PA, 1965, pg. 194.

3. Ibid., pg. 150.

4. Ibid., pg. 154.

5. *The Southern Banner*, February 12, 1862.

6. Brown, Rodney Hilton, *American Polearms, 1526–1865*, N. Flaaderman & Co., Inc., New Milford, CT, 1967, pg. 123.

7. Ibid., pg. 134.

8. Chandler, Allen D., *The Confederate Records of the State of Georgia*, vol. 2, Charles P. Byrd, State Printer, Atlanta, GA, 1909, pg. 199.

9. Ibid., pg. 350.

10. Ibid., pgs. 344–353.

11. Brown, pg. 250.

12. Lord, pgs. 57–58.

13. Gordon, John B., *Reminiscences of the Civil War*, Charles Scribner's Sons, New York, NY, 1905, pg. 5.

CHAPTER 4

1. Hedberg, Jonas, *Kungliga Artilleriet: Det Ridande Artilleriet*, Stockholm, Sweden, 1987, pgs. 11–13.

2. Graham, C. A. L., *The Story of the Royal Regiment of Artillery*, Royal Artillery Institution, Woolwich, UK, 1939, pgs. 24–25.

3. Von, R., "About the Use of Horse Artillery," *Nues Militarisches Magazin*, 1802, pgs. 10–14.

4. Johns Hopkins, Baltimore Heritage, "Henry Thompson's Clifton Mansion," *Explore Baltimore Heritage*, accessed January 1, 2014.

5. Johnson, Jameson Riley, "The Birth of Modern Artillery in the 1846–48 War Against Mexico," *The Artilleryman*, Winter 1998, vol. 20, no. 1.

6. Boatner, Mark M., III, *The Civil War Dictionary*, David McKay Company, Inc., New York, NY, 1959, pg. 121.

7. Hassler, William W., "John Pelham of the Horse Artillery," *Civil War Times Illustrated*, August 1964, vol. 3, no. 5.

8. Ibid.

9. Hassler, "John Pelham of the Horse Artillery"; and Wise, Jennings Cropper, *The Long Arm of Lee; or, The History of the Artillery of the Army of Northern Virginia*, J. P. Bell Company, Inc., Lynchburg, VA, 1915, pgs. 262, 298–300.

10. Hassler, "John Pelham of the Horse Artillery."

11. Ibid.

12. McDonald, William, *A History of the Laurel Brigade, Originally the Ashby Cavalry of Northern Virginia and Chew's Battery*, Sun Job Printing Office, Baltimore, MD, 1907, pgs. 31–33.

CHAPTER 5

1. Peterson, Harold L., *Arms and Armor in Colonial America, 1526–1783*, Currier Dover Publications, Mineola, NY, 2000, pgs. 217–218.

2. Davis, Burke, *The Civil War: Strange & Fascinating Facts*, Fairfax Press, New York, NY, 1960, pg. 56.

3. Lord, pg. 159.

4. Chin, George M., *The Machine Gun: History, Evolution, and Development of Manual, Automatic, and Airborne Repeating Weapons*, U.S. Government Printing Office, Washington, DC, 1951, pgs. 39–40.

5. Davis, *The Civil War: Strange & Fascinating Facts*, pgs. 57–58.

6. Ibid., pg. 58.

7. Ibid., pgs. 59–60.

8. Ibid., pg. 60.

9. Kling, Warren, "The Story of Josephus Requa (1833–1910), a Dentist, and His Civil War Machine Gun," *Epitaph*, Rochester, NY, vol. 19, no. 4, Fall 1999.

10. Ibid.

11. Chin, pg. 42.

12. Ibid., pgs. 42–43; and Hegsted, Lyle, "Retired Engineer Keeps Busy When He Sets Out to Make Williams Gun," *The Artilleryman*, Spring 2002.

13. Chin, pg. 45.

14. Chin, pgs. 48–54; and Davis, *The Civil War: Strange & Fascinating Facts*, pg. 60.

CHAPTER 6

1. Phisterer, Frederick, *New York in the War of the Rebellion 1861–1865*, J. B. Lyon Company, Albany, NY, 1912, pgs. 247–249.

2. Ibid.

3. Wise, Jennings Cropper, *The Long Arm of Lee; or, The History of the Artillery of the Army of Northern Virginia*, vol. 1, J. P. Bell Company, Inc., Lynchburg, VA, 1915, pgs. 212–213.

4. Wise, pg. 233; Davis, Burke, *Jeb Stuart: The Last Cavalier*, Fairfax Press, New York, NY, 1967, pg. 145; and Wert, Jeffry D., *Cavalryman of the Lost Cause: A Biography of J. E. B. Stuart,* Simon & Schuster, New York, NY, 2008, pg. 112.

5. Kerr, Jeffrey S., "The Yankees Are Coming!" *Austin Post*, December 5, 2012.

6. Kellersberger, Getulius, The First (and Last) Rocket Battery of the Confederate Army in Texas, *Civil War Times Illustrated*, vol. 2, no. 3, June 1963, pgs. 26–27; and Sundstrom, Helen, *Memoirs of an Engineer in the Confederate Army in Texas*, privately printed, 1957, pgs. 33–34.

7. Ibid.

8. Davis, Burke, *The Civil War: Strange & Fascinating Facts*, Fairfax Press, New York, NY, 1960, pgs. 245–246.

CHAPTER 7

1. Croddy, Eric, Perez-Armendariz, Clarissa, and Hart, John, *Chemical and Biological Warfare: A Comprehensive Survey for the Concerned Citizen*, Copernicus Books, Gottingen, Germany, 2002, pg. 86.

2. Coleman, Kim, *A History of Chemical Warfare*, Palgrave MacMillan, New York, NY, 2005, pg. 7.

3. Wyndham, Miles, "The Idea of Chemical Warfare in Modern Times," *Journal of the History of Ideas*, vol. 31, no. 2, 1970, pgs. 297–304.

4. Smart, Jeffrey K., "Chemical & Biological Warfare Research & Development During the Civil War," *CBIAC Newsletter*, vol. 5, no. 2, 2004.

5. Ibid.

6. Ibid.

7. Ibid.

8. Ibid.

9. Ibid.

10. Wiley, Bell I., "Drop Poison Gas From a Balloon," *Civil War Times Illustrated*, August 1997.

11. Bell, Andrew McIlwaine, *Mosquito Soldiers: Malaria, Yellow Fever, and the Course of the American Civil War*, Louisiana State University Press, Baton Rouge, LA, 2010, pg. 104.

12. Clarke, Albert, *Stories of Our Soldiers*, Journal Newspaper Company, Boston, MA, 1893, pg. 229.

13. Sherman, William T., *Memoirs of General W. T. Sherman: Written by Himself*, vol. 1, D. Appleton and Company, New York, NY, 1875, pg. 331.

CHAPTER 8

1. Griffith, Thomas Walters, *Annals of Baltimore*, William Woody, Baltimore, MD, 1833, pg. 257.

2. Field, Ron, *The Confederate Army 1861–65: Missouri, Kentucky & Maryland*, Osprey Publishing, Oxford, UK, 2008, pg. 33.

3. Round, Harold F., "Hooker's Light Division," *Civil War Times Illustrated*, Harrisburg, PA, July 1966, pg. 21.

4. Ibid., pgs. 22–23.

5. Ibid.

6. Brewer, A. T., *History of the Sixty-First Regiment Pennsylvania Volunteers 1861–1865*, Regimental Association, Art Engraving & Printing Co., Pittsburgh, PA, 1911, pg. 48.

7. Round, pg. 23.

8. Sears, Stephen W., *Chancellorsville*, Houghton Mifflin Company, Boston, MA, 1996, pgs. 352, 355.

9. Round, pg. 223; and Sears, pgs. 256–257.

10. Round, pgs. 23, 25.

CHAPTER 9

1. Chandler, Charles deForest, and Lahm, Frank P., *How Our Army Grew Wings: Airmen and Aircraft Before 1914*, Ronald Press Company, New York, NY, 1943, pgs. 6–8.

2. Chandler, pgs. 10–11; and Davis, *The Civil War: Strange & Fascinating Facts*, pg. 51.

3. Chandler, pgs. 16–17.

4. Haydon, F. Stansbury, *Military Ballooning During the Early Civil War*, Johns Hopkins University Press, Baltimore, MD, 2000, pgs. 39–56.

5. Davis, *The Civil War: Strange and Fascinating Facts*, pgs. 51–52.

6. Crouch, Tom D., *The Eagle Aloft: Two Centuries of the Balloon in America*, Smithsonian Institution Press, Washington, DC, 1983, pgs. 362–368; Evans, Charles M., *War of the Aeronauts: A History of Ballooning in the Civil War*, Stackpole Books, Mechanicsburg, PA, 2002, pg. 133; and Jaeger, Michael, and Lauritzen, Carol, *Memoirs of Thaddeus S. C. Lowe, Chief of the Aeronautic Corps of the Army of the United States During the Civil War: My Balloons in Peace and War*, Edwin Mellen Press, Lewistown, NY, 2004, pg. 73.

7. Hassler, William W., "Professor T. S. C. Lowe," *Civil War Times Illustrated*, vol. 6, no. 5, August 1967, pgs. 12–14.

8. Haydon, pg. 175.

9. Chandler, pg. 25.

10. Ibid., pgs. 25–26.

11. Hassler, pg. 16.

12. Ibid.

13. Evans, pgs. 179–180.

14. Jaeger, pgs. 119–121.

15. Hassler, pgs. 17–18.

16. Davis, *The Civil War: Strange & Fascinating Facts*, pgs. 54–55.

17. Davis, *The Civil War: Strange & Fascinating Facts*, pg. 55; and Hoehling, Mary, *Thaddeus Lowe: America's One-Man Air Corps*, Julian Messner, Inc., New York, NY, 1958, pg. 164.

CHAPTER 10

1. Heidler, David S., and Heidler, Jeanne T., *Encyclopedia of the American Civil War: A Political, Social and Military History*, W. W. Norton & Company, New York, NY, 2000, pgs. 1380–1381; and Brown, J. Willard, *The Signal Corps, U.S.A. in the War of the Rebellion*, Arno Press, New York, NY, 1974, pg. 20.
2. Brown, J. Willard, pgs. 20–21.
3. Heidler, pg. 20–21.
4. Raines, Rebecca Robbins, *Getting the Message Through: A Branch History of the U.S. Army Signal Corps*, United States Army Center of Military History, Washington, DC, 1996, pgs. 7–8; and Brown, J. Willard, pgs. 43–44.
5. Raines, pgs. 9–11.
6. Foster, G. Allen, *The Eyes and Ears of the Civil War*, Criterion Books, New York, NY, 1963, pg. 10.
7. Ibid., pgs. 10–12.
8. Bates, David Homer, *Lincoln in the Telegraph Office: Recollections of the United States Military Telegraph Corps During the Civil War*, D. Appleton, New York, NY, 1907, pg. 25; and Plum, William Rattle, *The Military Telegraph During the Civil War in the United States*, Arno Press, New York, NY, 1974, vol. 1, pg. 67.
9. Raines, pgs. 13, 17–22.
10. Ibid., pgs. 22–23.
11. Brown, J. Willard, pgs. 241–242.
12. Sears, Stephen W., *Landscape Turned Red: The Battle of Antietam*, Ticknor and Fields, New Haven, CT, 1983, pg. 286.
13. Sears, Stephen W., *Chancellorsville*, Houghton Mifflin, Boston, MA, 1996, pgs. 194–196.
14. *War of the Rebellion: A Compilation of the Official Records of the Union and Confederate Armies*, Government Printing Office, Washington, DC, 1891, Series 1, vol. 27, pt. 3, pg. 488. Hereafter referred to as *O.R.*
15. Raines, pg. 26.
16. Brown, J. Willard, pg. 367.
17. Foster, pgs. 11–12.
18. Raines, pg. 29.
19. Galligher, Gary W., *The Personal Recollections of General Edward Porter Alexander*, University of North Carolina Press, Chapel Hill, NC, 1989, pgs. 37–39, 50.
20. Raines, pg. 30.

CHAPTER 11

1. Eicher, John H., and Eicher, David J., *Civil War High Commands*, Stanford University Press, Stanford, CA, 2001, pg. 129.

2. Stevens, C. A., *Berdan's United States Sharpshooters in the Army of the Potomac 1861–1865*, Morningside House Inc., Dayton, OH, 1984, pgs. 1–5.

3. Ibid., pgs. 9–11.

4. Kurtz, Henry I., "Berdan's Sharpshooters Most Effective Union Brigade?" *Civil War Times Illustrated*, February 1963, vol. 1, no. 10.

5. Edwards, William B., *Civil War Guns*, Stackpole Company, Harrisburg, PA, 1962, pg. 212.

6. McAulay, John D., *Civil War Breech Loading Rifles: A Survey of the Innovative Infantry Arms of the American Civil War*, Andrew Mowbray Inc., Lincoln, RI, 1991, pg. 77.

7. Kurtz.

8. Lasswell, Mary, *Rags and Hope: The Recollections of Val C. Giles, Four Years with Hood's Brigade, Fourth Texas Infantry, 1861–1865*, Coward-McCann, New York, NY, 1961, pg. 180.

9. Dyer, Frederick H., *A Compendium of the War of the Rebellion*, vol. 3, Thomas Yoseloff, New York, NY, 1959, pgs. 1280–1281.

10. National Archives Records Group 393, Washington, DC, pg. 304–305.

11. Edwards, pgs. 142–143.

12. Coffin, Charles, *My Days and Nights on the Battlefield*, Dana Estes Co., Boston, MA, 1887, pgs. 92–93.

13. Dillahunty, Albert, *Shiloh*, National Park Service, Government Printing Office, Washington, DC, 1955, pg. 12.

14. Billby, Joseph G., *A Revolution in Arms: A History of the First Repeating Rifles*, Westholm Publishing, Yardley, PA, 2006, pg. 133.

15. Dyer, vol. 2, pg. 1076.

16. Sifikas, Stewart, *Compendium of the Confederate Armies: Mississippi*, Facts on File, New York, NY, 1992, pg. 79.

17. Bergeron, pgs. 167–168.

18. Buck, Irving, *Cleburne and His Command*, Morningside Press, Dayton, OH, 1985, pg. 128.

19. Leon, Louis, *A Diary of a Tar Heel Confederate Soldier*, Eastern Digital Resources, Clearwater, SC, 2003, pg. 30.

20. McClure, Alexander K., *Annals of War*, Blue and Grey Press, Edison, NJ, 1996, pgs. 270–271.

21. McKinney, Tom, "Jack Hinson's One Man War," *The Kentucky Civil War Bugle*, April–June 2010, vol. 4, no. 2.

CHAPTER 12

1. Breeden, James O., "Field Medicine at Antietam," *Caduceus: A Museum Quarterly for Health Sciences*, 1994, vol. 10, no. 1, pgs. 10–14.

2. Adams, George W., *Doctors in Blue: The Medical History of the Union Army in the Civil War*, Henry Schuman, Inc., New York, NY, 1952, pgs. 61–62.

3. Freeman, Frank R., *Gangrene and Glory: Medical Care During the American Civil War*, Associated University Press, Cranbury, NJ, 1998, pg. 76.

4. Billings, John D., *Hard Tack and Coffee: Soldier's Life in the Civil War*, Konecky & Konecky, New York, NY, 2005, pg. 299.

5. Wilbur, C. Keith, *Civil War Medicine 1861–1865*, Globe Pequot Press, Guilford, CT, 1998, pgs. 33–34.

6. Ibid., pgs. 36–37.

7. Ibid.

8. Price, William H., *The Civil War Centennial Handbook*, Prince Lithographic Co., Inc., Arlington, VA, 1961, pg. 67.

9. Breeden, pg. 12.

10. Denney, Robert E., *Civil War Medicine: Care and Comfort of the Wounded*, Sterling Publishing Co., Inc., New York, NY, 1994, pg. 162.

11. Miller, Francis Trevelyan, *The Photographic History of the Civil War*, vol. 2, Review of Reviews Co., New York, NY, 1911, pg. 308.

12. Ibid., pg. 310.

13. Ibid., pg. 308.

14. *O.R.*, vol. 36, pgs. 550–552.

15. Freeman, pg. 162.

16. Musto, R. J., "The Treatment of the Wounded at Gettysburg: Jonathan Letterman, the Father of Modern Battlefield Medicine," *Gettysburg Magazine*, Issue 37, 2007.

17. Freeman, pgs. 31–32.

18. Ibid., pg. 41.

19. Gildersleeve, John R., "History of Chimborazo Hospital, Richmond, Va., and its Medical Officers During 1861–1865," *Virginia Medical Semi-Monthly*, July 8, 1904.

20. Jones, John W., *The Southern Historical Society Papers*, vol. 25, Southern Historical Society, Richmond, VA, 1897, pgs. 113–116.

21. Wilbur, pg. 63.

CHAPTER 13

1. Mosby, John Singleton, and Russell, Charles Wells, *The Memoirs of Colonel John S. Mosby*, Little, Brown and Company, New York, NY, 1917, pgs. 7–8; and Ramage, James A., *Rebel Raider: The Life of General John Hunt Morgan*, University Press of Kentucky, Lexington, KY, 1986, pgs. 20–24.

2. Longacre, Edward G., *Lee's Cavalrymen: A History of the Mounted Forces of the Army of Northern Virginia*, Stackpole Books, Mechanicsburg, PA, 2002, pg. 107.

3. Munson, John W., *Reminiscences of a Mosby Guerilla*, Zenger Publishing Co., Washington, DC, 1983, pg. 25.

4. Ibid., pgs. 24–25.

5. Wert, Jeffry D., *Mosby's Rangers: The True Adventures of the Most Famous Command of the Civil War*, Touchstone Books, New York, NY, 1990, pgs. 20–22.

6. Keen, Hugh C., and Mewborn, Horace, *43rd Battalion Virginia Cavalry: Mosby's Command*, H. E. Howard, Inc., Lynchburg, VA, 1993, pg. 11.

7. Williamson, James J., *Mosby's Rangers: A Record of the Operations of the Forty-Third Battalion Virginia Cavalry*, Ralph B. Kenyon, Publisher, New York, NY, 1896, pgs. 208–210.

8. Ibid., pgs. 261–263.

9. Alexander, John H., *Mosby's Men*, Neale Publishing Company, New York, NY, 1907, pgs. 140–148.

10. Wert, pgs. 249–250.

11. Munson, pg. 228.

12. Jones, Virgil Carrington, *Gray Ghosts and Rebel Raiders*, Holt, Rinehart and Winston, New York, NY, 1956, pg. 112.

13. *O.R.*, Series 1, vol. 21, pgs. 747–748.

14. Ibid., vol. 25, pt. 2, pgs. 642–643.

15. Ibid., vol. 25, pt. 1, pgs. 105, 134.

16. Ibid., vol. 29, pt. 1, pg. 106.

17. Lepa, Jack H., *The Shenandoah Valley Campaign of 1864*, McFarland Publishers, Inc., Jefferson, NC, 2003, pg. 28.

18. Jones, pgs. 305–307.

19. Ibid., pgs. 356–362.

20. Dupuy, Trevor N., Johnson, Curt, and Bongard, David L., *Harper Encyclopedia of Military Biography*, Castle Books, New York, NY, 1992, pg. 525.

21. Harper, Robert S., *Ohio Handbook of the Civil War*, Ohio Historical Society, Columbus, OH, 1961, pg. 23.

22. Dupuy, pg. 525.

CHAPTER 14

1. Beymer, William Gilmore, *Scouts and Spies of the Civil War*, University of Nebraska Press, Lincoln, NE, 2003, pg. 3.

2. Ibid., pg. 4.

3. Bakeless, John, *Spies of the Confederacy*, J. B. Lippincott Company, Philadelphia, PA, 1970, pgs. 314–315.

4. Simon, John Y., and Bridges, Roger D., *The Papers of Ulysses S. Grant, Volume 4: January 8–March 31, 1862*, Southern Illinois University Press, Carbondale, IL, 1972, pgs. 16–17.

5. Beymer, pgs. 12–14.

6. Mackey, Robert O., *The Uncivil War: Irregular Warfare in the Upper South, 1861–1865*, University of Oklahoma Press, Norman, OK, 2004, pg. 109.

7. Record Group 94, Regimental Order Book, 91st Ohio Volunteer Infantry, National Archives, Washington, DC.

8. Stephenson, Darl L., *Headquarters in the Brush: Blazer's Independent Union Scouts*, Ohio University Press, Athens, OH, 2001, pg. 27.

9. Ibid., pg. 45.

10. Record Group 393, vol. 106, pt. 2, West Virginia, entries 1158–1159, National Archives, Washington, DC.

11. Schmitt, Martin F., *General George Crook: His Autobiography*, University of Oklahoma Press, Norman, OK, 1946, pg. 135.

12. Munson, pg. 124.

13. Ramage, James A., *Gray Ghost*, The University Press of Kentucky, Lexington, KY, 1999, pg. 224.

14. Williamson, pgs. 226–227; and *O.R.*, Series 1, vol. 43, pt. 1, pg. 615.

15. Wert, *Mosby's Rangers,* pg. 252.

16. Williamson, pg. 302.

17. *O.R.*, Series 1, vol. 43, pt. 2, pg. 654.

18. Baker, Lafayette C., *The United States Secret Service in the Late War*, World Bible House, Philadelphia, PA, 1890, pgs. 45–74, 76.

19. Bakeless, pgs. 7–10.

CHAPTER 15

1. Freehling, William W., *The Road to Disunion*, vol. 2, Oxford University Press, New York, NY, 2007, pg. 212.

2. Asprey, Robert B., "The Assault on Fort Fisher," *The Marine Corps Gazette*, November 1965.

3. Lord, pgs. 315–318.

4. Sullivan, David M., "The Marine Battalion at the Battle of Bull Run: Emending the Record," *Leatherneck Magazine*, February 2002.

5. *O.R.*, vol. 2, pg. 383.

6. Sullivan.

7. Ibid.

8. Ibid.

9. Ibid.

10. Graham, C. R., *Under Both Flags: A Panorama of the Great Civil War*, W. S. Reeve Publishing Co., Chicago, IL, 1896, pgs. 395–396.

11. Alexander, Joseph H., "Civil War Marines: Four Frustrating Years," *Leatherneck Magazine*, November 2007.

12. Asprey.

13. Donnelly, Ralph W., *The Confederate States Marine Corps: The Rebel Leathernecks*, White Mane Publishing, Shippensburg, PA, 1989, pg. 4.

14. Lord, pg. 289.

15. Rawson, Edward K., and Woods, Robert H., *Official Records of the Union and Confederate Navies in the War of the Rebellion*, Series II, vol. 1, Government Printing Office, Washington, DC, 1898, pg. 308. Hereafter referred to as *O.R. Navy*.

16. Naval History Division, Navy Department, *Civil War Naval Chronology 1861–1865*, Government Printing Office, Washington, DC, 1971, pt. 4, pgs. 12–13. Hereafter referred to as *Civil War Naval Chronology*.

17. Ibid., pg. 67.

18. Broadwater, Robert P., "Fort Fisher: Gibraltar of the Confederacy," *Confederate Veteran Magazine*, vol. 1, 1998.

19. *Civil War Naval Chronology*, pt. 5, pg. 78; and Salmon, John S., *The Official Virginia Battlefield Guide*, Stackpole Books, Mechanicsburg, PA, 2001, pg. 480.

CHAPTER 16

1. Dyer, pgs. 1280, 1321, 1345, 1577, 1709, 1717, 1718.

2. Johnson, Robert Underwood, and Buel, Clarence Clough, *Battles and Leaders of the Civil War*, vol. 2, Century, New York, NY, 1881, pg. 2. Hereafter referred to as *Battles and Leaders*.

3. Ibid., pgs. 2–3.

4. Ibid., pgs. 8–10.

5. Grant, Ulysses S., *Personal Memoirs of U.S. Grant*, vol. 1, Charles L. Webster & Company, New York, NY, 1885, pgs. 374–380.

6. Cozzens, Peter, and Girardi, Robert I., *The New Annals of the Civil War*, Stackpole Books, Mechanicsburg, PA, 2004, pg. 96.

7. Bailey, Ronald H., *Forward to Richmond: McClellan's Peninsula Campaign*, Time-Life Books, Alexandria, VA, 1983, pg. 94.

8. *O.R.*, Series 1, vol. 14, pg. 477.

9. Fishel, Edwin C., *The Secret War for the Union: The Untold Story of Military Intelligence in the Civil War*, Houghton Mifflin, Boston, MA, 1996, pg. 152.

10. *Battles and Leaders*, vol. 3, pgs. 539–542.

11. Pleasants, Henry, Jr., and Straley, George H., *Inferno at Petersburg*, Chilton Company, Philadelphia, PA, 1961, pg. 10.

12. *Battles and Leaders*, vol. 4, pgs. 545–547.

CHAPTER 17

1. Davis, *The Civil War: Strange & Fascinating Facts*, pgs. 63–64.

2. Swanberg, W. A., *First Blood: The Story of Fort Sumter*, Charles Scribner's Sons, New York, NY, 1957, pg. 146.

3. Cohn, Scotti, *Beyond Their Years: Stories of Sixteen Civil War Children*, Twodot, Guilford, CT, 2003, pg. 119.

4. Broadwater, Robert P., *Boy Soldiers and Soldier Boys: Children in the Civil War Armies*, Dixie Drams Press, Bellwood, PA, 2006, pg. 25.

5. Coffey, Michael W., "North Carolina's Youngest Soldiers: The Junior Reserves," *Tar Heel Junior Historian*, Spring 2011.

6. Ibid.

7. Broadwater, Robert P., "Walter Clark: Rebel for All Time," *North South Trader's Civil War*, vol. 25, no. 4.

8. Gragg, Rod, *Confederate Goliath: The Battle of Fort Fisher*, Harper Collins Publishers, New York, NY, 1991, pgs. 91–92.

9. *O.R.*, vol. 47, pg. 1087

10. Hughes, Nathaniel Cheairs, Jr., *Bentonville: The Final Battle of Sherman & Johnston*, University of North Carolina Press, Chapel Hill, NC, 1996, pgs. 174–175.

CHAPTER 18

1. Martin, David G., *Gettysburg July 1*, Combined Publishing, Conshohocken, PA, 1996, pgs. 372, 374; and Pfanz, Harry W., *Gettysburg: The First Day*, University of North Carolina Press, Chapel Hill, NC, 2001, pgs. 357–358.

2. *North Carolina Argus*, December 1, 1864.

3. *Battles and Leaders*, vol. 4, pg. 479.

4. Hinkley, Julian, *Service With the Third Wisconsin Infantry,* History Committee, Madison, WI, 1912, pgs. 171–172.

5. Hughes, Nathaniel Cheairs, Jr., *General William J. Hardee: Old Reliable*, Louisiana State University Press, Baton Rouge, LA, 1965, pgs. 282–283.

6. McLaws Letter Book Journal, March 16, 1865, General Lafayette McLaws Papers, Southern Historical Collection, University of North Carolina, Chapel Hill, NC.

7. *O.R.*, Series 1, vol. 52, pt. 1, pgs. 1020–1021.

8. Gragg, pg. 188.

9. Bradley, Mark L., *Last Stand in the Carolinas: The Battle of Bentonville*, Savas Publishing Company, Campbell, CA, 1996, pg. 296.

10. McClurg, Alexander C., *The Last Chance of the Confederacy*, Military Order of the Loyal Legion of the United States, A. C. McClurg and Company, Chicago, IL, 1891, pgs. 385–386.

11. *O.R.*, Series 1, vol. 47, pt. 2, pgs. 1450–1451.

CHAPTER 19

1. Rhodes, Neil, Richards, Jennifer, and Marshall, Joseph, *King James VI & I: Selected Writings*, Ashgate Publishing, Surrey, UK, 2003, pg. 1.

2. Delgado, James P., *Silent Killers: Submarines and Underwater Warfare*, Osprey Publishing, Oxford, UK, 2011, pgs. 52–53.

3. Davis, *The Civil War: Strange & Fascinating Facts*, pg. 175.

4. *O.R. Navy*, 1898, Series 1, vol. 7, pg. 477.

5. Davis, *The Civil War: Strange & Fascinating Facts*, pg. 175.

6. Veit, Chuck, "The Innovative Mysterious Alligator," *Naval History Magazine*, August 2010, vol. 24, no. 4, pg. 26.

7. Delgado, James P., *Misadventures of a Civil War Submarine: Iron Guns and Pearls*, Texas A&M University Press, College Station, TX, 2012, pg. 99.

8. "The Untold Story of the Intelligent Whale," *Undersea Warfare: The Official Magazine of the U.S. Submarine Force*, Summer 2008, no. 38.

9. Ibid.

10. Veit, Chuck, "Submarines: There More Than the H. L. Hunley," *Civil War Navy: The Magazine*, Winter 2013, vol. 1, issue 2, pgs. 7–8.

11. Naval History Division, Navy Department, *Civil War Naval Chronology 1861–1865*, Government Printing Office, Washington, DC, 1971, pt. 5, pg. 283; and Chaffin, Tom, *The H. L. Hunley: The Secret Hope of the Confederacy*, Hill and Wang, New York, NY, 2008, pgs. 15–16.

12. *Civil War Naval Chronology*, pgs. 283, 286.

13. Ibid., pg. 286.

14. Davis, *The Civil War: Strange and Fascinating Facts*, pgs. 169–170.

15. Ibid., pg. 170.

16. Ibid.

17. Ibid., pg. 171.

18. *Civil War Naval Chronology*, pg. 245.

19. Ibid., pgs. 245–246.

20. Chaffin, Tom, *The H. L. Hunley: The Secret Hope of the Confederacy*, Hill and Wang, New York, NY, 2008, pgs. 247–249.

21. Ibid., pg. 258.

CHAPTER 20

1. Sondhaus, Lawrence, *Naval Warfare 1815–1914*, Routledge Books, London, UK, 2001, pg. 61.

2. Ibid., pgs. 73–76.

3. Symmonds, Craig L., *The Civil War at Sea*, Praeger Books, Santa Barbara, CA, 2009, pg. 15.

4. Hearn, Chester G., *Naval Battles of the Civil War*, Thunder Bay Press, San Diego, CA, 2000, pgs. 65–66; and Hearn, Chester G., *The Capture of New Orleans 1862*, Louisiana State University Press, Baton Rouge, LA, 1995, pgs. 86–91.

5. Hearn, *Capture of New Orleans*, pgs. 210–236.

6. Donovan, Frank R., *Ironclads of the Civil War*, American Heritage Publishing Co., Inc., New York, NY, 1964, pgs. 74–76.

7. Gibbons, Tony, *Warships and Naval Battles of the Civil War*, Gallery Books, New York, NY, 1989, pg. 17.

8. Donovan, pgs. 76–80.

9. Ibid., pgs. 80–83.

10. Freeman, Fred, *Duel of the Ironclads*, New York, NY, 1969, pgs. 7–8; and Egan, Robert S., "Thoughts and Speculation on the Conversion of USS *Merrimack* into CSS *Virginia*," *Warship International*, vol. 42, no. 4, pgs. 362–373.

11. Freeman, pgs. 9, 18, 29.

12. Ibid., pg. 28.

13. Ibid., pgs. 12–13.

14. Pratt, Fletcher, *The Monitor and the Merrimac, and Other Naval Battles*, Landmark Books, New York, NY, 1951, pgs. 73–76.

15. Freeman, pg. 28.

16. Ibid., pgs. 30–31.

17. Ibid., pgs. 35–38.

18. Ibid., pgs. 42–49.

CHAPTER 21

1. Garrison, Webb, *Amazing Women of the Civil War: Fascinating True Stories of Women Who Made a Difference*, Rutledge Hill Press, Nashville, TN, 1999, pgs. 30–31; and Leonard, Elizabeth D., *All the Daring of the Soldier: Women of the Civil War Armies*, Penguin Books, New York, NY, 2001, pgs. 106–110.

2. Leonard, pgs. 114–117; and Broadwater, Robert P., *Daughters of the Cause: Women of the Civil War*, Daisy Press, Martinsburg, PA, 1996, pgs. 14–15.

3. Broadwater, pgs. 12–13.

4. Leonard, pgs. 146–147.

5. Garrison, *Amazing Women of the Civil War*, pgs. 13–20.

6. Broadwater, *Daughters of the Cause*, pgs. 13–14.

7. Ibid., pg. 17.

8. Zeinert, Karen, *Those Courageous Women of the Civil War*, Millbrook Press, Brookfield, CT, 1998, pgs. 24–25.

9. Ibid., pg. 25.

10. Broadwater, *Daughters of the Cause*, pg. 16.

11. Frank, Lisa Tendrich, *An Encyclopedia of American Women at War: From the Home Front to the Battlefields*, ABC-CLIO, Santa Barbara, CA, 2013, vol. 2, pgs. 411–412.

12. Ibid., pg. 412.

13. Rice, Charles, "All-Girl Rhea County Spartans," *America's Civil War*, July 1996, pgs. 8, 77–79.

CHAPTER 22

1. Broadwater, Robert P., *Desperate Deliverance: The Story of African Americans in the Civil War*, Daisy Publications, Martinsburg, PA, 1998, pgs. 3–5.

2. Ibid., pgs. 5–6; and Quarles, Benjamin, *The Negro in the Civil War*, Little, Brown and Company, Boston, MA, 1953, pg. 37.

3. Jordan, Ervin L., Jr., *Black Confederates and Afro-Yankees in Civil War Virginia*, University Press of Virginia, Charlottesville, VA, 1995, pgs. 222–223.

4. *New York Herald*, July 11, 1863.

5. Broadwater, *Desperate Deliverance*, pg. 7.

6. Trudeau, Noah A., *Like Men of War: Black Troops in the Civil War 1862–1865*, Castle Books, Edison, NJ, 2002, pgs. 14–16.

7. Quarles, pgs. 113–114.

8. Wilson, Joseph T., *The Black Phalanx: African American Soldiers in the War of Independence, the War of 1812 & the Civil War*, Da Capo Press, New York, NY, 1994, pgs. 192–196; and Broadwater, *Desperate Deliverance*, pgs. 13–15.

9. Gladstone, William A., *United States Colored Troops 1863–1867*, Thomas Publications, Gettysburg, PA, 1990, pg. 9.

10. Emilio, Luis F., *A Brave Black Regiment: The History of the Fifty-Fourth Regiment of Massachusetts Volunteer Infantry, 1863–1865*, Da Capo Press, New York, NY, 1995, pgs. 1–5.

11. Cox, Clinton, *Undying Glory: The Story of the Massachusetts 54th Regiment*, Scholastic Books, New York, NY, 1991, pg. 90.

12. Broadwater, *Desperate Deliverance*, pgs. 21–22.

13. Rose, Willie Lee, *Rehearsal for Reconstruction: The Port Royal Experiment*, University of Georgia Press, Athens, GA, 1999, pgs. 248–253.

14. Hewitt, Laurence, *Port Hudson: Confederate Bastion on the Mississippi*, Louisiana State University Press, Baton Rouge, LA, 1987, pgs. 140–149.

15. Broadwater, *Desperate Deliverance*, pgs. 19–20.

16. Gladstone, pgs. 9–11; and Broadwater, Robert P., *Civil War Medal of Honor Recipients: A Complete Illustrated Record*, McFarland & Company, Publishers, Inc., Jefferson, NC, 2007, pgs. 243, 252.

17. Wilson, pgs. 444–446.

18. Gragg, pgs. 213, 227.

19. *Battles and Leaders*, vol. 4, Century, pg. 473.

20. Wilson, pgs. 491–494.

21. Broadwater, *Desperate Deliverance*, pg. 66.

CHAPTER 23

1. Hauptman, Laurence M., *Between Two Fires: American Indians in the Civil War*, Free Press, New York, NY, 1995, pg. 66.

2. Broadwater, Robert P., *From Beyond the Battlefields: Civil War Side Shows and Little Known Events*, Dixie Dreams Press, Bellwood, PA, 2003, pgs. 64–65.

3. Ibid., pgs. 78–80.

4. Hauptman, pgs. 125–126, 138–142.

5. Broadwater, Robert P., "The Thomas Legion of North Carolina," *Confederate Veteran Magazine*, vol. 2, 1997, pgs. 32–34.

6. Ibid., pgs. 34–35.

7. Ibid., pgs. 35–36.

8. Ibid., 38–40.

9. Hatch, Thom, *The Blue, the Gray, & the Red: Indian Campaigns of the Civil War*, Stackpole Books, Mechanicsburg, PA, 2003, pgs. 1–8.

10. Ibid., pgs. 8–10.

11. Ibid., pgs. 13–15.

12. Ibid., pgs. 17–21.

13. Shea, William L., and Hess, Earl J., *Pea Ridge: Civil War Campaign in the West*, University of North Carolina Press, Chapel Hill, NC, 1992, pgs. 23–25.

14. Ibid., pgs. 25–27.

15. Hauptman, pgs. 31–32.

16. Ibid., pgs. 33–35.

BIBLIOGRAPHY

MANUSCRIPT COLLECTIONS

The National Archives
University of North Carolina
General Lafayette McLaws Papers

NEWSPAPERS, MAGAZINES, AND PERIODICALS

America's Civil War
The Artilleryman
Austin Post
Baltimore Heritage
Caduceus: A Museum Quarterly for Health Sciences
CBIAC Newsletter
Civil War Navy: The Magazine
Civil War Times Illustrated
Columbiad Journal
Confederate Veteran Magazine
East Texas Historical Journal
Epitaph
Gettysburg Magazine
Journal of the History of Ideas
The Kentucky Civil War Bugle
Leatherneck Magazine
The Marine Corps Gazette
Military Collector and Historian

The National Tribune
Naval History Magazine
New York Herald
North Carolina Argus
North South Trader's Civil War
Nues Militarisches Magazin
The Southern Banner
Tar Heel Junior Historian
Undersea Warfare: The Official Magazine of the U.S. Submarine Force
Warship International

BOOKS

Adams, George W., *Doctors in Blue: The Medical History of the Union Army in the Civil War*, Henry Schuman, Inc., New York, NY, 1952.

Albaugh, William A. III, *Confederate Edged Weapons*, Harper & Brothers, New York, NY, 1960.

Alexander, John H., *Mosby's Men*, The Neale Publishing Company, New York, NY, 1907.

Amann, William, *Personnel of the Civil War*, 2 vols., Thomas Yoseloff, New York, NY, 1968.

Bailey, Ronald H., *Forward to Richmond: McClellan's Peninsula Campaign*, Tine Life Books, Alexandria, VA, 1983.

Bakeless, John, *Spies of the Confederacy*, J. B. Lippincott Company, Philadelphia, PA, 1970.

Baker, LaFayette C., *The United States Secret Service in the Late War*, World Bible House, Philadelphia, PA, 1890.

Bates, David Homer, *Lincoln in the Telegraph Office: Recollections of the United States Military Telegraph Corps During the Civil War*, D. Appleton, New York, NY, 1907.

Bates, Samuel P., *History of Pennsylvania Volunteers, 1861–5*, 5 vols., B. Singerly, Harrisburg, PA, 1869–71.

Bell, Andrew McIlwaine, *Mosquito Soldiers: Malaria, Yellow Fever, and the Course of the American Civil War*, Louisiana State University Press, Baton Rouge, LA, 2010.

Bergeron, Arthur W., Jr., *Guide to Louisiana Confederate Military Units 1861–1865*, Louisiana State University Press, Baton Rouge, LA, 1989.

Beymer, William Gilmore, *Scouts and Spies of the Civil War*, University of Nebraska Press, Lincoln, NE, 2003.

Billby, Joseph G., *A Revolution in Arms: A History of the First Repeating Rifles*, Westholm Publishing, Yardley, PA, 2006.

Billings, John D., *Hard Tack and Coffee: Soldier's Life in the Civil War*, Konecky & Konecky, New York, NY, 2005.

Blanton, DeAnne, and Cook, Lauren M., *They Fought Like Demons: Women Soldiers in the Civil War*, Vintage Books, New York, NY, 2002.

Boatner, Mark M., III, *The Civil War Dictionary*, David McKay Company, Inc., New York, NY, 1959.

Bowley, Freeman S., *A Boy Lieutenant: The 30th United States Colored Troops*, Sergeant Kirkland's Museum, Fredericksburg, VA, 1997.

Boynton, Charles B., *The History of the Navy During the Rebellion*, Appleton Books, New York, NY, 1867–68.

Bradley, Mark L., *Last Stand in the Carolinas: The Battle of Bentonville*, Savas Publishing Company, Campbell, CA, 1996.

Brewer, A. T., *History of the Sixty-First Regiment Pennsylvania Volunteers 1861–1865*, Regimental Association, Art Engraving & Printing Co., Pittsburgh, PA, 1911.

Broadwater, Robert P., *The Battle of Fair Oaks: Turning Point of McClellan's Peninsula Campaign*, McFarland & Company, Inc., Publishers, Jefferson, NC, 2011.

Broadwater, Robert P., *Boy Soldiers and Soldier Boys: Children in the Civil War Armies*, Dixie Dreams Press, Bellwood, PA, 2006.

Broadwater, Robert P., *From Beyond the Battlefields: Civil War Side Shows and Little Known Events,* Dixie Dreams Press, Bellwood, PA, 2003.

Brockett, L. P., and Vaughan, Mary C., *Woman's Work in the Civil War: A Record of Heroism, Patriotism and Patience*, Zeigler, McCurdy & Co., Philadelphia, PA, 1867.

Brooksher, William R., and Snider, David K., *Glory at a Gallop: Tales of the Confederate Cavalry*, Brassey's, Washington, DC, 1993.

Brown, Dee Alexander, *Morgan's Raiders*, Konecky & Konecky, New York, NY, 1959.

Brown, J. Willard, *The Signal Corps, U.S.A. in the War of the Rebellion*, Arno Press, New York, NY, 1974.

Brown, Jacob, *Brown's Miscellaneous Writings Upon a Great Variety of Subjects*, J. J. Miller, Cumberland, MD, 1896.

Brown, Rodney Hilton, *American Polearms, 1526–1865*, N. Fladerman & Co., Inc., New Milford, CT, 1967.

Buck, Irving, *Cleburne and His Commands*, Morningside Press, Dayton, OH, 1985.

Cabot, Stephen, *Report of the Draft Riot in Boston, July 14, 1863*, Veterans Association of the 1st Massachusetts Heavy Artillery, Boston, MA, 1863.

Campbell, R. Thomas, *Fire & Thunder: Exploits of the Confederate States Navy*, Burd Street Press, Shippensburg, PA, 1997.

Chandler, Allen D., *The Confederate Records of the State of Georgia*, vol. 2, Charles P. Byrd, State Printer, Atlanta, GA, 1909.

Chandler, Charles deForest, and Lahm, Frank P., *How Our Army Grew Wings: Airmen and Aircraft Before 1914*, The Ronald Press Company, New York, NY, 1943.

Chin, George M., *The Machine Gun: History, Evolution, and Development of Manual, Automatic, and Airborne Repeating Weapons*, 5 vols., Government Printing Office, Washington, DC, 1951.

Clarke, Albert, *Stories of Our Soldiers*, Journal Newspaper Co., Boston, MA, 1893.

Cochran, Hamilton, *Blockade Runners of the Confederacy*, Bobbs-Merrill Company, Inc., Indianapolis, IN, 1958.

Coffin, Charles, *My Days and Nights on the Battlefield*, Dana Estes Co., Boston, MA, 1887.

Cohn, Scotti, *Beyond Their Years: Stories of Sixteen Civil War Children*, Twodot, Guilford, CT, 2003.

Coleman, Kim, *A History of Chemical Warfare*, Palgrave MacMillan, New York, NY, 2005.

Cornish, Dudley Taylor, *The Sable Arm: Negro Troops in the Union Army 1861–1865*, W. W. Norton & Co., New York, NY, 1966.

Cox, Clinton, *Undying Glory: The Story of the Massachusetts 54th Regiment*, Scholastic Books, New York, NY, 1991.

Cozzens, Peter, and Girardi, Robert I., *The New Annals of the Civil War*, Stackpole Books, Mechanicsburg, PA, 2004.

Croddy, Eric, Perez-Armendariz, Clarissa, and Hart, John, *Chemical and Biological Warfare: A Comprehensive Survey for the Concerned Citizen*, Copernicus Books, Gottigen, Germany, 2002.

Crouch, Tom D., *The Eagle Aloft: Two Centuries of the Balloon in America*, Smithsonian Institution Press, Washington, DC, 1983.

Dannett, Sylvia G. L., *Noble Women of the North*, Thomas Yoseleff, New York, NY, 1959.

Davis, Burke, *The Civil War: Strange & Fascinating Facts*, Fairfax Press, New York, NY, 1960.

Davis, Burke, *Jeb Stuart: The Last Cavalier*, Fairfax Press, New York, NY, 1967.

DeKay, James Teritus, *The Rebel Raiders: The Astonishing History of the Confederacy's Secret Navy*, Ballantine Books, New York, NY, 2002.

Delgado, James P., *Misadventures of a Civil War Submarine: Iron Guns and Pearls*, Texas A&M University Press, College Station, TX, 2012.

Delgado, James P., *Silent Killers: Submarines and Underwater Warfare*, Osprey Publishing, Oxford, UK, 2011.

Denney, Robert E., *Civil War Medicine: Care & Comfort of the Wounded*, Sterling Publishing Co., Inc., New York, NY, 1994.

Dillahunty, Alfred, *Shiloh*, National Park Service, Government Printing Office, Washington, DC, 1955.

Donnelly, Ralph W., *The Confederate States Marine Corps: The Rebel Leathernecks*, White Mane Publishing, Shippensburg, PA, 1989.

Donovan, Frank R., *Ironclads of the Civil War*, American Heritage Publishing Co., Inc., New York, NY, 1964.

Dupuy, Trevor N., Johnson, Curt, and Bongard, David L., *Harper Encyclopedia of Military Biography*, Castle Books, New York, NY, 1992.

Dyer, Frederick H., *A Compendium of the War of the Rebellion*, 3 vols., Thomas Yoseloff, New York, NY, 1959.

Edwards, William B., *Civil War Guns*, Stackpole Company, Harrisburg, PA, 1962.

Eicher, John H., and Eicher, David J., *Civil War High Commands*, Stanford University Press, Stanford, CA, 2001.

Eller, Ernest M., and Knox, Dudley W., *The Civil War at Sea*, Naval Historical Foundation, Washington, DC, 1961.

Emilio, Luis F., *A Brave Black Regiment: The History of the Fifty-Fourth Regiment of Massachusetts Volunteer Infantry*, Da Capo Press, New York, NY, 1995.

Evans, Charles M., *War of the Aeronauts: A History of Ballooning in the Civil War*, Stackpole Books, Mechanicsburg, PA, 2002.

Field, Ron, *The Confederate Army 1861–65: Missouri, Kentucky & Maryland*, Osprey Publishing, Oxford, UK, 2008.

Fishel, Edwin C., *The Secret War for the Union: The Untold Story of Military Intelligence in the Civil War*, Houghton Mifflin Company, Boston, MA, 1996.

Foster, G. Allen, *The Eyes and Ears of the Civil War*, Criterion Books, New York, NY, 1963.

Fowler, William M., Jr., *Under Two Flags: The American Navy in the Civil War*, W. W. Norton & Company, New York, NY, 1990.

Frank, Lisa Tendrich, *An Encyclopedia of American Women at War: From the Home Front to the Battlefields*, 2 vols., ABC-CLIO, Santa Barbara, CA, 2013.

Freehling, William W., *The Road to Disunion*, Oxford University Press, New York, NY, 2007.

Freeman, Frank R., *Gangrene and Glory: Medical Care During the American Civil War*, Associated University Press, Cranbury, NJ, 1998.

Freeman, Fred, *Duel of the Ironclads*, Time-Life Books, Alexandria, VA, 1969.

Garrison, Webb, *Amazing Women of the Civil War: Fascinating True Stories of Women Who Made a Difference*, Rutledge Hill Press, Nashville, TN, 1999.

Garrison, Webb, *Civil War Schemes and Plots,* Gramercy Books, New York, NY, 2001.

Gibbons, Tony, *Warships and Naval Battles of the Civil War*, Gallery Books, New York, NY, 1989.

Gladstone, William A., *United States Colored Troops 1863–1867*, Thomas Publications, Gettysburg, PA, 1990.

Gordon, John B., *Reminiscences of the Civil War,* Charles Scribner's Sons, New York, NY, 1905.

Gorman, Ed, *The Blue and the Gray Undercover: All New Civil War Spy Adventures*, Tom Dougherty Associates, New York, NY, 2001.

Gragg, Rod, *Confederate Goliath: The Battle of Fort Fisher*, Harper/Collins Publishers, New York, NY, 1991.

Graham, C. A. L., *The Story of the Royal Regiment of Artillery*, Royal Artillery Institution, Woolwich, UK, 1939.

Graham, C. R., *Under Both Flags: A Panorama of the Great Civil War*, W. S. Reeve Publishing Co., Chicago, IL, 1896.

Grant, Ulysses S., *Personal Memoirs of U. S. Grant*, 2 vols., Charles L. Webster & Company, New York, NY, 1885.

Griffith, Thomas Walters, *Annals of Baltimore*, William Woody, Baltimore, MD, 1833.

Gwin, Alexander Crawford, *Marching Orders: A Civil War Diary*, Daisy Publishing, Altoona, PA, 1999.

Hall, Richard, *Patriots in Disguise. Women Warriors of the Civil War*, Paragon House, New York, NY, 1993.

Harper, Robert S., *Ohio Handbook of the Civil War*, Ohio Historical Society, Columbus, OH, 1961.

Hatch, Thom, *The Blue, the Gray, & the Red: Indian Campaigns of the Civil War*, Stackpole Books, Mechanicsburg, PA, 2003.

Hauptman, Laurence M., *Between Two Fires: American Indians in the Civil War*, Free Press, New York, NY, 1995.

Hayden, F. Stansbury, *Military Ballooning During the Early Civil War*, Johns Hopkins University Press, Baltimore, MD, 2000.

Hearn, Chester G., *The Capture of New Orleans 1862*, Louisiana State University Press, Baton Rouge, LA, 1995.

Hearn, Chester G., *Naval Battles of the Civil War: The Ships, the Men, and the Epic Naval Battles of America's War of the Rebellion*, Thunder Bay Press, San Diego, CA, 2000.

Hedberg, Jonas, *Kungliga Artilleriet: Det Ridande Artilleriet*, Stockholm, Sweden, 1987.

Heidler, David S., and Heidler, Jeanne T., *Encyclopedia of the American Civil War: A Political, Social and Military History*, W. W. Norton & Company, New York, NY, 2000.

Hewitt, Laurence, *Port Hudson: Confederate Bastion on the Mississippi*, Louisiana State University Press, Baton Rouge, LA, 1987.

Higginson, Thomas Wentworth, *Army Life in a Black Regiment*, Collier Books, New York, NY, 1962.

Hill, Jim Dan, *Sea Dogs of the Sixties: Farragut and Seven Contemporaries*, A. S. Barnes & Company, Inc., New York, NY, 1961.

Hinkley, Julian, *Service with the Third Wisconsin Infantry*, History Committee, Madison, WI, 1912.

Historical Sketch of the Chicago Board of Trade Battery, Andrew Finney Co., Chicago, IL, 1902.

Hoehling, A. A., *Damn the Torpedoes: Naval Incidents of the Civil War*, Gramercy Books, New York, NY, 1989.

Hoehling, Mary, *Thaddeus Lowe: America's One-Man Air Corps*, Julian Messner, Inc., New York, NY, 1958.

Horan, James D., *The Pinkertons: The Detective Dynasty That Made History*, Crown Publishers, Inc., New York, NY, 1967.

Hughes, Nathaniel Cheairs, Jr., *Bentonville: The Final Battle of Sherman & Johnston*, University of North Carolina Press, Chapel Hill, NC, 1996.

Ingraham, Charles A., *Elmer E. Ellsworth and the Zouaves of '61*, University of Chicago Press, Chicago, IL, 1925.

Jaeger, Michael, and Lauritzan, Carol, *Memoirs of Thaddeus S. C. Lowe, Chief of the Aeronautic Corps of the Army of the United States During the Civil War: My Balloons in Peace and War*, Edwin Mellen Press, Lewistown, NY, 2004.

Johnson, Robert Underwood, and Buel, Clarence Clough, *Battles and Leaders of the Civil War*, 4 vols., Century, New York, NY, 1880–81.

Jones, John W., *The Southern Historical Society Papers*, 49 vols., Southern Historical Society, Richmond, VA, 1876–1943.

Jones, Virgil Carrington, *Gray Ghosts and Rebel Raiders*, Holt, Rinehart and Winston, New York, NY, 1961.

Jones, Virgil Carrington, *Ranger Mosby*, University of North Carolina Press, Chapel Hill, NC, 1976.

Joslyn, Mauriel Phillips, *Valor and Lace: The Roles of Confederate Women 1861–1865*, Southern Heritage Press, Murfreesboro, TN, 1996.

Lamb, William, *Colonel Lamb's Story of Fort Fisher*, Blockade Runner Museum, Carolina Beach, NC, 1966.

Lasswell, Mary, *Rags and Hope: The Recollections of Val C. Giles, Four Years with Hood's Brigade, Fourth Texas Infantry, 1861–1865*, Coward-McCann, New York, NY, 1961.

Lavine, Sigmund A., *Allan Pinkerton: America's First Private Eye*, Dodd, Mead & Company, New York, NY, 1963.

Leon, Louis, *A Diary of a Tar Heel Confederate Soldier*, Eastern Digital Resources, Clearwater, SC, 2003.

Leonard, Elizabeth D., *All the Daring of the Soldier: Women of the Civil War Armies*, Penguin Books, New York, NY, 2001.

Leonard, Elizabeth D., *Yankee Women: Gender Battles in the Civil War*, W. W. Norton & Company, New York, NY, 1994.

Lepa, Jack H., *The Shenandoah Valley Campaign of 1864*, McFarland Publishers, Inc., Jefferson, NC, 2003.

Leslie, Edward E., *The Devil Knows How to Ride: The True Story of William Clarke Quantrill and His Confederate Raiders*, Random House, New York, NY, 1996.

Longacre, Edward G., *Lee's Cavalrymen: A History of the Mounted Forces of the Army of Northern Virginia*, Stackpole Books, Mechanicsburg, PA, 2002.

Lord, Francis A., *Civil War Collector's Encyclopedia: Arms, Uniforms, and Equipment of the Union and Confederacy*, Stackpole Books, Harrisburg, PA, 1965.

Mackey, Robert R., *The Uncivil War: Irregular Warfare in the Upper South, 1861–1865*, University of Oklahoma Press, Norman, OK, 2004.

Mahan, A. T., *The Navy in the Civil War*, Charles Scribner's Sons, New York, NY, 1883.

Martin, David G., *Gettysburg July 1*, Combined Publishing, Conshohocken, PA, 1996.

McAulay, John D., *Civil War Breech Loading Rifles: A Survey of the Innovative Infantry Arms of the American Civil War,* Andrew Mowbray Inc., Lincoln, RI, 1991.

McCarthy, Agnes, and Reddick, Lawrence, *Worth Fighting For: A History of the Negro in the United States During the Civil War and Reconstruction*, Zenith Books, Garden City, NJ, 1965.

McClure, Alexander K., *The Annals of War*, Blue and Grey Press, Edison, NJ, 1996.

McClurg, Alexander C., *The Last Chance of the Confederacy*, Military Order of the Loyal Legion of the United States, A. C. McClurg and Company, Chicago, IL, 1891.

McDonald, William, *A History of the Laurel Brigade, Originally the Ashby Cavalry of the Army of Northern Virginia and Chew's Battery*, Sun Job Printing Office, Baltimore, MD, 1907.

Meade, George, *The Life and Letters of George Gordon Meade*, 2 vols., Charles Scribner's Sons, New York, NY, 1913.

Miller, Francis Trevelyan, *The Photographic History of the Civil War*, 10 vols., Review of Reviews Co., New York, NY, 1911.

Mosby, John Singleton, and Russell, Charles Wells, *The Memoirs of Colonel John S. Mosby*, Little, Brown and Company, New York, NY, 1917.

Munson, John W., *Reminiscences of a Mosby Guerilla*, Zenger Publishing Co., Washington, DC, 1983.

Murphy, Jim, *The Boy's War: Confederate and Union Soldiers Talk About the Civil War*, Clarion Books, New York, NY, 1990.

Murray, R. L., *"They Fought Like Tigers": The 11th New York Fire Zouaves, 14th Brooklyn and the Irish 69th New York at First Bull Run,* Benedum Books, Wolcott, NY, 2005.

Naval History Division, Navy Department, *Civil War Naval Chronology 1861–1865*, Government Printing Office, Washington, DC, 1971.

Orrmont, Arthur, *Master Detective: Allan Pinkerton*, Julian Messner, New York, NY, 1966.

Peterson, Harold L., *Arms and Armor in Colonial America, 1526–1783*, Currier Dover Publications, Mineola, NY, 2000.

Pfanz, Harry W., *Gettysburg: The First Day*, University of North Carolina Press, Chapel Hill, NC, 2001.

Phisterer, Frederick, *New York in the War of the Rebellion 1861–1865*, 6 vols., J. B. Lyon Company, Albany, NY, 1912.

Pinkerton, Allan, *The Spy of the Rebellion: Being a True History of the Spy System of the United States Army During the Late Rebellion*, G. W. Dillingham Co., Publishers, New York, NY, 1883.

Pleasants, Henry, Jr., and Straley, George H., *Inferno at Petersburg*, Chilton Company—Book Division Publishers, Philadelphia, PA, 1961.

Plum, William Rattle, *The Military Telegraph During the Civil War in the United States*, 2 vols., Arno Press, New York, NY, 1974.

Poland, Charles P., Jr., *The Glories of War: Small Battles and Early Heroes of 1861*, AuthorHouse, Bloomington, IN, 2006.

Pratt, Fletcher, *The Monitor and the Merrimac and Other Naval Battles*, Random House, New York, NY, 1951.

Price, William H., *The Civil War Centennial Handbook*, Prince Lithograph Co., Inc., Arlington, VA, 1961.

Quarles, Benjamin, *The Negro in the Civil War*, Little, Brown and Company, Boston, MA, 1953.

Ramage, James A., *Rebel Raider: The Life of General John Hunt Morgan*, University Press of Kentucky, Lexington, KY, 1986.

Randall, Ruth Painter, *Colonel Elmer Ellsworth*, Little, Brown and Company, Boston, MA, 1960.

Rawson, Edward K., and Stewart, Charles W., *Official Records of the Union and Confederate Navies in the War of the Rebellion*, 31 vols., Government Printing Office, Washington, DC, 1894–1922.

Rhodes, Neil, Richards, Jennifer, and Marshall, Joseph, *King James VI & I: Selected Writings*, Ashgate Publishing, Surrey, UK, 2003.

Rose, Willie Lee, *Rehearsal for Reconstruction: The Port Royal Experiment*, University of Georgia Press, Athens, GA, 1999.

Salmon, John S., *The Official Virginia Battlefield Guide*, Stackpole Books, Mechanicsburg, PA, 2001.

Schmitt, Martin F., *General George Crook: His Autobiography*, University of Oklahoma Press, Norman, OK, 1946.

Sears, Stephen W., *Chancellorsville*, Houghton Mifflin Company, Boston, MA, 1996.

Sears, Stephen W., *Landscape Turned Red: The Battle of Antietam*, Ticknor and Fields, New Haven, CT, 1983.

Sensing, Thurman, *Champ Ferguson: Confederate Guerilla*, Vanderbilt University Press, Nashville, TN, 1994.

Shea, William L., and Hess, Earl J., *Pea Ridge: Civil War Campaign in the West*, University of North Carolina Press, Chapel Hill, NC, 1992.

Sherman, William T., *Memoirs of General W. T. Sherman: Written by Himself*, 2 vols., D. Appleton and Company, New York, NY, 1875.

Siepel, Kevin H., *Rebel: The Life and Times of John Singleton Mosby*, St. Martin's Press, New York, NY, 1983.

Sifikas, Stewart, *Compendium of the Confederate Armies: Mississippi*, Facts on File, New York, NY, 1992.

Silber, Nina, *Daughters of the Union: Northern Women Fight the Civil War*, Harvard University Press, Cambridge, MA, 2005.

Simon, John Y., and Bridges, Roger D., *The Papers of Ulysses S. Grant, Volume 4: January 8–March 31, 1862*, Southern Illinois University Press, Carbondale, IL, 1972.

Smith, Charles R., *Marines in the Revolution: A History of the Continental Marines in the American Revolution 1775–1783*, History and Museums Division Headquarters, U.S. Marine Corps, Washington, DC, 1975.

Sondhaus, Lawrence, *Naval Warfare 1815–1914*, Routledge Books, London, UK, 2001.

Stephenson, Darl L., *Headquarters in the Brush: Blazer's Independent Union Scouts*, Ohio University Press, Athens, OH, 2001.

Stern, Philip Van Doren, *Secret Missions of the Civil War*, Wings Books, New York, NY, 1990.

Stevens, C. A., *Berdan's United States Sharpshooters in the Army of the Potomac*, Morningside Bookshop, Dayton, OH, 1984.

Stevens, Michael E., *As If It Were Glory: Robert Beecham's Civil War from the Iron Brigade to the Black Regiments*, Bowman & Littlefield Publishers, Inc., Lanham, MD, 1998.

Straubing, Harold Elk, *In Hospital and Camp: The Civil War Through the Eyes of Its Doctors and Nurses*, Stackpole Books, Harrisburg, PA, 1993.

Swanberg, W. A., *First Blood: The Story of Fort Sumter*, Charles Scribner's Sons, New York, NY, 1957.

Symonds, Craig L., *The Civil War at Sea*, Praeger Books, Santa Barbara, CA, 2009.

Taylor, Frank H., *Philadelphia in the Civil War*, published by the author, Philadelphia, PA, 1879.

Trudeau, Noah Andre, *Like Men of War: Black Troops in the Civil War 1861–1865*, Castle Books, Edison, NJ, 2002.

Turner, George Edgar, *Victory Rode the Rails: The Strategic Place of the Railroads in the Civil War*, Greenwood Press, Publishers, Westport, CT, 1975.

U.S. Officer of Military Records, *The War of the Rebellion: A Compilation of the Official Records of the Union and Confederate Armies*, U.S. Department of War, Washington, DC, 1880–1901.

U.S. Office of Naval Records and Library, *Official Records of the Union and Confederate Navies in the War of the Rebellion*, Government Printing Office, Washington, DC, 1894–1922.

Wert, Jeffry D., *Cavalryman of the Lost Cause: A Biography of J. E. B. Stuart*, Simon & Schuster, New York, NY, 2008.

Wert, Jeffry D., *Mosby's Rangers: The True Adventures of the Most Famous Command of the Civil War*, Touchstone Books, New York, NY, 1990.

Wiley, Bell Irvin, *Confederate Women: Beyond the Petticoat*, Barnes & Noble Books, New York, NY, 1994.

Williamson, James J., *Mosby's Rangers: A Record of the Operations of the Forty-Third Battalion Virginia Cavalry*, Ralph B. Kenyon, Publisher, New York, NY, 1896.

Wilson, Joseph T., *The Black Phalanx: African American Soldiers in the War of Independence, the War of 1812, & the Civil War*, Da Capo Press, New York, NY, 1994.

Wise, Jennings Cropper, *The Long Arm of Lee; or, The History of the Artillery of the Army of Northern Virginia*, 2 vols., J. P. Bell Company, Inc., Lynchburg, VA, 1915.

Zeinert, Karen, *Those Courageous Women of the Civil War*, Millbrook Press, Brookfield, CT, 1998.

INDEX

Mansfield, Robert K., 29
Marine Battalion, 136
Marine Brigade, 143, 144
Mason, A. P., 159
Massachusetts National Guard, 11
Maury, Matthew Fontaine, 46
McCaw, James B., 112
McClellan, George B.: and Ager's machine
    guns, 35; and Ambulance Corps,
    106–7; and Peninsula Campaign, 35,
    42–43, 73, 81, 117; and rockets,
    42–43; and Rush, 14; and signalmen,
    81; and West Point class, 12
McClintock, James, 183–85
McCulloch, Ben, 233
McDonald, Caroline, 212
McDonald, Mary, 212
McDowell, Irvin, 65, 71, 134
McIntosh, Chilly, 231
McIntosh, Daniel, 231
McIntosh, James M., 231, 232, 234
McIntosh, Lachlan H., 20
McLaws, Lafayette, 171
McNeill, Jesse, 122
McNeill, John Hanson, 120–22
McNeill's Rangers, 119, 120–22
Meade, George G.: counterattacking
    Longstreet, 83; and Jackson, 30; and
    114th Pennsylvania, 6
Meade, George G., Jr., 14
Merriam, Scovel S., 181
Mexican-American War: deaths during,
    103; and horse artillery, 25–27, 32;
    and Rush, 12, 16; and use of
    rockets, 42
Meyer, Albert J.: background, 77–78; and
    Beardslee telegraph, 80; and
    development of Signal Corps,
    78–80; reinstated as chief signal
    officer, 84; signal system, 78; and
    use of observation balloon, 65–66
Milroy, Robert, 126
Mine Explosion battle, 228
Miner, Brinkerhoff N., 81
Miners, 145–56
Minié, Claude, 87–88
Minié ball, 88
Mitchell, John G., 176

Mitchell, Sallie, 212
Moe, Seth, 212
Montgomery, James, 219
Montjoy, R. P., 120
Moore, Samuel Preston, 111–12
Morgan, Daniel, 171
Morgan, James D., 175
Morgan, John Hunt, 94, 123
Morgan, Nancy Hill, 210–11
Morris, Robert, Jr., 14, 16
Morris, Robert H., 14
Mosby, John Singleton: and execution of
    Union army soldiers, 119–20; and
    Fairfax Court House, 117–18; and
    Greenback Raid, 119; overview,
    116–17; and partisan rangers
    command, 117, 129
Mosby's Rangers, 116–17, 127–30. *See
    also* Partisan rangers
Mound City, 193
Mower, Joseph, 177
Munson, James, 117
Murphy, J. McLeod, 149

Nancy Harts, 132, 202, 211
Napoleonic Wars, 11, 17, 24, 42
Nashville Campaign, 165
National Cemetery, 168
National Detective Police, 131
National Guard Cadets, 1
National Guard Militia
    Museum, 181
National Lancers, 11
Native Americans, 225–36
Nautilus, 178
Naval Artillery Battery, 142
Naval Brigade, 143, 144
Navy Department, 179
Neafie & Levy, 179
Neutrality Act, 12
New Era, 193
A New Sign Language for Deaf Mutes
    (Meyer), 77
Newton, John, 60
New York Draft Riots, 39
New York Fire Zouaves, 3
New York Rocket Battalion, 42
New York State Telegraph Company, 77

ABOUT THE AUTHOR

ROBERT P. BROADWATER is an independent scholar and historian. He has authored or contributed to more than 30 books on the American Revolution and the Civil War, including ABC-CLIO's *William T. Sherman: A Biography* and *Ulysses S. Grant: A Biography*.